Pink Think

W · W · NORTON & COMPANY
NEW YORK · LONDON

Pink Think

Becoming a Woman in Many Uneasy Lessons

Lynn Peril

For information about permission to reproduce selections from
this book, write to Permissions, W. W. Norton & Company, Inc.,
500 Fifth Avenue, New York, NY 10110.

The text of this book is composed in Fairfield
with the display set in Pike and Sign Painter House Casual
Desktop composition by Tom Ernst
Manufacturing by The Haddon Craftsmen, Inc.
Book design by Rubina Yeh
Production manager: Amanda Morrison

Library of Congress Cataloging-in-Publication Data
Peril, Lynn.
  Pink think : becoming a woman in many uneasy lessons / by Lynn Peril.
    p. cm.
  Includes bibliographical references.
  ISBN 0-393-32354-4 (pbk.)
  1. Women—Socialization. 2. Femininity. 3. Femininity—History—20th century.
4. Etiquette for women—History—20th century. 5. Pink—Social aspects. I. Title.

HQ1221 .P445 2002
305.42—dc21   2002070255

W. W. Norton & Company, Inc.
500 Fifth Avenue, New York, N.Y. 10110
www.wwnorton.com

W. W. Norton & Company Ltd.
Castle House, 75/76 Wells Street, London W1T 3QT

1 2 3 4 5 6 7 8 9 0

To Johnny
who taught me to believe in myself

Contents

Acknowledgments

Fortunately, I had a lot of support during the almost three years I spent working on this book. Many thanks to Johnny Bartlett, Katherine Cluverius, Catherine Coxe, Bob D'Olivo, Karen Finlay, Rita Haskin, Timothy J. Halloran, Mary Ann Irwin, Eileen Lenihan, Jim Malloy, John Marr, Elizabeth McKenna, Donna Mae Mims, Mark Perelman, Mimi Pond, Mary Ricci, Chip Rowe, Jessica Rudin, Rich Stim, Deb Stoller, Jane Townley, Anne Treistman, V. Vale, Pete Wentz, Michele Lee Willson, Tomiko Wood, Michael Zadoorian, the librarians at San Francisco's Mechanic's Institute Library and the Minneapolis Public Library, Dennis Preisler at the Sears Archive, Mickey McGowan at the Unknown Museum, Ron and Maria at Kayo Books, all the gals at the Ladies Lit List, and everyone in the Payerl/Voorhorst/Komie/Bartlett clans—especially my very patient mom!

I'd like to thank loyal *Mystery Date* readers everywhere. You don't know how much your support has meant to me over the years. I especially appreciate the items of femoribilia many of you have donated to my collection—they helped form the basis of this book.

Joshua Glenn, editor of *Hermenaut,* has not only supported my writing at every turn but also suggested I contact Alane Mason at a particularly dire point in *Pink Think*'s protracted gestation.

At a time when a handful of multinational megacorporations are changing the face of the publishing industry, I am proud to claim one of the remaining independents as my publisher. At W. W. Norton, Alane

Mason and her assistant, Stefanie Diaz, provided insightful editorial input as well as boundless enthusiasm for this project. They made me write a better book, and I am profoundly grateful to them both.

Finally, *Pink Think* really would not exist without the efforts of Faye Bender, cheerleader, friend, and agent extraordinaire. All writers should be so lucky.

Pink Think

An Introduction

Long before it's time for Mom to help plan the wedding
dress or Dad to give the bride away, it's time to be raising
a future wife in your home. Because wives aren't born—
they are made. Your daughter is born a female, but she
has to learn how to be feminine.

Constance J. Foster,
"Raise Your Girl to Be a Wife,"
Parents magazine, 1956

The full-page ad that graced women's magazines in 1958 was so discreet as to be mysterious: a pink-suited socialite posed atop San Francisco's Russian Hill, while her servants carried a bevy of pink gift-wrapped boxes from her car to her fashionable apartment building. "Pink is a very special mood" read the large and flowing type beneath the picture. One had to investigate the smaller print to discover that the ad was for "Serena, the luxury sanitary napkin" by Modess. In addition to its other fancy attributes, Serena was "softly pink to please" the most discriminating woman, its pastel color as much an homage to femininity as the use to which it was put. Serena was not the only pink pad to grace drugstore shelves: the "soft pink covering" on Kotex's Miss Deb napkins made sixties-era preteens "feel feminine and dainty—just the way a young lady wants to feel."

With such strong associations between femininity and the color pink, it may come as a surprise to discover that pink was not originally considered a "girl color" at all. Until the nineteenth century, most babies wore white; and if baby clothing incorporated color, boys were just as likely to wear pink as girls. The identification of girls with pink and boys with blue was apparently a French innovation, the exact origins of which remain unclear.[1] It soon found its way into popular culture on this side of the Atlantic, however. In 1868, Louisa May Alcott included a scene in her phenomenally successful novel *Little Women* wherein Amy March (the artsy sister, remember?) puts "a blue ribbon on the boy and a pink on the girl, French fashion," to differentiate between newborn twins.[2] But color-coding babies pink and blue according to their gender didn't become widespread until the post–World War II baby boom, when the arbitrary color assignment of a century or so before turned into a new mass habit and established a modern "fact." By the time a 1952 series of poise and beauty booklets called *The Charming Woman* urged readers to "Ask yourself why a baby has to wear pink and blue," its answer suggested that the conflation of color and gender sprang directly from the womb: "[T]hese are the young delicate colors which actually *look like* the baby."[3]

There's more to the story of pink than baby booties and blankets. A 1948 fad among coeds for pink Brooks Brothers shirts assumed such proportions that a year later the venerable menswear retailer began manufacturing a version specifically for women. The new shirt was only slightly modified from the original (or, as a *New Yorker* article smirkingly noted, "the body of the shirt is—ah—fuller") and immediately clicked with the college crowd.[4]

The shirt craze was just the tip of the iceberg, however. The sight of so many girls and women clamoring for that particular item, cash clenched in sweaty fists, buoyed the hope of manufacturers everywhere. Then again, maybe we were simply a nation literally "in the pink" with postwar prosperity, giddy that the war was over and ready for some serious shopping.

Responding to the resounding demand of consumers, pink products became more and more visible in magazine ads and on the shelves of all manner of stores. Did you want to coordinate an outfit around your Brooks Brothers shirt? Start from the inside out with a Playtex "Pink-Ice" girdle, packaged in a "slim, shimmering pink tube." It was guaranteed to be both "cool as a frosty drink" and "invisible beneath your briefest swimsuit"— though a look at the size of the garment quickly confirms that "brief" was a relative term. Were you tired of your antiseptic hospital-white kitchen and bathroom? Then the newly popular pastel lines of appliances and plumbing fixtures were for you! Little did pink-crazed shoppers realize they'd actually been available since the late 1920s.

It was Mamie Eisenhower's passion for pink that brought the color a new prominence. From the rhinestone-spattered, pink silk ball gown she wore to hubby Ike's inaugural in 1953 to the decor of her White House boudoir and vacation cabin, Mamie surrounded herself with a pale shade soon marketed as "First Lady Pink." A few short years later, Americans were in the throes of what can only be described as pinkmania. Pink-besotted consumers could purchase pastel products ranging from pots, pans, and hand mixers to automobiles and golf balls. Housewives washed their Tickled Pink cups and plates in Dreft, a dishwashing powder that turned the water a gentle shade of pink while leaving the suds a fluffy white. Up-to-date gals got "fashion's fresh, young 'in the pink' look" by using one of three shades of Pond's powdered makeup, each available in an "adorable pink Date Case." A 1955 fashion layout devoted to Pink Party Dresses got to the heart of the color's appeal: "It makes the stag line giddy, it's the toast of gala occasions . . . and it's a legitimate feminine wile."[5]

Turning Pink into Pink Think

From the moment she's wrapped in a pink blanket, long past the traumatic birthday when she realizes her age is greater than her bust measurement, the human female is bombarded with advice on how to wield those feminine wiles. This advice ranges from rather vague proscriptions along the lines of "nice girls don't chew gum/swear/wear pants/fill-in-the-blank," to obsessively elaborate instructions for daily living. How many women's lives, for example, were enriched by former Miss America Jacque Mercer's positively baroque description of the proper way to put on a bathing suit, as it appeared in her guide *How to Win a Beauty Contest* (1960)?

> [F]irst, roll it as you would a girdle. Pull the suit over the hips to the waist, then, holding the top away from your body, bend over from the waist. Ease the suit up to the bustline and with one hand, lift one breast up and in and ease the suit bra over it. Repeat on the other side. Stand up and fasten the straps.[6]

Instructions like these made me bristle. I formed an early aversion to all things pink and girly. It didn't take me long to figure out that many things young girls were supposed to enjoy, not to mention ways they were supposed to behave, left me feeling funny—as if I was expected to pound my square peg self into the round hole of designated girliness. I didn't know it at the time, but the butterflies in my tummy meant I had crested the first of many hills on the roller coaster ride of femininity—or, as I soon referred to it, the other f-word. Before I knew what was happening, I was hurtling down its track, seemingly out of control, and screaming at the top of my lungs.

After all, look what I was up against. The following factoids of femininity date from the year of my birth (hey, it wasn't *that* long ago):

✷ In May of 1961, Betsy Martin McKinney told readers of *Ladies' Home Journal* that, for women, sexual activity commenced with intercourse and was completed with pregnancy and childbirth. Therefore, a woman who used contraceptives denied "her own creativity, her own sexual role, her very femininity." Furthermore, McKinney asserted that "one of the most stimulating predisposers to orgasm in a woman may be childbirth followed by several months of lactation." (Mmm, yes, must be the combination of episiotomy and sleep deprivation that does it.) Politely avoiding personal examples, she neglected to mention how many little McKinneys there were.

* During the competition for the title of Miss America 1961, five finalists were given two questions to answer. First they were asked what they would do if "you were walking down the runway in the swimsuit competition, and a heel came off one of your shoes?" The second question, however, was a bit more esoteric: "Are American women usurping males in the world, and are they too dominant?" Eighteen-year-old Nancy Fleming, of Montague, Michigan, agreed that "there are too many women working in the world. A woman's place is in the home with her husband and children." This, along with her pragmatic answer to the first question ("I would kick off both shoes and walk barefooted") and her twenty-three-inch waist (tied for the smallest in pageant history), helped Nancy win the crown.

* In 1961, toymaker Transogram introduced a new game for girls called Miss Popularity ("The True American Teen"), in which players competed to see who could accrue the most votes from four pageant judges—three of whom were male. Points were awarded for such attributes as nice legs, and if the judges liked a contestant's figure, voice, and "type." The prize? A special "loving" cup, of course! Who, after all, could love an unpopular girl?

These are all prime examples of "pink think." Pink think is a set of ideas and attitudes about what constitutes proper female behavior; a groupthink that was consciously or not adhered to by advice writers, manufacturers of toys and other consumer products, experts in many walks of life, and the public at large, particularly during the years spanning the mid-twentieth century—but enduring even into the twenty-first century. Pink think assumes there is a standard of behavior to which all women, no matter their age, race, or body type, must aspire. "Femininity" is sometimes used as a code word for this mythical standard, which suggests that women and girls are always gentle, soft, delicate, nurturing beings made of "sugar and spice and everything nice." But pink think is more than a stereotyped vision of girls and women as poor drivers who are afraid of mice and snakes, adore babies and small dogs, talk incessantly on the phone, and are incapable of keeping secrets. Integral to pink think is the belief that one's success as a woman is grounded in one's allegiance to such behavior. For example, a woman who fears mice isn't necessarily following the dictates of pink think. On the other hand, a woman who isn't afraid of mice but pretends to be because she thinks such helplessness adds to her appearance of femininity is toeing the pink think party line. When you hear the words "charm" or "personality" in the context of successful womanhood, you can almost always be sure you're in the presence of pink think.

While various self-styled "experts" have been advising women on their "proper" conduct since the invention of the printing press, the phenomenon defined here as pink think was particularly pervasive from the 1940s to the 1970s. These were fertile years for pink think, a cultural mindset and consumer behavior rooted in New Deal prosperity yet culminating with the birth of women's liberation. During this time, pink think permeated popular books and magazines aimed at adult women, while little girls absorbed rules of feminine behavior while playing games like the aforementioned Miss Popularity. Meanwhile, prescriptions for ladylike dress, deportment, and mindset seeped into child-rearing manuals, high school home economics textbooks, and guides for bride, homemaker, and career girl alike.

It was almost as if the men and women who wrote such books viewed proper feminine behavior as a panacea for the ills of a rapidly changing modern world. For example, myriad articles in the popular press devoted to the joys of housewifery helped coerce Rosie the Riveter back into the kitchen when her hubby came home from the war and expected his factory job back. During the early cold war years, some home economics texts seemed to suggest that knowing how to make hospital corners and a good tuna casserole were the only things between Our Way of Life and communist incursion. It was patriotic to be an exemplary housewife. And pink-thinking experts of the sixties and seventies, trying to maintain this ideal, churned out reams of pages that countered the onrushing tide of both the sexual revolution and the women's movement. If only all women

"Let's Face It"

Pink think assumed not only that the "average American woman" was Caucasian but that those who weren't white aspired to be. This was especially apparent in *Let's Face It*, a 1959 "Guide to Good Grooming for Negro Girls." While some of the book's illustrations portrayed girls with vaguely African-American features, other sketches might well have come from any other guide aimed at white teens. Juxtaposed over chapter titles that appealed directly to the reader herself ("The Clothes You Wear," "The Way You Act"), the images strongly suggested that the way "you" wanted to be was white.

behaved like our Ideal Woman, the experts seemed to say through the years, then everything would be fine.

You might even say that the "problem with no name" that Betty Friedan wrote about in *The Feminine Mystique* (1963) was a virulent strain of pink-thinkitis. After all, according to Friedan, "the problem" was in part engendered by the experts' insistence that women "could desire no greater destiny than to glory in their own femininity"—a pink think credo.

Becoming a Woman in Many Uneasy Lessons

Pink think was, and remains, an active agent in the lives of many women who internalized its contradictory messages and struggled to meet its illusory goals. Even I, a pants-wearing, dress-hating tomboy, was not immune to its tyranny. Miss Popularity and Miss America failed to imprint a big pink "G"-for-girl on my forehead, but still, trying to hold myself up to the rigid standards of pink think caused me no end of distress.

Long Before Pink Think, There Was True Womanhood

Experts have long expounded on what makes an ideal woman. As defined by historian Barbara Welter in an influential 1966 essay, the True Woman was a nineteenth-century paradigm of feminine virtues described in women's magazines, gift annuals, religious literature, and cookbooks.

The True Woman was pious. Not only was she responsible for her own spiritual life, but her "purifying, passionless love" could bring "an erring man back to Christ."[*] She was pure and virtuous. "Sit not with another in a place that is too narrow; read not out of the same book; let not your eagerness to see anything induce you to place your head close to another person's," wrote Mrs. Eliza Farrar in *The Young Lady's Friend* (1842).[†]

Above all, she was submissive. Welter quoted a Mrs. Sandford on the subject of womanly self-abnegation: "A really sensible woman feels her dependence. She does what she can, but she is conscious of inferiority. . . . "[‡] Finally, she cherished the domestic state. As Mrs. S. E. Farley wrote in 1846, "the true dignity and beauty of the female character seem to consist in a right understanding and faith and cheerful performance of social and family duties."[§]

According to Welter, the "cult of True Womanhood" flourished from 1820 to 1860. But as one contemplates twentieth-century pink think, it's obvious that the True Woman has had a long-lasting influence.

---

[*] Barbara Welter, "The Cult of True Womanhood," *American Quarterly* 18 (Summer 1966), 153.
[†] Ibid., 155.
[‡] Ibid., 159.
[§] Ibid., 162.

It all started with an incident in kindergarten when we girls made Easter bonnets out of paper plates and fabric scraps. My mom's contribution to the project was a couple of yards of pink net leftover from a beautiful Barbie ball gown she had made a few weeks before. I imagined a beautiful hat with the net covering my face, and tried my best to convey this desire to the adult in charge of the pointy scissors and stapler. I don't remember why I wanted a veil, an item of apparel generally associated with nuns and widows—perhaps pink think had already compromised my fashion sense. More likely, I had seen a veiled woman on the street and wanted to claim some of her mysterious sophistication for myself. But the word "veil" was not yet in my vocabulary, and the resulting monstrosity resembled nothing so much as a puffy pink cloud. Instead of a veil, the hat sported a couple of fake violets the scissors lady had thrown in for good measure. I was mortified. And when one of my teachers referred to me and my hideous hat as "dainty," I resolved I would never be that again—whatever it meant.

Over thirty years have passed since that unfortunate incident, and I have grown up to be many things, but dainty sure as hell isn't one of them. Instead, inspired by the many absurdities and contradictions of pink think, I have become a connoisseur and collector of what *Bust* magazine editor Debbie Stoller describes as "femoribilia": books, games, and other objects infused with pink think expectations and proscriptions— what an anthropologist might call the material culture of femininity.

Some of these artifacts are easy to spot, even by amateurs. Would anyone really disagree that a certain eleven-and-a-half-inch fashion doll packs a pink think wallop with her pneumatic breasts, minuscule waist, and pointed feet just waiting for tiny stiletto heels? Other objects are more subtle in their approach—the box for a Modess sanitary belt, for example.[7] Not only does the little pink box contain a remnant of an age gone by, it features a photo of a statuesque beauty, elegantly coiffed and gowned in pink. In her gloved hand she holds a feather fan (which uncannily resembles a giant pink mop head), and she stands against an ethereal painted backdrop of grand stairway and chandelier. In short, she is a picture of poised perfection even while having her period. "You there," the little box seems to say, "you in the baggy jeans and the stained underpants, you too could be this woman. In fact, you *should* be this woman. She isn't bothered by cramps or swollen with bloat, and she certainly didn't throw the toilet brush at her husband or boyfriend this morning in a fit of PMS-induced frenzy. What's wrong with you? Buy me, and be like her." The belt itself is—of course!—a tender shade of pink.

My own collection of femoribilia started with the purchase of a 1962 text called *Health and Safety for Teen-Agers* in a Seattle used-book store.

"It's important to you to be considered a 'real boy' or a 'real girl' by others . . . " Health and Safety for Teenagers, 1962.

I identified with Gretchen. I dated a lot of Dicks, too. Illustration from Health and Safety for Teenagers, *1962.*

Its cover featured wonderful mid-century modern graphics and typography, as well as a photo of two studious teens conscientiously poring over a textbook. Tucked inside were plastic transparencies of the human body—the kind that always reminded me of the cadaver slices on display at Chicago's Museum of Science and Industry, which amazed and terrified me as a little girl. What delighted me now were the book's beautiful, color-saturated illustrations of stylishly dressed teens in vintage clothing, every last one of them beset by either the quaintest of problems ("I'm not sure how to act at a class party") or the smarmiest of personalities ("Our group has prepared a summary of our best ideas about how you can learn to concentrate. We'll have copies mimeographed later so each of you can have one").

It was the section devoted to dating do's and don'ts that really rang my bell, as it carefully outlined behavior for both girls and boys. "As a rule, a girl does not ask a boy for a date—even though she would very much like to do so." "When you are 'eating out' on a date, the girl's order is always given first." Such regulations seemed absolutely bizarre, especially since my own experiences with a long line of musician boyfriends rather uncomfortably resembled the book's examples of dating don'ts. After a long day at work, I found it comforting to follow along with "Dick" and "Gretchen" as they bumbled their way through an ice-skating date, or commiserate with "Vic Schultz," who "became very much discouraged" a few weeks after his transfer to Lake High School. When I found an old home economics textbook in a thrift store several weeks later I bought it immediately. Chock-full of antiquated instructions on cooking, sewing, and clean living, the book mesmerized me with its audacious assumptions about female behavior. I was hooked. Before I knew it, I was actively seeking out items that were prime examples of pink think pedantry.

During the golden age of pink think, the ideal of femininity was so deeply interwoven in the American psyche that even seemingly gender-less items were marketed specifically to women. By simply affixing the word "lady" in front of its product's name, a manufacturer created a whole new set of expectations. For example, according to a 1962 catalogue, Papermate's Lady Capri pen had a soft pastel finish and was "practical for women who demand heavy duty pen elegance." Other Papermate Capri pens were guaranteed to write over greasy spots. But only the "completely feminine" Lady Capri could write—elegantly, one surmises—"even over cold cream," just the thing for the gal hastily scribbling down important phone numbers during her nightly beauty ritual.

With some products, though, manufacturers went even further to impress feminine suitability on the public. Razors and shaving were by and large considered the domain of men, despite the fact that women, too, had been removing their unwanted hair since time immemorial. So when Norelco introduced a new product in the early 1960s, it went for the one-two punch of feminizing prefix plus color: no one could possibly mistake a woman's pastel pink Lady Norelco for the more "masculine" (i.e., beige) version sold to her husband.

Using the color pink as a symbol of femininity didn't work as well for the Lionel Toy Company in 1957, when, hankering after a whole new group of consumers, it tried to market a toy train to little girls. Their solution—and imagine, if you will, the board meetings that led up to this decision—was to manufacture a train identical in all respects to their regular models, except for its color. After all, how could it lose? The Lady Lionel featured not only real smoke and a working headlight, but what the company's 1958 catalogue referred to as "a beautiful pink frosted locomotive." The rest of the train was done up in the equally "fashion-right" colors of robin's egg blue and buttercup yellow. The boys in marketing assumed that girls would flock to the color pink like moths to a flame, but sales were meager. The pink train was in production for only two years—leading, of course, to its present-day status as a highly valued collectible.

What worked for products also worked for people. The color pink could always be trusted to help those women engaged in activities not traditionally associated with their gender to maintain an aura of femininity. Donna Mae Mims, a driver who won a Sports Car Club of America National Championship in 1964, dubbed herself the "Pink Lady." She drove a pink Austin Healey Sprite with the words "Think Pink" emblazoned on the rear deck, and wore pink coveralls and a pink crash helmet. Ms. Mims may have had the audacity to compete against men and win, but pink helped to deflect criticism and reminded observers that she was, at heart, a girl like any other. (Her appearances in a provocative men's magazine, *The Millionaire*, didn't hurt either.)

Pink lady Donna Mae Mims in 1969. She was "described by one hard-as-nails sportswriter as a 'yummy blonde.'"

The Patron Saint of Pink Think

Perhaps no one used the color pink as effectively as fifties movie star and patron saint of pink think, Jayne Mansfield. "Pink was my color," she later reflected, "because it made me happy":

> [Pink] is bright and gay. "Mansfield pink" will become famous, I'd tell anyone who called it "Mansfield Madness." Now I had something to

The Patron Saint of Pink Think's guide to life, 1963.

intrigue the photographers. Come up for a drink and paint me pink. I'd invite anyone who had a camera. I'd add I would be happy to pose for any layouts they'd like. I was desperate.[8]

But not for long. As her star rose in the Hollywood firmament, she indulged her penchant often. She owned a pink Jaguar and was married in a skin-tight pink lace gown. Her Sunset Boulevard home was called the "Pink Palace" in honor of its decorating scheme. When Mansfield invited all and sundry to a party celebrating her new pink swimming pool, it was filled to the brim with pink champagne for the occasion. But pink was more than a chromatic theme for Mansfield. It was a visual short-hand for her ideas of femininity and female sexuality. "Men want women to be pink, helpless and do a lot of deep breathing," she advised. "If a girl has curviness, exciting lips and a certain breathlessness, it helps. And it won't do a bit of harm if she has a kittenish, soft cuddly quality."[9]

Eventually, however, Mansfield was trapped by this very philosophy. Losing her bikini top was a playful way of calling attention to her sexy self. But ten years later an unending series of broken bra straps, split dresses and errant boobs that leapt out when least expected seemed pathetic and, worse yet from Mansfield's publicity-loving point of view, boring. As Mansfield biographer Martha Saxon pointed out, there was a sea change in attitudes toward female sexuality from the not-before-you're-married 1950s to the Pill-fueled coffee-tea-or-me 1960s, and Mansfield's leering, innuendo-filled approach to sex was passé before she knew what hit her.[10]

Mansfield clung to the precepts of pink think even as they proved a shaky scaffold for public acceptance. Yet her instincts were unerring in at least one way: surrounding herself with the color pink was an effective confirmation of her hyper-feminine status. Mansfield, of course, pushed femininity far past its natural boundaries. A frequently married mother of five, there was little question of her public devotion to women's most tra-ditional roles. But even her beloved pink couldn't help her out when Mr. Blackwell, naming her as one of the worst dressed women of 1964, called her a "stuffed sausage" whose "baby pink look—the baby doll shorties and darling pink bows for her multicolored hair"—was more suitable for

A Few Helpful Words from the Patron Saint of Pink Think

The following rules to "help a girl be physically attractive" are listed in *Jayne Mansfield's Wild, Wild World* (1963):

1. Yes, think sexy, that is important. It makes you walk, talk and be sexier.

2. Dress sexy—not obvious, but teasing.

3. Create sexy incidents and conversations. Again not obvious but subtle. [Of course, subtlety—just what Jayne was known for!]

4. Be careful who you are with and where. They are your frame.

5. Never hurry.

6. Work towards good health.

7. Stay away from competition that's too rugged.

8. Learn all you can about the subject of being attractive.

9. Use artificial devices if necessary.

10. If you build a better man-trap, you'll catch a better man.

her young daughter. No one came to Mansfield's defense when Paul McCartney, riding high on the Beatles' successes of 1965, called her "an old bag" right in the middle of a Playboy interview.[11] It was, after all, only what everybody else had been thinking for years. Mansfield was only thirty-four in June 1967, when she was reputedly decapitated in a horrendous car wreck on her way from a nightclub engagement.

Femininity: The Other F-Word

One of pink think's supreme ironies is that even so-called experts couldn't agree on what constituted femininity—while all the while they preached the imminent fall of western civilization if women wore pants on the street. Not that femininity has ever been easy to define. Even a 1987 dictionary I consulted fell into pink think when it followed up its definition of feminine ("having qualities characteristic of or suitable to women") with the words "gentle, delicate, etc."

When it came right to down to it, women in the golden age of pink think were bombarded from all sides with conflicting advice. Consider, for example, the origin of femininity. Was it something women were born with or something learned as they grew up? Teen advice doyenne Evelyn Millis Duvall briefly touched on both sides of this question in her *Facts of Life and Love for Teenagers*, a teen advice classic that went into multiple editions throughout the 1950s and 1960s. My copy is a pink-and-black beauty from 1957, but you'll find one at your neighborhood thrift or used-book store with little difficulty. Duvall wrote:

> Girls are born female. Nature endows girls with the physical potentialities of becoming women. The basic physical characteristics that make girls forever different from boys and women different from men . . . these things are her essential *femaleness*.
>
> *Femininity*, on the other hand, is learned. Most of what goes into making a woman act and behave and feel like a woman is learned as she grows up—as a little girl, as a budding young woman, and as the mature, full-grown woman.[12]

Of course, Duvall was not immune to pink think (among other things, she advised menstruating girls to "Dress just a little more prettily [and] smile a little wider than usual"), but her definition got straight to what she thought was the crux of the matter: femininity needed to be learned.

Conversely, *Good Housekeeping* magazine told readers in a 1960 article called "How to Know When You're Really Feminine" that the "grass-roots fact about woman [on] which experts agree" was that her psychology was based firmly on her biology. According to one of the fourteen specialists in feminine behavior consulted by *Good Housekeeping*, woman's real character was by nature "womb-centered"—a description that brings to mind the pesky wandering uterus held responsible for so many female troubles centuries before *Good Housekeeping*'s panel reached its conclusions. At any rate, women couldn't avoid being feminine any more than they could avoid blood pressure or urine production.

Whether they thought femininity innate or learned, the experts agreed that proper feminine behavior required constant, vigilant reinforcement. Women who didn't follow the experts' rules—whether through inattention or wanton disregard—were often assigned to the gulag of gender nonconformity as malcontents and deviants. *Good Housekeeping*'s experts darkly hinted at the unnamed "emotional penalty" paid by women who tried to avoid their biological destiny. Juvenile delinquency and lesbianism were but two of the outcomes for women (if you could even call them that) who ignored the standards of femininity. Even married women who were otherwise impeccably feminine in their appearance and behavior could become suspect if they didn't "fulfill" their sexuality by bearing children. The key to avoiding such tragedies, of course, was found between the covers of the latest guides to charm, beauty, and personality.

Always Ask a Man

Red-haired former B-movie actress (*Journey to the Center of the Earth*) Arlene Dahl is perhaps best known as the mother of Fabio-like studmuffin Lorenzo Lamas, but she was also a firm believer in the "delicacy and refinement" of female behavior. "Shocked" at the discovery that some women dressed for themselves or other women and not for men, Dahl wrote *Always Ask a Man*, a 1965 beauty guide and pink think classic. Beauty for beauty's sake served no purpose, Dahl maintained. Instead, her book was for women who longed "to be beautiful for and be loved by a man." To that end, she cautioned women against wearing pants; men "with few exceptions . . . do not like them." As for cosmetics, Dahl wore "a touch of lipstick to bed . . . a pale peach or pink to match my sheets." Perhaps there's truth to the rumor that husband Fernando Lamas never saw her naked face during their marriage.

Ladylike behavior was at least as important as, if not more so than, lady-like appearance. Dahl laid down some specific rules (emphasis is hers):

> NEVER upstage a man. Don't top his joke even if you have to bite your tongue to keep from doing it. Never launch loudly into your own opinions on a subject—whether it's petunias or politics . . .
>
> If you don't give a man a chance to look after you, he'll soon give up and let you look after yourself! Men have a naturally protective attitude about women, so don't keep trying to prove how self-sufficient you are.
>
> Keep your femininity in focus and you can overcome all handicaps. Let yourself be frankly and fabulously female and you'll have men fighting for your smiles. Remember the secret ingredient of fascination— *femininity*.

Among the many celebrities whose thoughts on femininity Dahl went on to quote, the professionally tan George Hamilton had the most— ahem—interesting take on the subject: "A woman is often like a strip of film—obliterated, insignificant—until a man puts the light behind her." Beginning to get the picture?

As we shall see in the coming pages, the pink think of the 1940s to 1970s held that femininity was necessary for catching and marrying a man, which was in turn a prerequisite for childbearing—the ultimate feminine fulfillment. This resulted in little girls playing games like Mystery Date long before they were ever interested in boys. It made home economics a high school course and college major, and suggested a teen girl's focus should be on dating and getting a boyfriend. It made beauty, charm, and submissive behavior of mandatory importance to women of all ages in order to win a man's attention and hold his interest after marriage. It promoted motherhood and housewifery as women's only meaningful career, and made sure that women who worked outside the home brought "feminine charm" to their workplaces lest a career make them too masculine.

Not that pink think resides exclusively alongside antimacassars and 14.4 modems in the graveyard of outdated popular culture. Shoes, clothing, and movie stars may go in and out of style with astounding rapidity, but attitudes have an unnerving way of hanging around long after they've outlived their usefulness—even if they never had any use to begin with.

How Do You Rate as a Girl?

What's your pink appeal? Take this simple test, courtesy of the February 1960 issue of *Seventeen* magazine. (My score? Let's just say there's room for improvement.)

1. Do you wait for a boy to open a car door, even though you both know you are quite capable of managing it yourself?

2. Do you listen responsively to a story you have heard before rather than squash the pleasure of the boy who is telling it?

3. If you are going to the movies with another girl, do you look presentable enough to cope with an unexpected encounter?

4. If your bureau drawers or closets were open to view without warning, could you stand the inspection without apologies?

5. In a serious discussion which includes both sexes, can you keep from being overpowering even though you know a great deal on the subject?

6. If a boy forgets his manners, can you restrain yourself from correcting him?

7. Are you able to refuse a kiss without hurting a boy's pride and sending him home in a huff?

8. If that special boy told you he liked your long hair, would you keep it long to please him?

9. Have you the courage to be nice to a boy whom the other girls consider a bore?

10. In stores, are you apt to moon over pretty lingerie and perfume?

Scoring: Seven or more yeses: you are a veritable flower of femininity! Five to seven yeses: there are a few thorns. Under five: ouch!

Chapter 1

Kiddie Pink

It's up to you to create a female aura around her before she can even say "goo." . . . *Ribbons and ruffles and other "pretties" will not only subliminally impress her with the specialness of her own gender but will also influence the behavior and attitude of family and friends who hover around the cradle.*

Eve Nelson,
Take It from Eve (1967)

E ven though a baby couldn't read and she might not like the opposite sex until some time after puberty (and maybe not even then), that didn't mean she couldn't start learning how to get a date while she was still in her crib. According to the dictates of pink think, early childhood set the stage for dating and mating that would occur later in a girl's life. It was up to her parents, ably assisted by the experts, to see that she followed the proper path.

It was as if a baby girl's character was as soft, impressionable, and fast setting as plaster of paris. If her parents didn't get the proper examples in

25

front of her as soon as possible, her little mind would quickly solidify for
good or evil.

What Is a Girl?

Alan Beck's phenomenally popular but unrepentantly schmaltzy 1950
essay "What Is A Girl?" didn't offer direct advice to parents or their
daughters, but it did reflect a predominant view of little girls in the middle
of the twentieth century. The editor of an insurance company's in-house
magazine, Beck first published a brief homily on the joys of boys in 1949.
No sooner had it hit the mailboxes of New England Mutual Life's
employees than Beck was receiving phone calls from teary-eyed readers
telling him how moved they were by "What Is a Boy?" When Beck's
bosses at New England Mutual quickly reprinted the essay in an advertisement, the "Boy" "was off like a greased bat through a pneumatic
tube," as its author so colorfully put it. No fool, Beck immediately sat
down and wrote a companion piece titled "What Is a Girl?"[1]

Chances are good that somewhere along the line you've either read or
heard Beck's masterwork. By 1957, New England Mutual had sent out
millions of reprints, and that doesn't count the other ways in which it was
reproduced. Perhaps it was embossed on a plaque that hung over your
crib, or maybe you found one of three spoken-word renditions (Jackie
Gleason, Arthur Godfrey, or Jan Peerce) on a 45- or 78-rpm record at the
thrift store.

Mostly cutesy and innocuous in its assertions that little girls liked
"new shoes, party dresses, . . . dolls, make-believe, dancing lessons . . .
kitchens . . . make up . . . tea parties," the usual girly stuff, "What Is A
Girl?" also harbored a darker, more anthropomorphic view of moppet-
hood. Girl children were sly as foxes, stubborn as mules, squealed like
pigs, and above all were equipped with the "mysterious" minds of women.
As if that wasn't flattering enough, Beck declared little girls to be a
delightful combination of "Eve, Salome and Florence Nightingale"—the

temptress, the seductress, and the nurse! The scenario's got porn script written all over it. With Eve and Salome as her role models, Beck's Girl knew the importance of charm and beauty before she was even out of her frilly white pinafore, while her future husband and children could expect the same motherly care Florence Nightingale gave to wounded soldiers.

Now, before you jump all over me for elevating this snippet of banality from pop cult doggerel to feminist screed, consider this: "What Is a Girl?" was not only used in a Voice of America broadcast back when the Iron Curtain was more than just a good name for a band, but, according to *Good Housekeeping*, it was also read into the Congressional Record. [2] "Girl" was kitsch, but during the cold war years, she was presented as an American ambassador of democracy. It may have been a slow day in world politics, but that's still a high accolade for the sort of prose generally relegated to greeting cards and needlepoint pillows.

To mold a tiny daughter into the sort of girl Beck's essay praised required quick work. As beauty expert Eve Nelson noted in *Take It from Eve* (1967), "a tiny girl's personality begins to form at once":

> Her environment and the way she is treated by others will play a big part in how she eventually thinks of herself. While it's true that she can't actively appreciate a pink ribbon in a wisp of hair or a gay, flowered ruffle on her bassinette, these things set the mood. [3]

Visitors who saw these "feminine fripperies" immediately realized the baby's gender, and began "crooning over her in honeyed words: 'What a beautiful little daughter! . . . What a pretty little girl . . . !'" According to Nelson, flattery sowed at this early age flowered in adulthood, for "be[ing] told you are pretty goes a long way toward making you pretty."

Physical attractiveness ranked high in the pink think canon, and not only because beauty (or at least good grooming) was crucial for catching a man. Good beauty habits were also important after marriage, when prettiness and charm helped a wife to "hold her husband's interest," as the women's magazines euphemistically described it, as well as to cajole a recalcitrant breadwinner into providing luxury items as well as house-

hold necessities to his stay-at-home wife. Thus, forward-thinking mothers got their daughters off on the right foot. "Start your baby, especially if
it is a girl, on a lifelong beauty and grooming program," advised *Family
Circle's Complete Book of Charm and Beauty*. A little petroleum jelly not
only kept baby's eyelids from sticking together but also "pave[d] the way
to good beauty habits," and a happy marriage.

Thus, there was little time to lose when training a future bride. In a
1956 *Parents* magazine article called "Raise Your Girl to Be a Wife," Constance J. Foster (the mother of "two handsome, utterly masculine sons")
told anxious parents there was "a lot they can do from the moment of . . .
birth to lay the groundwork" for their newborn daughter's happy marriage. This consisted of helping daughters develop what Foster called the
inner patterns of femininity. She recommended that mothers of successful future brides help their daughters understand that the kitchen was
"as important a room as the boudoir," just as fathers needed to "rave over
their [daughters'] first fumbling attempts to bake a cake and make
dresses for their dolls." Parental praise for these nascent homemaking
skills reinforced "the ability to be a real woman and like it."[4] Daddy especially needed to be involved; he was the surrogate husband for whom his
daughter, grown to adulthood skilled in both erotic and culinary arts,
would one day make cakes and clothing.

Danger! Boyish Girl!

As any gal who lived vicariously through Jo March will tell you, not every
little girl wanted to waste her time baking and sewing while there were
trees to climb, bikes to ride, and adventures to pursue. The heroine of
Little Women, fifteen-year-old Josephine March, is girl literature's original tomboy. "Boys' games and work and manners" appealed to Jo—itself a
boyish abbreviation of her given name, as well as a foil for the girlish
moniker given to her best friend, Theodore "Laurie" Laurence. Repri-
manded by her ladylike sister as too old for "such boyish tricks" as using

"Little Women"

While one of *Little Women*'s themes was how girls grow into Christian womanhood, marriage, and maternity, author Louisa May Alcott's classic girls' novel doesn't quite fall into the proto-pink-think category of True Womanhood. Alcott's alter ego, Jo March, finds freedom in boyish hi-jinks and written expression, even though she fears later life as "a literary spinster with a pen for a spouse."[*] Married off at the last minute to the ghastly Professor Bhaer, Jo can't escape her future as a "little woman," but the author clearly identified more with her high-spirited days as a tomboy. Perhaps such undertones reflected the complexities of Alcott's life: in an inversion of contemporary mores, Louisa, her mother, and sisters supported their philosopher father, a burden that increasingly fell on Louisa's shoulders when death and marriage removed her sisters from the family home. Both parents urged her to write a moralistic story for girls, even though Alcott much preferred writing thrilling stories of romance and intrigue for adults. In light of *Little Women*'s resounding success and her role as breadwinner, Alcott all but gave up writing the stories she truly enjoyed. Her heroine Jo isn't allowed what looks like real happiness to modern eyes, either (marriage to the soulful, sexy Laurie and further access to her writing skill), but she retained much more spirit than preached by other proponents of the True Woman.

[*]Alcott, *Little Women*, 478.

slang and whistling, Jo explodes in a speech dear to the hearts of many readers on the cusp of adolescence: "I hate to think I've got to grow up, and be Miss March, and wear long gowns, and look as prim as a China-aster . . . I can't get over my disappointment in not being a boy."[5]

By the middle of the twentieth century, most experts agreed that it was all right for girls to follow in Jo's footsteps, but only to a certain point—usually adolescence. Childhood tomboyism was "freeing and fine," Constance Foster said, as long as parents also fussed over their daughter's appearance at times, the better to "help her to enjoy being a girl and acting like one."

It was a matter of balance between appropriate girlishness and the threat of too much masculinity. A "piquant amount of tomboyishness was not undesirable," wrote Dr. Leslie B. Hohman, M.D., whose article on "Girlish Boys and Boyish Girls" appeared in a 1941 issue of *Ladies' Home Journal*, but girls who took boyishness too far were playing with fire. Wise parents didn't permit these problem children "to dress boyishly, or to play as an equal in boys' games." They knew, as sure as Dr. Hohman did, that too much masculinity in their daughters would "lessen the chances for happy adjustment to some extent—even if it is not followed to the ultimate extremes" (the "ultimate" being that old bugaboo homosexuality, of course). A touch of boyish behavior was a little mustard on an otherwise bland sandwich, but any more made the whole recipe unpalatable. After all, the real work of girlhood was becoming a woman, not a man.

Even so, masculine influence exerted by a little girl's father played an important role when it came to her gender role development. This went further than praising her early attempts at baking and sewing. Girls needed the boundaries of their father's masculinity in order to fully define themselves as feminine, not to mention help them understand their future position as women in relation to men. In other words, a little girl practiced her arsenal of womanly skills on her father, and his reactions to such behavior either helped her to accept or drove her to reject her future role as wife, mother, and homemaker. "Noted authorities on women's life cycle" Lawrence K. and Mary Frank wrote in their booklet *How to Be a Woman* (1954) that a girl achieved true femininity "only by giving and getting honest responses in her associations with men." Even a small girl would "sense and respond" to Daddy's masculinity by acting more feminine. But if she felt rebuffed in her attempts, if Daddy reacted with less than admiring attention or, worse, if he treated her like a boy, the consequences were immediate, jarring, and out of her control. She might become "more athletic than she wants to be, more Spartan than she feels about her cuts and bruises," in short, less like a girl than a boy. Later in her life, this conflict would make dating and contact with the opposite sex difficult. Shying from her traditional role in pursuit of masculinity, she would be forced to compete with men in the job force, with disastrous results. Sociologist L. Guy Brown quoted one of these "deserters from the marriage process" in a 1949 article:

> My father wanted a son, since he felt that great contributions to scientific progress can be made only by men. . . . I am a research chemist, but a poor female specimen. . . . I want to be a woman.[6]

Chickie's Story—A Tomboy Makes Good

To get our minds off that tragic tale, let's look at the story of one girl's "happy adjustment" to femininity. Surely the experts smiled on Patricia Crossman's "Walk Toward Tomorrow," which appeared in the October 1966 issue of *Good Housekeeping* magazine. The poignant story of a tomboy "taking her first step toward growing up to be a treasured woman," twelve-year-old Charlotte, called "Chickie" by almost everyone but her mother, dresses in "loose sweat shirts and dungarees" and is embarrassed by "the developing bulges in her figure." She is a "dependable bunter, a so-so shortstop, a natural at broad jumping, and the best tree climber" in her neighborhood. One day, her best friend, Stewart, confesses that he and his brother, Douglas, plan to walk the narrow railing on the bridge when the three of them go to the movies that Saturday. So Chickie secretly practices walking the rail herself. The big day dawns foggy and wet. Despite Chickie's protests, her mother makes her wear "really neat pants and a clean sweater." The rail is slippery, but the boys climb up anyway. They take no notice of Chickie, following on the rail some twenty feet behind. Startled by the blast of a ship's horn from the river below, the boys tumble to the pedestrian walkway. "They couldn't

make it," Chickie realizes in a burst of self-awareness and growing confidence. "But I can!" Alas, she doesn't. Instead, she hesitates before the
boys see her, "sensing that to beat the boys would somehow be losing
instead of winning." Following the rules given in practically every midcentury dating guide, she jumps down to cheer them on: "You guys were
going great! That crazy siren is enough to throw anybody off balance! Are
you going back up?" Thus challenged, the boys take to the railing once
again, while Chickie walks on ahead. Nearing the end of the walkway,
she looks back in time to see the boys trot to the end of the railing in tri-
umph: "Chickie felt rockets bursting in her chest. It's better than if I did
it myself, she thought wonderingly."

Better than if I did it myself?!? Oh, Chickie, how could you? But her
transformation from brave, athletic tomboy to formless glob of femininity
isn't over yet. "Wow!" she gushes. "That was great. You guys getting up
there again. I couldn't look. I mean—I was scared!" Such self-effacement
has to be rewarded, of course, and so Douglas holds her elbow firmly as
they cross the street: "You're quite a girl, Charlotte. . . . You look great.
You know that? The way you ought to—like a girl."

One can only assume Chickie ran right home and threw all those icky
boy clothes away forever, in favor of fluffy petticoats, a full arsenal of
foundation garments, and dreams of a teenage marriage.

Oh, Daddy! Flirtation and Other Games for Girls

Thus, by story's end, Chickie learned to exploit an important attribute of
femininity: the ability to flirt. According to the Franks, this was a natural
trait, one of the ways in which little girls responded to their father's masculinity. "You probably have seen little girls of 2 or 3 playing up to their
fathers. They flirt. They coax." The Franks weren't the only ones who
noticed this phenomenon. Arlene Dahl didn't have any fancy diplomas,
but as we've already seen in her book *Always Ask a Man*, she considered

herself an expert on the subject of femininity, and encouraged young women to play up their "natural" aptitude for flirtation:

> Every woman is an actress. (Admit it!) Her first role is that of a coquette. (If you have any doubts, just watch a baby girl with her father.) . . . If you are a schoolgirl, flatter your father. Discard those blue jeans and dress up for him when he comes home.

Thank heaven for little girls, indeed! Beauty expert Eve Nelson also commented on the coquettish nature of girl children: "Even before a tiny 'she' begins to walk, the first man she makes a beeline for is her Daddy." Perhaps this was the logic behind Ideal's Saucy Walker doll. While the 1952 ad proclaimed she "Does Everything!" a closer reading made it clear the palette of Miss Saucy Walker's activities was rather limited after all: mostly, she walked and flirted. Not to underestimate the power of flirtation, of course. Just as Daddy found it impossible to resist his tiny flirt's demands, so too could a future husband be coaxed into all sorts of useful behaviors, from asking her out on a date to buying her a new Frigidaire.

Bearing in mind how important it was for little girls to learn their first lessons in womanhood at an early age, it's not surprising that board games that encouraged prepubescent girls to play at dating were so popular. What better way to learn the ropes when it came to the opposite sex than with a game like Mystery Date—the bestselling girls' game of the 1960s?

Chances are if you were anywhere near a television set on a Saturday morning in 1966 or so, you too harbor a memory of this game's devilishly catchy advertising jingle: "Mystery Date / Are you ready for your Mystery Date? / Don't be late / It must be great / Open the door for your [sigh] Mystery Date."

The big moment, and the stroke of genius behind this game, came when one landed on the space marked "OPEN THE DOOR?" If you were holding a complete outfit of matching clothing and accessories, it was time to open the plastic three-dimensional "Mystery Door" in the center of the game board. Behind the door was a photograph of the

Beach Date (in shorts and Hawaiian shirt, with cooler, towel, and beach umbrella), the Ski Date (in form-fitting ski pants that cannot hide his muscular thighs . . .), the Formal Date (in white dinner jacket and red carnation—could that be a corsage for you in the box he's holding?), or the Bowling Date (alas, this guy looks like he's a member of the Future CPAs of America club). There was also what the instructions refer to as "The Pest," colloquially known as "The Dud." Dressed in a thermal shirt and work pants and boots, he was supposed to be the bad date, the one who could, according to the directions, cause a player to "lose valuable time getting rid of him." However, the Dud kind of resembled a bus-and-truck version of Mel Gibson. I'd much rather take my chances with him than the Bowling Geek any day—but only if Mr. Hunky Thighs Ski Date was unavailable.

I doubt if I'm the only female who felt this way about the Dud. I'm sure that millions of young girls the world over formed their first romantic fantasy around him. Certainly more than one bad relationship has been explained away by an early attraction to the Dud.

This wasn't the only problem caused by the Dud's inclusion in the game. Milton Bradley received so many complaints from mothers who felt their sons resembled the Dud that he and the other dates were replaced with drawings in the 1970s.

So there you are—you've opened the door to find Mr. Ski Date waiting for you, and, horror of horrors, you're holding a bathing suit, formal bag and shoes, and a parka. You're not ready. Damn. You roll the die and continue to move around the game board, picking up, discarding, and swapping accessory cards and opening the door. The first girl to open the door to the appropriate date while holding the proper three accessory cards wins!

Sadly, I never owned the Mystery Date game, but every day at lunch I carried a Campus Queen lunchbox. Not only did the lunch box and its matching thermos feature a freshly bouffanted debutante and her fratboy date, but the back of the box was printed with a game. I wasn't the least bit interested in boys or dating at that age, but thanks to the back of my lunchbox, I knew that having your boyfriend call was a very good thing (you got to spin again) and that having your hem come down on your prom dress was something you didn't want to happen (you had to wait one turn to fix it). And, of course, becoming campus queen was the best thing of all, because that meant you won the game!

There were still other board games that revolved around dating. There was Miss Popularity, where the player who filled her bulletin board with the most social events won. Barbie Queen of the Prom had similarities to Mystery Date in that it involved buying clothes in order to get ready for a date. Shopping, dating, and "school activities" all figured prominently. These games were tailor-made for girls going through that hideous first flush of adolescence, when everybody looks weird, with braces and glasses and bodies that grow too much in one direction and not enough in another, and everyone begins to wonder, "Am I normal?" Therein lies the games' appeal: they are the armchair version of dating, a much less

Wow! Pillow Fight Game for Girls

Wow! was a rare bird in the world of girls' games, as its object was neither dating nor consumerism. Instead, it featured good old-fashioned American aggression. The locale was a pretend pajama party, with the game board divided into one pink and one blue "room." Players used plastic bed-shaped catapults to lob tiny pink or blue fabric pillows over the divider at each other in an attempt to knock down the greatest number of cardboard "girls" and/or the "housemother" from the other side. The first player to capture all the opponent's girls and housemother was the winner.

Wow! was "safe" for girls, as the box copy noted, because its "fast action" was one step removed from the real thing. It may have been dangerously tomboyish to whomp your pal with a pillow in real life, but tossing a miniature fake pillow at a miniature fake girl was simply good, clean fun.

frightening version of real life. Of course, by placing all the emphasis on looks and the all-important boyfriend, these games also had the potential to make awkward social misfits feel even more alienated. We knew, after all, from playing the little kids' card game of the same name, that one never wanted to get stuck with an Old Maid.

Dating was not the only womanly skill board games taught little girls. Games like Cut-Up (a "shopping spree game") and Park and Shop (the object was to find a parking place, shop the fastest, and get back home first) taught both the American way of consumerism and another time-honored feminine role: that of shopper. At mid-century, the ideal house-wife was responsible for the efficient budgeting of her family's money. Why, you couldn't even win the Miss Popularity game unless you retained possession of the credit card issued to each player at the start!

I Want to Be . . . a Housewife or a Career Girl? Part 1

Of course, being a woman wasn't all dating and shopping. There was serious work—housework!—to be done. From toy toasters to child-sized carpet sweepers, homemaking toys have long provided what the 1962 catalogue copy for the Little Sweetheart Ironing Board Set called "safe fun for little house wives-to-be." Colonial girls played with tea sets imported from England, and readers of Louisa May Alcott's 1870 novel *Little Men* will recall Daisy's cunning play kitchen (complete with wood-burning stove and a host of other now-too-dangerous details). Toy train maker Lionel advertised a "real electric range" in 1930, while fashionable girls of the mid-1950s played with a miniature plastic version of designer Russel Wright's American Modern dinnerware.

In 1964, Kenner introduced perhaps the most well-known of all homemaking toys: the lighbulb-heated Easy-Bake Oven. An immediate success, the oven sold more than 500,000 units in its first year on the market and opened the door for copy-cat products like the aqua and white Suzy Homemaker line of toys. In fact, open any 1960s-era toy cat-

Housework Is Child's Play !

Housework is child's play . . . so get to work! Housekeeping toys, 1966.

alogue, and you will see pages of happy little homemakers playing with a full range of miniaturized cleaning tools and kitchen appliances—some fully functional, others make-believe, but all of them claiming to be "just like mother's."

Again, proper training in early childhood was the key to success in later life—and these toys were an important part of the scenario. When essayist Louise Paine Benjamin asked readers in 1947, "Is Your Little Girl a Good Wife?" she equated "good wife" with "good housekeeper." According to Benjamin's scenario, a child's curiosity trapped her in a life of drudgery: "Almost as soon as babyhood is over, a little girl's natural interest in what her mother is doing all day paves the way for the first steps in a homemaking partnership." Child-sized pots and pans, brooms, dust mops, and vacuum cleaners made it fun for girls to go from playing alongside Mommy to performing real housekeeping chores on their own—at least in theory. However, the benefits were more than a clean house, according to Benjamin, who demonstrated that housekeeping skills increased a young woman's value in the marriage market:

> They will know how to whip up a tasty meal, a new dress, knit a sweater, clean a chicken, turn a shirt collar or paint a living room. Better yet, they will probably be gay and workman-deft about it—proving, as always, that a woman's skill and interest in her home life can be just as stimulating and ego-rewarding as a successful profession in the business world.[7]

Stimulating, ego-rewarding, and, not coincidentally, husband-pleasing.

The same lessons girls learned with their tiny pots, pans, and brooms were reinforced in a 1961 storybook for young girls. Carla Greene's *I Want to Be a Homemaker* tells the story of Jane, who moves into her brand-new playhouse with her dog and three dolls. "I sweep and dust and wash and iron," says Jane. "I try to be a good homemaker." In the pages that follow, Jane learns about cooking, first-aid, and interior decorating. The denouement? When little Tom from next door asks her what she wants to be when she grows up, Jane answers, "I'm going to be a cook, cleaner, nurse, teacher and an artist" because "a good homemaker is all of those things."

Of course, in the pink-thinking past homemaker was considered the only "true" career for a woman. If a woman had to work outside the home due to money woes or preference (some of the advice writers grudgingly admitted this was possible), then she could best retain her womanliness by bringing femininity to the job site or choosing a career that otherwise exploited feminine traits. For example, *I Want to Be a Telephone Operator* (1958) explained that when "girls learn to be operators . . . they must be polite," and make a career asset out of the sort of subservient behavior pink think rewarded. Other jobs represented in the *I Want to Be* series included professions that were generally considered to be "woman's work" because they drew on feminine skills and servitude usually associated with housewifery and childcare: *I Want to Be a Teacher* (1957), *I Want to Be a Librarian* (1960), *I Want to Be a Nurse* (1957), *I Want to Be an Airline Hostess* (1960).

I Want to Be a Beauty Operator (1970) explained the ins and outs of a mostly female occupation and reinforced the importance of personal appearance with another case of tomboy turned Girl. "How can a plain potato girl have any fun at a girl-boy party?" asks jeans-wearing, tree-climbing Jane. "I am a mess," she tells Mother (who is glad to know Jane "at last" cares about how she looks). Luckily, Miss Kay, a beauty operator, is coming to lunch. Difficult Jane doesn't want to go to the beauty parlor and "be made over into something that I am not." Nevertheless, cooler heads prevail, and before you know it, she's back from the salon wearing full girl-drag: dress, mary janes, and a ribbon in her newly cut hair. Just in case there was any question, the text pointed out that "she looked much better" that way. Her makeover complete, little Jane has seen the light. "It must be wonderful to help people like this," she says ecstatically.

Little Girl Glamour: First Lessons in Charm and Beauty

A gal's beauty problems began early—with skin ailments like baby acne and cradle cap. But that was only the start. In her *Guide to Glamor* (1957), Eleanore King recommended training girls in "correct posture and proper standing and sitting habits . . . *as early as they can understand, usually around three years of age*" (italics in the original). Female children between the ages of six and twelve, King reported, "were as eager to do the graceful thing as their older sisters or mothers," especially if they were properly rewarded:

> If your child seems nervous or fidgety, teach her to assume one standing position in the middle of the room, away from furniture, and to hold it for several minutes at a time. Give her a special reward or merit for each

accomplishment. Oh! the wonder a ten cent package of gold stars can create when awarded star by star for deserved and earned merit. This is the finest poise training you can give her.[8]

When good little girls finished standing in the middle of the room, they could play with Ideal's "Doll of Beauty," which taught beauty care with its "exclusive 'Magic Flesh'—specially made for doll make-up." The Doll of Beauty was just one of an assortment of girls' toys and dolls dedicated to the cosmetic arts, as amply illustrated by numerous department store toy catalogues of the era. There were vanity tables whose drawers bulged with play lipsticks and nail polishes, the perfect complements to an afternoon of make-believe in the child-sized prom dresses or wedding gowns advertised on the same pages. Hair care seemed to be a particular favorite: toy beauty parlors came sized to fit both dolls and their owners, and if a girl's hair care skills were less than perfect, well, there were always those helmet-like plastic wigs.

While brand allegiance training for future housewives of America really took off during high school home economics classes, the beauty toys provided an opportunity to begin instilling loyalty in young consumers-to-be. Many of these toys, for example, featured miniaturized versions of real products. A special pajama party overnight case might contain tiny packages of brand-name cold cream and tissues, or a toy home permanent set include the same type of chemicals that Mom used.

But why play at beauty when you could study it? Charm schools offered girls and women classes in grooming, make-up, dress, deportment, and poise. They were separate from modeling schools, though some charm schools taught modeling skills, and vice versa. Some offered training in secretarial skills and offered job placement to their graduates. While most students were between their teens and early thirties, it wasn't unusual to find preteens attending special classes just for them. There were franchised charm schools like the John Robert Powers School, as well as local enterprises such as New York's Fifth Avenue School of Modeling and Charm (which offered "Special Pre-Teen Courses" in the mid-1960s).[9] Charm schools weren't cheap. In 1960, a seven-week charm course for preteen girls based in Tampa, Florida, cost $50—roughly $300 in 2001 dollars.[10]

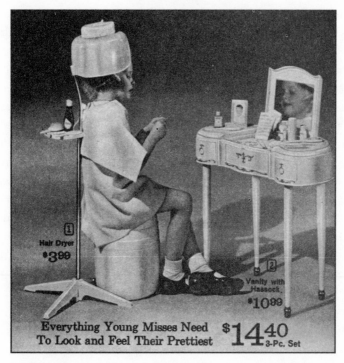

Everything Young Misses Need
To Look and Feel Their Prettiest $14.40 3-Pc. Set

Lessons in beauty and branding, 1966. The vanity came with a "children's cosmetic set" featuring the same products Mom used.

Charm school proper wasn't the only place for girls to receive instruction in the arcane arts of femininity and brand allegiance. In the mid-1950s, the Breck shampoo corporation, in conjunction with the Girls Clubs of America, developed a program of good grooming and manners for girls aged nine to twelve. The course's *Handbook of Charm* emphasized "lustrous, well-kept hair" as "a must at any age to feminine beauty and charm. The earlier in life a girl comes to realize this, the better." Therefore, the book devoted a great deal of its content to hair care—"one of the most important phases of the entire Charm Course. Unless the girls can be impressed with this fact and become really interested in learning the principles of proper hair care, they cannot hope to 'graduate' from the course with a full measure of satisfaction." The course's altruistic aim was to make sure girls learned "to conform to the accepted social pattern of appearance and behavior."

Department stores also took advantage of the opportunity to direct young minds and pocketbooks, offering fashion shows and charm courses on occasion. Pity the poor preteens who spent weekends or vacation time learning to "take one giant step from the never-never land of make believe into the ever-ever land of charm and beauty," in Montgomery Wards' "Crossroads to Charm" course. According to the course handbook, "authored" by corporate spokesgirl Wendy Ward, the "growing-up road" led straight ahead; a wrong turn meant you might become that horror of horrors, a "late charmer." The course emphasized ladylike deportment, good grooming, and, of course, the proper wardrobe.

For those who preferred listening to records in the privacy of their rooms to a trip to the local Wards store, there was also "The 20 Day Wendy Way to Charm," a vinyl version of the course narrated by the mascot herself. "Hello there . . . I'm Wendy Ward. Beauty is learned . . . and earned . . . you'll never find it sitting on a mushroom" is the cryptic slogan printed on side two's label. Girls were supposed to listen to the record every morning for twenty days, consulting the accompanying "Passport to Charm." According to Wendy and crew, charm is "a perfect blend of outer and inner graciousness." Their advice runs from a recommendation that fattening foods be thought of as "ugly pills," to the suggestion that "the next time you feel the urge to be rude, remember that rudeness is the devil's gift to a self-conscious girl, and you don't want people to think you're self conscious." The advice started getting a little thin around Day Number 8, when the daily assignment was to "try a new food." Although the record is from 1963, Wards held the in-store version of the course for another twenty years or so.

Perhaps the experts were so obsessive because puberty loomed ahead. The teen years were the experts' last best chance to mold young minds before surging hormones completely disrupted the process.

Chapter 2

Adolescence: The Magic Years of Pink

[Y]ou can and should pursue your own interests and always do your best, but not to the disadvantage of that boy in your life, whether he be your date, your steady or someday . . . your husband.

From "The Secret of Being Feminine," *For Teens Only, February 1963*

T he pinnacle of the semester-long martyrdom that was my junior high school home economics class was reached the day that a girl from the local John Robert Powers modeling school came to class to talk to us about "charm"—an elusive quality that apparently involved posture as well as personality. This perky young woman assumed I cared so much about ladylike deportment that she chose me to help demonstrate the portion of the lecture devoted to "How to Properly Seat One-self." "Go ahead," she said, "and sit down." I obliged her, seating myself at the table the teacher had helpfully provided at the front of the room.

"Now," she chortled triumphantly, "if you lean forward like that, he'll see everything!"

At the time I wanted to die. In retrospect, however, I think several current obsessions can be traced to this traumatic moment in my adolescence—for example, my love of Rusty "Bounce Your Boobies" Warren, my fascination with pinup girl June "The Bosom" Wilkinson, and my desperate need to find a perfectly pointy 1950s bra. Oh, yes, and my collection of home ec textbooks, begun with a thrift shop copy of *Homemaking for Teen-Agers* (1966).

What I was supposed to have taken away from my experience in front of the class was its intended lesson in femininity. After all, the teen years were an especially important time for girls to develop the proper attitude toward womanhood. Because heterosexual relationships, marriage, and motherhood were first among pink think's goals, it was important to guide girls' behavior regarding boys and dating before nature took its course. Young women needed to understand their roles as soon-to-be wives and mothers and act accordingly. "Girls must," a 1955 home economics text called *Family Living* told its teen readers, "learn the feminine role and feel positive about approaching womanhood if their adult lives are to be completely satisfying."[1]

The Secrets of Being Feminine

I suspect that "Am I progressing satisfactorily toward womanhood?" was a question teens rarely asked themselves. It was, nonetheless, an opening salvo in a "revealing personality test" which appeared in the October 1962 issue of *For Teens Only* magazine. Of course, girls have always worried about when they'd get their first period or when their breasts would appear, but this question and the ones that followed it had little to do with bodily changes. Instead, a reader was to rate herself from 1 to 10 on a series of statements, such as "She is friendly with boys, but she's not too forward" or "She does her best (by grooming, diet, exercise, etc.) to make herself attractive." Once she had done that, the next step was to ask four friends to rate her, anonymously, on the same thirty-five questions. The resulting data pinpointed a girl's strong and weak points, according to the magazine. Why put yourself through such an ordeal? Because "[t]he better you understand yourself . . . the better a girl you will be—and the happier a woman you will become!"

Being feminine was the cornerstone of female success and happiness (that is, marriage and mating), and the sooner girls learned its rules, the better. Femininity was important, Bernice Bryant explained in *Miss Behavior* (1948), because *"the normal boy is attracted to the completely feminine girl"* while the normal girl liked *"a man who is completely masculine, the direct opposite of you"* (emphasis in original). Sharp gender role divisions made for happy future marriages because "[t]he more the young woman has been trained to be feminine and to abstain from activities regarded as masculine, and the more the groom has been reared to be masculine and protected from the values of the world of women, the greater the cleavage between the two in marriage."[2]

It wasn't enough just being born female. True femininity "meant thinking like a girl even when you're not with a boy on a date," knowing how to "fix broken hems and missing buttons," and helping out at parties by picking up an "overflowing ashtray, or dripping drink."[3] Men expected a certain level of competence in the kitchen, too. What if "your date turned up proudly one day with a fish he had just caught? And if he asked you to cook it?" wondered *The Co-Ed Cookbook* (1967). You might laugh off that incident, but not knowing how to cook might have serious future consequences; after all, "someday it will be your job to get *him* off to work every morning, and he won't be able to do his best work on a cup of coffee and a donut."

According to the experts, feminine girls were popular girls. While boys had to do little more than be polite and go out for sports to attain the holy grail of high school life known as popularity, girls had to be self-effacing in a way that was often equated with femininity. "Like a competent secretary, the popular girl anticipates the needs and requests of her friends," wrote Alfred Murray in *Youth's Courtship Problems* (1940). A popular girl was always "understanding and sympathetic," "good-natured and cheerful," and considered others "at all times in all circumstances."[4] She was "helpful and considerate" and said "only nice things" about friends and classmates.[5] Likewise, the feminine girl felt "her own emotions more sharply" and was "quick to sense the reactions of others," which allowed her to "spare hurt feelings."[6]

Cleanliness and daintiness reflected a girl's femininity and self-esteem: "Any girl who slops around in dirty sneakers, cuts her hair with the kitchen shears, and fastens her skirt with a safety pin is broadcasting the fact that she doesn't think much of herself. Maybe she really *is* too busy reading Jean-Paul Sartre and dissecting frogs to bother with mundane little things like pushing back her cuticles—but I doubt it," griped the author of *A New You* (1965).

Femininity required a specific set of behaviors—girls who followed the rules were feminine, and those who didn't, weren't. Take, for example, the story of petite, bright-eyed Kit and tall, capable Dinah, as related in *Miss Behavior*. The girls were dishing up ice cream, milk, and candy at a special French Club party to honor new members, when three boys entered the kitchen. "Please come help me," called Dinah. "I can't open the milk can." The boys rushed to help, but before they reached her, "Kit, the nitwit, ran to the can and said, 'I'll open it.'"

> No sooner had she pried off the lid than she hoisted the heavy container to the table, heaved it to its side and poured the contents into a giant pitcher.
>
> And those three big males turned away helpless and hurt.
>
> Where did they turn? Guess?
>
> Dinah had moved to another table where she was struggling with the cellophane candy wrappers . . .[7]

In helping Dinah unwrap and serve the candy, the boys "began to act like men." This was one of the cardinal rules where femininity was concerned: boys needed girls to be feminine in order for them to feel masculine.

One-third of the boys contacted by *Teens Today* for a special 1959 issue devoted to "What Boys Think About You" asked a girl for a first date based on her femininity. "Lots of times," one of their respondents noted, "I ask a girl out because she has a way of acting like I'm eight feet tall and strong as a bull." One "Secret of Being Feminine" as revealed in a 1963 article in *For Teens Only* magazine was that "when a boy finds the girl he wants to marry, it will be because he feels manly with her. He knows that with her, he will be 'head of the house.' " Similarly, boys enjoyed being with a popular girl because "in her company, they feel more manly, cleverer, or better than they feel with other girls."[8]

Boys also brought out the femininity in girls:

> The girl who is feminine *wants* the man to lead her—it's as simple as that. She craves being a helpmate to him, and these are the qualities that make her so desirable. She likes being with a boy because he brings out these feelings in her.[9]

Perhaps this is why boys' opinions weighed so heavily. Teen magazines devoted pages and pages to what boys did and didn't like about girls' appearance and behavior. Boys reported they liked "neat, clean-looking . . . well-scrubbed" girls.[10] Ninety percent of the boys contacted by *Teens Today* said that a girl who "really overdoes both make-up and the too-tight-sweater bit" appeared "easy." Of course, eighty percent admitted looking at these girls, "but none of them wanted their own girls to wear [tight sweaters]. Besides, as an Iowa senior said, 'Let's face it: if a girl's got a body that's worth showing off, fellows will notice. She doesn't have to try to knock a guy's eyes out!' "[11]

On the other hand, boys didn't want girls wearing sweaters that were too loose, either. In February 1961 *Teens Today* presented a meticulously detailed, rhyming description of the "Boys *Dis*approve Look," which noted that "a girl who wishes his varsity letter, doesn't appear in a stretched-out sweater!"[12]

Even frankly fictitious boys' opinions found their way into the maga-

"You can spread the word that a little fancy frosting never hurt a cake." Thoughts on girlish glamour from "Chuck," 1947.

zines. Chuck, a "dark hunk of muscle with a slow motion grin," sold girls Arrid deodorant in a 1947 ad headlined "Take it from THE BOYS":

> Jeepers, says Chuck, . . . I like to date the Eye Tonics. You can spread the word that a little fancy frosting never hurt a cake. And take it from me, it's strictly a dumb play for a girl to skip her glamour homework. Those now-and-theners don't rate with me . . . I'm for the filly with an even pace.

Chuck's words were no less improbable than some of those presented as coming from the mouths of honest-to-goodness boys. Did these panels of oh-so-appropriate young men really exist, or were they just a good excuse to reinforce adult ideals of teen girl behavior? The "mature high school senior" quoted in *Thresholds to Adult Living* certainly didn't sound like any adolescent males I knew. When asked what "the average seventeen or eighteen year old boy expects from a girl on a date," he responded:

> For myself, I'm looking for a good time—good companionship. . . . Of course, I'm a human being. I have certain physical desires, and if I can quench that desire with a good night kiss, that's all right as far as I'm concerned—until I'm ready to get married. . . . Actually, the requirements for a good time on a date are practically the same as for a wife.[13]

Who could have guessed that when it came to girls, housewifery skills were uppermost in the minds of America's teenage boys? "Sure, I look for a good time on a date," *Teens Today* quoted a boy in 1959, "but I look for something else, too. Like is the girl still a giddybrain, or could she manage a house and a couple of kids." The purpose of dating, after all, was not to see the latest movie or learn the latest dance craze but to "learn a little more about your femininity and your date's masculinity," the better to assess a partner for marriage.[14]

Contradictory information was a hallmark of pink think. For example, in one 1961 issue of *TEEN* magazine, readers were told that wearing tight sweaters and dresses was a tactic employed only by the desperately boy crazy. A few pages later, however, the repentant tomboy protagonist of a story called "Act Like a Girl!" not only puts on a form-fitting swimsuit in a hopeful ploy to dazzle the boy of her choice but does so with her mother's blessing: "As a mother I suppose I should say, 'Penny, you're not being very ladylike.' But as a woman I'm going to say, 'Go get 'im, honey.'"[15] The result? Penny comes home from the pool having snagged both a Friday night movie date and one to next week's club picnic.

Because a really feminine girl knew "a boy feels good" when he took out a girl who looked and acted nice, she would "go out of [her] way to give him this feeling."[16] But what if the girl in question didn't quite fit into the experts' restrictive definition of femininity?

Fatty Fiction

Even if a girl followed all the rules of femininity, she still might find herself excluded from the experts' ideal. Being overweight, for example, called one's femininity into question. "It's hard to picture a girl of large build being quite feminine, yet many chubby girls have very pleasing tendencies," wrote advice columnist Dolly Martin, as if she couldn't quite believe it herself.[17] Adah Broadbent taught a high school course in which girls "learn[ed] to redesign themselves and others." Imagine, if you will, the pecking party that resulted when Broadbent opened season on the less-than-slender with the following edict from her book *Teen-Age Glamor* (1955): "If you are a fatty, you aren't a beau-catcher."

Fictional fat girls were also subject to the consequences of not fitting the mold. My first encounter with "fatty fiction" occurred when I was in grade school. I can't remember much of the story I read in a children's magazine, but the ending has stayed with me ever since: The chunky young protagonist, having cut out her daily after-school milkshake, is slated to appear at her sister's wedding as a "slim young junior bridesmaid." I may have been all of eight years old, but I was instantly horrified and ashamed. All those fountain treats I so skillfully whipped up with my Suzy Homemaker blender had had an unintended effect, and now the kids at school sang out "Fatty, fatty, two by four, can't get through the kitchen door" when they saw me coming. Unlike the girl in the story, however, I wasn't losing any weight. She was a slim, young junior bridesmaid. I was a lumpy, grumpy preadolescent hiding out from the real world in children's fiction, a refuge that was cruelly snatched away by this impertinent story. Its moral, after all, was clear: Thin was better.

Almost thirty weight-obsessed years later, I picked up a copy of Marguerite Vance's *Secret for a Star* (1957) in a used-book store, and the memory came flooding back. After all, *Secret for a Star* shared the earlier story's basic plot: A fat girl loses weight and all of her problems are solved. But there was more. Its subtly judgmental cover copy billed *Secret for a Star* as the "warm, touching story of a girl's recognition of her own responsibility in controlling her weight," as if to do otherwise was somehow a reprehensible moral lapse.

Secret for a Star is a prime example of fatty fiction. Aimed at teens and preteens, this genre generally focuses on a female protagonist who is unhappy or otherwise socially maladjusted because she is fat. The plot hinges on her struggles to lose weight, and the denouement is reached when the young girl achieves her goal. Along the way, her emotional and social problems are resolved, the result (overtly or not) of her weight loss. Fatty fiction flourished from the 1950s to the early 1980s, when anorexia nervosa became the malady du jour for teen novels.

A random reading of fatty fiction produces many similarities. For example, fictional fat girls often have dead or otherwise missing parents. The short stories "The Size 10 Dress," by Cynthia Lawrence (which appeared in a 1962 children's book called *Here's Barbie*), and "Good-bye, Old Laura," by Lucile Vaughan Payne (published in the June 1955 issue of *Seventeen*), featured motherless girls. In the course of Isabelle Holland's *Heads You Win, Tails I Lose* (1973), Melissa's father walks out on her mother, who immediately reverts to alcoholic behavior. The suggestion here seems to be that with "proper" (two-parent, male-head-of-household) parenting, the children wouldn't be fat in the first place. Instead, these young protagonists veer from the accepted course of alimentary self-control just as their broken families deviate from the nuclear standard. On the other hand, orphanhood sometimes acts as a punishment for obesity. Nowhere is this more clear than in *Secret for a Star*, where poor plump Prudence's mother and father are killed in a car accident while she spends the afternoon making cookies!

Another coincidence is the frequency with which fat girl protagonists long for careers on the stage. After practically offing her parents with her baking, *Secret for a Star*'s Prudence wows the audience at her high school play, then loses weight and becomes an overnight Broadway sensation. Meanwhile, in *Heads You Win*, Melissa is at a rehearsal for her school's production of *Antigone* when her prolonged popping of mom's diet pills finally catches up with her ("Wild colors were swirling around inside and outside my head . . ."). These girls live out a fantasy life onstage, restricted as they are in "real life" by the contours of their bodies.

There's also the implication that fat girls shouldn't be the center of attention, no matter how much they would like to be. Melissa's stage appearance is a debacle, and Prudence chooses to lose weight only after a talent scout tells her she must do so in order to live up to her innate thespian talents. Similarly, Big Bertha of "The Size 10 Dress" doesn't appear on the school fashion show stage until she's lost weight and been humiliated in the eyes of her fellow students for presuming to wear the same dress and hairstyle as Barbie. But even that isn't punishment enough, and Bertha finds herself eclipsed at the penultimate moment of the show by Her Nibs. After a last-minute makeover during which "the fabulous Barbie" changes Bertha's hair-do and accessories, her copycat look is partially defused. Depending on your level of cynicism, this either "saves the day" or puts poor Bertha squarely back in her place. As she and Barbie walk hand in hand down the fashion show aisle, sewing class teacher Miss Salinger notes that it "only goes to show that any smart girl can take a style and make it her own." We know she's not talking about Bertha, whose unsuccessful attempt to unseat Barbie as top doll suggests once a fat girl, always a fat girl.

Works of fatty fiction, and the teen-interest magazines in which they were likely to appear, did little to resolve conflicting messages about weight. "Good-bye, Old Laura" appeared in the same issue of *Seventeen* as a weight-loss plan that included a daily one-third pint of ice cream. And readers left positively famished by reading about Prudence's diet in *Secret for a Star* could run to the kitchen and whip up a batch of her Old Sailor's Fudge, using the recipe helpfully printed on page 185.

Just as in real life, fictional fatties suffer taunts and insults from classmates, strangers, and parents. Alas, they rarely fight back. (True, *Secret for a Star*'s Prudence throws a catsup-smeared shrimp at vile society jerk Laura Van Duzen when she insults Prue's dead parents, but Prue later writes a formal note of apology.) In "Good-bye, Old Laura," the titular heroine adopts the persona of "funny fat girl" and throws party after party for her gang as a ploy to stay close to Jim Roberts, who hasn't a clue of her romantic daydreams. Luckily, Laura's repressed emotions burst to the surface in a most entertaining fashion.

> "Golly, I'm thirsty!" Sue Price laughed [and] let the dazzle of her blond hair brush Jim Roberts' shoulder. "Jim, you are the most *marvelous* dancer—I need a Coke—hey, Fatsy, dear, how about a Coke?"
>
> . . . [Laura] felt nothing but rage, pure rage, and her hand around the glass was as cold as the icy drink she poured.
>
> "You wanted a Coke—" The liquid seemed to spring through the air, a carbonated arc, straight at the pretty, astonished face, the tempting red mouth, fizzing and spattering as it hit the white dress. "Try that," said Laura. "And keep your cute nicknames to yourself after this!"

Alas, more frequently, the heroines of fatty fiction don't lash out, no matter how big the insult. When the chubby protagonists lose their weight, they lose their anger. They become thin and nondisruptive, the better to "fit in," both literally and otherwise. *Heads You Win* ends with a newly slender heroine figuratively joining the patriarchy, walking into the sunset with her estranged father. In "The Size 10 Dress," Bertha's appearance at the school fashion show signals the end of her attempt to usurp Barbie's dominant position. And while lesser girls couldn't be blamed for using their newfound fame to teach a well-deserved lesson to all those who had insulted them in the past, *Secret for a Star*'s Prudence simply murmurs, "Isn't life strange? Goodness, I guess I'll try to go to sleep now."

Home Economics: Indoctrinating Homemakers

As a real-life fat girl in 1974, I might have been less perturbed at being called to the front of the home ec classroom had I known a little of the discipline's history. Although my experience with the Powers girl that day seems to indicate otherwise, the course of study that eventually became known as home economics was originally a nineteenth-century effort to raise the status of women's work within the home. With the publication of books like *A Treatise on Domestic Economy* (1841), writer and educator Catharine Beecher defined domesticity for generations to come. Reflecting the prevailing nineteenth-century gender ideology that men and women inhabited "separate spheres," Beecher's writings suggested that women be educated for the "honors and duties of the family state" just as men were "trained for their trades and professions."[18] In 1869, Beecher described these social roles in *The American Woman's Home; or Principles of Domestic Science*, a revised and expanded version of the earlier *Treatise*:

> The family state then, is the aptest earthly illustration of the heavenly kingdom, and in it woman is its chief minister. Her great mission is self-denial, in training its members to self-sacrificing labors for the ignorant and weak: if not her own children, then the neglected children of the Father in heaven. . . .
>
> To man is appointed the out-door labor—to till the earth . . . toil in the foundries, traverse the ocean, transport merchandise . . . conduct

civil, municipal and state affairs, and all the heavy work, which, most of the day, excludes him from the comforts of a home.[19]

Woman's role was all the more important because the "great stimulus" to a man's job performance was the "desire for a home of his own, and the hopes of paternity."[20] Consequently, if the little woman didn't shoulder her duty to bear children and maintain the home, the national economy was threatened.

Beecher's ideas about domesticity echoed throughout midcentury home ec texts (not to mention articles in women's magazines and advice books), but it was Ellen Richards who helped mold nineteenth-century domestic science into twentieth-century home economics. A research chemist who was the first female to receive a degree from the Massachusetts Institute of Technology, Richards was interested in both women's education and the field of domestic science.[21] The author of, among other books, *The Chemistry of Cooking and Cleaning* (1880), she put her theories to work at the Boston School of Housekeeping, a former school for servants revamped by Richards into a training ground for household and institutional management.[22] In 1909, Richards and a group of educators founded the American Home Economics Association (AHEA), its object "to improve the conditions of living in the home, the institutional household, and the community."[23]

Such noble ideals faded away with the Progressive Era, and by the 1920s, home economics was increasingly identified with the sort of housewife-in-training courses many of us remember from our teenage years. Hence you might have been stuck in class with a text like *Young Living* (1959), which intended to help students "develop the right attitude toward sharing the responsibilities as well as the pleasures of the home."[24] Clues to this attitude were found in a chapter entitled "What Homemaking Means to Everyone":

"Homemaking" has a lot of meanings. . . . It means learning about yourself so that you can make your home more pleasant, attract more friends, add something special to your home life—just as important as your study, in other classes, of mathematics, your native language and your beloved America and its place in the world. . . . We cannot take our home life for granted. We must all learn the skills of working together to keep our way of living in America the way we want it to be.

It was as if proper homemaking was the only thing standing between Our Way of Life and Godless Communism. What if Nikita Khrushchev came to dinner and you couldn't whip up a batch of cheese-stuffed Glamour Dogs or a Baked Noodle Ring? Would you want to be responsible for our losing the cold war?

Even seemingly innocuous textbooks like *Mealtime* (1960) could be just as dogmatic in their lesson plans. "Family mealtime, with all its associations, is an American tradition that must not be lost," stated author Bess Oerke. She continued to forge the link between home, family, and country in a philosophic chapter entitled "The Meaning of Mealtime":

This chapter is different from the usual first chapter in a foods textbook. . . . It begins with personal feelings and attitudes—so important to any homemaking success. It continues with the subject of "snacks," and their place in today's social plan.

And you thought I was being facetious about the connection between Baked Noodle Ring and patriotism, didn't you?

Sex segregation was a hallmark of home economics classes in the 1950s and 1960s. That didn't exactly mean a "no boys allowed" sign hung on the classroom door but, in 1960, only 2.5 percent of home economics students were male.[25] So, while many home economics texts included boys in their targeted audience, there was no mistaking whom the books were really aimed at. While the preface to the 1967 edition of *Teen Guide to Homemaking* noted that it was "generally agreed that experiences in homemaking education should be made available to both boys and girls," only girls' clothing appeared in the sewing section, and a diagram called "Hair Arrangements for Different Shaped Faces" showed only female heads and faces. In fact, chapters on sewing, cooking, and "good grooming" often dropped the pretense of coeducation altogether, along with any use of masculine pronouns.

It wasn't until the 1970s that traditional almost-girls-only home economics courses disappeared from the curriculum. In fact, I was in one of the last classes of sex-segregated home ec in my junior high school. The following year, in belated response to the passage of Title IX of the Civil Rights Act in 1972 (which prohibited sex segregation in educational programs), both home ec and its boys-only sibling, shop, were coed.[26]

Coeducation wasn't home ec's only response to the changing gender politics of the era. Mindful of the popular conflation of home economics with homemaking, as well as the proto-feminist roots of the profession, in 1973 the AHEA asked radical feminist Robin Morgan to address its national meeting. It must have seemed like a good idea, but imagine the attendees' shock when Morgan excoriated their profession from the podium. Citing home economics' reinforcement of traditional marriage and the nuclear family, along with its "incredible manipulation of women as consumers" as antithetical to the radical women's movement, Morgan declared she was "addressing the enemy" and labeled home economics "the final icing on the cake, the nail in the coffin, after which [a female student] is a limp, gibbering mass of jelly waiting for marriage."[27]

Just as Robin Morgan argued, consumerism had always been a big component of home economics. Indeed, in 1994, the American Home Economics Association changed its name to the American Association of Family and Consumer Sciences. Prudent shopping and wise spending have always been useful skills, but often classroom materials were little more than blatant advertising from corporations once again seeking early brand allegiance from a captive audience. Manufacturers of flour, baking soda, thread, fabric, and toothpaste all produced teaching materials that were advertised in trade publications like *What's New in Home Economics* or *Practical Home Economics*. For example, a 1946 student handout called "Look Lovely Angel" gave helpful hints on "face, figure, fashion, fella(s)," all courtesy of Arrid Cream Deodorant. Procter & Gamble's "Through the Looking Glass to Good Grooming" (1961) was a thick booklet of beauty tips, but its last page advertised P&G's soap, shampoo, deodorant, and laundry products. Procter's pamphlet devoted to "Cakes and Cookies" even went so far as to suggest students bake one cake with butter, another with its Crisco-brand shortening and compare the results. Audio-visual materials were another popular way for manufacturers to put brand names in front of students, as with the Del Monte film strip called "Pictorial Meal Planning" and its wall chart on "creative uses of fruits and vegetables," each of which was accompanied by student leaflets.

While brand allegiance was an important lesson, marriage was the goal to which midcentury home economics trained its students. Virtually all midcentury home ec texts contained sections on married life and child care, and some contained information about budgeting and interior design as well. *Family Living* put it bluntly, "You expect to get married and live happily ever after."[28] "Your own home is really not that far in the future—five or six years for many of you," asserted another text.[29] Even the 1972 edition of *Teen Guide to Homemaking* told its readers, after a discussion of women's changing roles in society, that "it remain[ed] true, and probably always will, that the aim of most girls is to learn to successfully play their roles as wives and mothers."[30]

As magazines and guidebooks for adult women liked to point out, one of a housewife's many duties was helping hubby meet his business potential. Sometimes the skills learned in home ec class directly affected a husband's trip up the corporate ladder. *Young Living* explained the connection between successful housewifery and a husband's professional advancement to its teenage readers:

> Many business firms realize how much people are affected by their home life. For this reason, they often interview the wife as well as the husband before they employ a promising man. The more you know about getting along with others, meeting people, looking your best, and taking care of a family, the better impression you will make.[31]

Thresholds to Adult Living presented a similar, though considerably more dire, scenario:

The importance of being a good wife cannot be emphasized too greatly. For instance, the Air Force has found "a direct correlation between aircraft mishaps and unsettled home life. . . . The husbands get to thinking about rows with the little woman while they are up there and the first thing you know they press the wrong button."

A "bad" wife, one who argued with her husband and caused problems at home, might thus be the cause of accidental nuclear annihilation. On the other hand, *Thresholds to Adult Living*'s author, home economist Hazel Craig, was a bit naïve, to say the least. Consider her suggestion in Chapter 9 ("Marriage Miracles and Mirages") that students correlate information from their English lit classes to "learn something about the childhood, courtship and marriage of some of the writers you are studying at present. Discuss your findings in relation to marriage predictions in this chapter. For instance, Charles Dickens and Oscar Wilde had very unhappy childhoods. Were their marriages affected by these experiences?" I think something other than an unhappy childhood had an effect on Oscar Wilde's marriage—he was, after all, flamboyantly gay.

I Want to Be . . . a Housewife or a Career Girl? Part 2

Despite the clear expectation that most girls would eventually be stay-at-home wives and mothers, there was always a chance that some women would work prior to marriage or perhaps afterward to supplement household income. *Managing Livingtime* (1966) suggested that a college education was a possibility "if you want [it] badly enough," even though it mitigated the statement with a suggestion that "unobtainable" goals be changed.[32] *McCall's Guide to Teen-Age Beauty and Glamour* (1959) even offered readers "the sad example of the isolated egghead. She isn't unpopular because she is brainy; it is because she's unpopular that she *is* so intensely intellectual."

"Whether in love or not, she's confident that a handsome breadwinner will come along . . ." Ad for U.S. Savings Bonds, 1950.

Most frequently, however, the expectation was that "[w]hen a young girl goes to work, she is apt to look on her job pretty much as a fill-in between maturity and marriage," as a 1950 ad for U.S. Savings Bonds expressed it. *Teens Today* bluntly told readers in 1959 that "[w]hether you're an airline hostess . . . or a secretary, you know that eventually you'll want a husband, a home, children. That's just how it is: you're a woman."

The assumption that no woman would choose career over home was so strong that when *American Girl* profiled a Ph.D. in physics for a daring 1956 article on "Science, the future career," they made sure she was presented in appropriately feminine terms. "Cosmic rays and cake baking are both lots of fun, says Dr. Summerfield, research physicist—and homemaker," was the caption under her picture.

The most suitable careers for women were found in the field of home economics—at least according to many home ec textbooks. Indeed, with a zeal to proselytize matched only by proponents of certain outré pseudo-scientific theories, almost every midcentury home ec text contained a chapter on "Career Opportunities in Home Economics." While the authors of these texts almost always billed themselves as some sort of professional ("Director of Social Conduct at South High School, Lima, Ohio" or the succinct yet magisterial "Family Life Consultant"), the careers presented to student readers were much less authoritative. For the most part, they involved the sorts of feminine skills taught in home economics class, and embraced the same sort of low-paid work that made "housewife" such a notoriously undervalued occupation. "Cake Decorator" ("You would decorate cakes, cookies, and sandwiches . . . for special occasions") is one such example from *Teen Guide to Homemaking*. The 1972 edition actually listed "Baby Food Specialist" as a career option. "Tests nutritional value, taste and appearance of baby food" was the job description provided, even though taste-testing strained peas doesn't seem to present much opportunity for advancement for anybody over the age of twenty-four months.

Date with a Career—Career Girl Romances

When she was too old for *I Want to Be a Beauty Operator* but too young for books like *Women Will Be Doctors* (1947) ("'You ought to be having babies, not delivering them,' growled old Doctor Scudder . . .'"), or *Surfing Nurse* (1971) ("'Too good to be true!' was how Nurse Kara Simmon felt about her temporary assignment away from St. Mark's. For she was on Surfari with the American Surfing Team as team nurse and as top competitor in the World Championships . . . "), the teen reader had her choice of what one publisher called "Career-Romance Novels for Young Moderns." Theoretically, these books taught young women about suitable occupations, but by and large they stressed the thrill of romance over the drudgery of work.

Goal in the Sky (1953) at least made an attempt to help young women understand some of the requisites for becoming a stewardess. Author Margaret Hill even acknowledged a list of "airline companies, school personnel and other individuals" who provided insight into the field. Not that Hill ignored romance in her story, however. When the family dude ranch goes belly up, Beth Dean is forced to leave college. A hopeless typist, the world of business is out of the question, but a joy ride with handsome veterinarian Kirk Arnold gives her some new ideas, even a few about work. A little research proved she didn't have to be "a regular glamour girl" or a nurse to be an airline stewardess. Beth met the physical requirements:

AGE: 21 through 26

HEIGHT: 5 feet 2 inches through 5 feet 7 inches

WEIGHT: 105 pounds through 125 pounds (in proportion to height)

MARITAL STATUS: Single. Never been married...

PHYSICAL CHARACTERISTICS: Clear complexion, attractive smile, straight even teeth, hair its natural color, good figure, slender legs.

Stewardesses also needed to be "pleasant, gracious, emotionally stable, ingenious, whole, self-controlled." In fact, Sky Lanes airline preferred the term "hostess," as it better described "the role we want our girls to play on the plane. A hostess should be gracious and charming whether in her own home or in the cabin of an airliner." Sky Lanes further required each of its "girls" to be "discriminating about her friends, about her conduct and about the places where she is seen." Wholesome, discriminating Beth almost fails the preliminary interview when a pencil mark on her jaw is mistaken for a tiny scar. After all, Sky Lanes couldn't "employ a hostess who has a visible scar," lest passengers think it resulted from a crash. Beth passes intelligence and psychological tests without mishap, as well as a face-to-face meeting with the frightening Mr. O'Dell (who surreptitiously records the applicants' voices for nefarious reasons of his own, which are never adequately explained), and a physical before she is finally accepted into Sky Lanes's training school. Of course, there's a great deal more—about Beth's training period in Texas; her rival, Dorothy Scott; her dates with boring Leo and flashy Lester; her demerits for coming in late at night; practice flights; and finally the exciting moment when she receives her wings. But what about her pilot, Kirk Arnold, and the tender feelings he and Beth have yet to explore?

These novels covered a wide array of professions. *Lynn, Cover Girl* (1950), *Kate Brennan, Model* (1957), and *Fashion for Cinderella* (1960) were all set amid the glamorous world of fashion. *Nina Grant, Pediatric Nurse* (1960) and *Medicare Nurse* (1967) were but two of a shelf devoted to nursing. There were plenty of titles devoted to less mundane occupations: *Polly Perry, TV Cook* (1959), *Nancy Runs the Bookmobile* (1956), *Sally's Real Estate Venture* (1954), to name but a few. *Pamela Lee, Home Economist* (1956) told the story of a young woman who, as a county home demonstration agent, shows young members of the 4-H Club how to make cookies, while she finishes her thesis on the chemistry of foods ("I've decided it's going to specialize in tomatoes, and I'm going to make it a humdinger!"). Along the way she meets and becomes engaged to the exceedingly dull Ben Potter, who postpones their wedding because "It's the sensible thing to wait until we're on our feet financially."

That's the plain fact behind these books—while they introduce girls to different occupations, they almost always end with the main character getting engaged or married. They were romance novels, of course, and the tension between career and marriage-as-career usually lurks just beneath the surface. Sometimes, readers were told outright how well a woman's work meshed with married life. After model Kate Brennan accepts Dr. Geoffrey Stewart's proposal, he reminds her, "You're the one

"*Aren't you the smart one—
majoring in Home Ec!*"
Pamela Lee, Home
Economist, 1956.

who convinced me that modeling is the kind of career just made to order
for marriage."[33] Other books were less clear about whether their career-
girl protagonists were going to stay that way after marriage. After the ceremony, Nina Grant leans against her new husband:

> "I like being Mrs. Enoc Halpern," she said with a glorious smile.
>   His smile matched hers. "I'm glad you do, my little nurse," he said.
> "For that is what you're going to be for the rest of your life."[34]

Can Mrs. Halpern and Nurse Grant coexist? There's no sequel, but
something in the groom's patronizing tone makes me think not.

Magazines, Matrimony, and the Marketplace

Long before they decided to attend college, get a job, or get married, teen girls were able to choose china patterns and diamond engagements rings from the pages of magazines like *Seventeen* and *Ingenue*. For example, an ad for Lenox china that appeared in the June 1960 issue of *Ingenue* magazine featured a photo of a young couple dressed for prom night or another formal dance. He, handsome in his tuxedo, sweeps her off her feet while she, pony-tailed and virginal in her fluffy white dress and red wrap, points one foot ecstatically in the air. "You get the license . . . I'll get the Lenox," reads the caption, neatly blending the lines between matrimony and consumerism in one fell swoop. The copy spelled out the bargain: "Lenox China just naturally goes with love and romance and planning for the future."

Chances are that a girl reading the June 1960 issue of *Ingenue* needed no further explanation of the ad because she had already been primed for its message. Just a page before the ad for china was one for Lane Sweetheart Chests. Here, a nicely dressed young couple blows kisses at one another. Linking the two of them spatially and figuratively is a hope chest, a wooden chest in which a girl gathered and stored linens, clothing, and other goods for an eventual home of her own.

But the Lane Sweetheart Chest was more than a storage unit; it was "your *first home* . . . before marriage, that you and your love can share!" Drawn together in a spiritual marriage of the marketplace, the chest was a chaste home quasi-married couples filled with "a blanket, a place setting, an heirloom." Another ad referred to the hope chest as a "pledge of love," and featured a photo of a girl looking dreamily into her future: "When Jim gave me this beautiful Lane Chest I knew how he really felt about me."[35] This was a recurring theme in Lane's advertising—when a boy gave you a hope chest, you knew he was ready for marriage. But since ads for hope chests didn't appear in magazines like *Boys' Life* or *Esquire*, it was up to his would-be fiancée to make sure Jim got the message about why and where to buy one.

Silverware manufacturers also urged teen girls to fill their hope chests with sterling place settings. These ads didn't always play overtly on matrimonial hopes and wishes. A 1958 ad for Gorham sterling told potential consumers that happy families enjoyed the "special, gracious glow" that only "fine solid silver" added to mealtime togetherness before asking, "Don't you want to have Gorham in *your own* happy home someday?" Acquiring silver was easy, the ad stressed, because a girl could begin buying teaspoons with the money she earned babysitting.[36] Gorham also manufactured sterling silver rings fashioned from salt spoons and set with cultured pearls. By wearing such a ring, a girl reminded herself and those around her of her silver pattern of choice.[37] As another ad noted, "it may be a little early to choose that man of your life, but it's not too early to decide about your Sterling Silver."[38]

Perhaps my favorite silver ad appeared in *Seventeen* magazine in May 1961. One of five advertisements for sterling that graced the issue, this one featured a young couple locked in an embrace, while the radiant young woman looks rapturously over her consort's shoulder at the sterling silver fork she holds in her hand. Clearly, this is a love affair between a girl and a fork—which is obviously much more important to her than the young man, who turns his face away from the camera. (Indeed, young men almost never show their faces in ads for china, stemware, and silver—their identity isn't really important, as the featured relationship is between woman and product.) The cause of her joy? "It's a happy time for any girl, when her groom-to-be tells her how much he likes the sterling they'll live with forever."[39]

Wedding iconography was also used to advertise products other than gift items, such as china, silver, and stemware. In 1960, a Bulova ad devoted to "The art of wearing a watch" featured a line drawing of a bride and a reader-submitted question: "Should you wear a watch with a wedding gown?" The answer was no, but the ad demonstrated many other appropriate ways of wearing watches.[40]

At the same time that their advertisers encouraged readers' matrimonial dreams, articles and editorial content within teen girls' magazines argued for chastity and against early marriage. In addition to the advertisement for

Bulova watches described above, the February 1960 *Seventeen* magazine contained two ads for sterling silver, two ads for china, one double-page ad for hope chests, and assorted ads for diamond engagement rings, wedding invitations, and something called the "Linen Hope Chest Club," which would send members towels, sheets, and table linens, "All From Famous Makers," for only $3.00 a week. In the same issue, however, an expert from the Marriage Counseling Service of Greater New York told readers that "teen-agers literally have not lived long enough to develop the basic maturity" demanded by marriage and imparted the grim statistic that teenage brides were three times more likely to be divorced than brides in their early twenties.[41] *Being Married*, a 1960 high school textbook that included chapters on "Your Wedding Plans" and "Being Newlyweds," cited studies ranking high school brides lower on "items of morale, family relations and emotionality" than their nonmarried female classmates.[42]

Even so, by 1959, 47 percent of brides were under the age of nineteen. In *What About Teen-age Marriage?* (1961), writer Jeanne Sakol tried to make early marriage and motherhood sound square next to the thrill of being a normal active teen. Nonetheless, her underlying message was that a girl would eventually settle down and get married. Being a Bachelor Girl for a few years could "be a healthy, exhilarating period of your life," but it was "not by any wild stretch of the imagination meant to be a substitute for marriage. Rather, it should be a profitable link between being a student and becoming a wife." Sakol said that expecting one's "husband to give up [his] outside interests after marriage would be foolish because he would feel 'trapped' and resent it," but she never explained how "Mommy should stay home to raise the children and run the household" without feeling the same. The peril of unwanted pregnancy was discussed in the chapter "Do You Have to Get Married?" The only mention of contraception, however, was in the glossary—where it was vaguely defined as "preventive measures against conception." Tales of girls who thought they were pregnant but were really virgins and young couples who "fearfully eloped only to find months later that the symptoms were false" were a strange way to start a chapter on unplanned pregnancy, but they probably reflected Sakol's profound hope that her readers didn't "have to" get married. Interestingly, she listed the Tampax Educational Department as one of the "leading associations of marriage counselors."

Teen Queens and Miss Congeniality

Girls who had to get married were obviously not the sort of role models the advice writers had in mind, but who could live up to the standards they presented? Beauty pageants offered prizes and praise to girls who best personified the sort of ideal teen glorified in guidebook and advice column alike. There were many titles for which they could compete: Miss Teenage America, America's Junior Miss, Miss American Teenager, Miss TEEN, and Miss TeenScreen, to name but a few. Pageant judges voted on such stalwart feminine qualities as personal appearance (though after the women's movement, the word "beauty" was banished), poise, grooming, posture, attitude, sincerity, and "the way you express yourself."[43] There were plenty of girls willing to face the judges: in 1965, 200,000 girls competed at local preliminary levels for the title of Miss American Teenager.[44] Winning entrants were the sort of perky, involved girls advice books and teen mags had long held up to readers as icons of teen life, or, as Miss American Teenager 1963 stressed to would-be contestants, she and her runner-ups were chosen "not only because we were attractive, but because we scored in every phase of teenage life." Citizenship and patriotism were also rewarded, what Miss American Teenager 1963 referred to as "the joy of representing the youth of America . . . upholding all the glories of serving your community and the entire nation."[45]

   "Serving one's community and the entire nation" often translated to "supporting the pageant's sponsors"—frequently businesses that targeted the teen market. Miss American Teenager was connected with the Palisades Amusement Park in New Jersey, the Miss TeenScreen and Miss Teen pageants were affiliated with the magazines whose names they carried, while the Dr Pepper soft drink company purchased the Miss Teenage America contest outright after years of sponsorship.[46]

Lincoln-Mercury Division Youth Safety Spokesmen pose beside a Comet Caliente convertible similar to the one each will drive during the coming year. Right to left they are: Miss Judy Doll of Navarre, Ohio, Miss Teenage America for 1964; Susan Rae Houghton, Miss Teenage America Modesto (California); Pat Hollis, Miss Teenage Houston (Texas) and Jeanine Zavrel of Falls Church, Virginia, Miss Teenage Washington, D. C. The Youth Safety Spokesmen will speak to teenage and adult groups across the country on the subject of traffic safety with emphasis on wearing seat belts at all times. Seventeen-year-old Judy Doll is five feet, four inches tall and weighs 104 pounds and has blue eyes and brown hair. She attends Fairless High School in Navarre where her major subjects are English and history. Susan Rae Houghton, 17, is a senior at Grace Davis High School in Modesto. She is five feet, five inches tall and weighs 118 pounds and has blue eyes and blond hair. Pat Hollis, 17, attends Bellaire Senior High School and is majoring in music and drama. She is five feet, seven inches tall and weighs 125 pounds, with hazel eyes and brown hair. Jeanine Zavrel, 16, is a junior at J. E. B. Stuart High School, in Falls Church, Virginia, and is majoring in English. She is five feet, four inches tall and weighs 115 pounds, with blue eyes and brown hair.

Judy Doll was Miss Teenage America 1964 and an auto safety spokesman.

Corporate sponsors donated pageant prizes, but strings were often attached. When Judy Doll was awarded the title of Miss Teenage America 1964, she also received the use of a brand-new convertible for a year. In return, she and three regional Miss Teenage Americas served as Lincoln-Mercury Division Youth Safety Spokesmen.[47] Judy's picture and a "personal" message from her appeared in a booklet called *How to Earn the Key to Dad's Car*:

[W]hen I was told my grand prize would be a lovely new Comet Caliente convertible, I realized I'd have the same responsibility facing me that any other teenager has when he or she wants to earn the privilege of driving a

car. I had to convince my parents that it would be safe for me to drive the
car on my own.

Judy and the other Youth Safety Spokesmen thoughtfully "asked
Lincoln-Mercury to help us put together this booklet" to share safe-driving
tips with other teens who wanted to earn the key to Dad's car—or, like
Judy, to their own. But the Youth Safety Spokesmen's responsibility as role
models didn't end there. The booklet noted (along with each girl's height,
weight, age, and hair and eye color) that they would be speaking on traffic
safety and seatbelt usage to adult and teen groups across the country.

A teen queen remained at the pageant sponsors' beck and call for a
year, but she was usually paid for such appearances. Indeed, pageantry
could be quite lucrative for the winners: In 1976, Miss Teenage America
received a minimum cash guarantee of $5,000 for personal appearances,
though some past titleholders earned as much $7,500. Combined with a
$12,000 scholarship to the college or university of her choice, plus prizes
including a complete wardrobe, a year's supply of cosmetics, and, surely
as a reminder that the pageant was "not a beauty contest," a set of ency-
clopedias, Miss Teenage America did all right, financially speaking.[48]

In terms of prizes and prestige, however, the big kahuna of beauty
contests was the Miss America pageant. Of course, Miss America was
not strictly a teen pageant, but its contestants and winners were usually
in their late teens or early twenties—a perfect age to be held up as the
perfect woman. In addition to the honors chosen by the judges (overall
titleholder, swimsuit, and talent competition winners), the contestants
themselves awarded one of their number the title of Miss Congeniality.
Just as the advice writers' ideal girl was helpful, considerate, cheerful,
and said only nice things about others, Miss Congeniality was the girl
everybody liked and got along with—at least in theory.

On the surface, being chosen Miss Congeniality appeared to be the
pageant's equivalent of being tagged a "good sport" in high school, a one-
way step to social oblivion and near-nerd status. Miss Congeniality was
the pageant's booby prize, given for the nebulous quality of "niceness," in
a contest where champion status was bestowed on the winners of the

swimsuit and talent competitions, and Miss America herself was adulated as near royalty. But Miss Congeniality was not all she appeared to be. Jeanne Swanner, who received the title in 1963, said that the title was given as much for "having a gimmick" as anything else. Hers was her height—she was over six feet tall. Miss Montana 1949's gimmick arrived when she and her horse fell off the stage during a dubious display of equestrian talent. Coincidentally or not, she was voted Miss Congeniality. The award came with a $1,000 scholarship, and unscrupulous girls often voted for themselves. Indeed, the plurality required to win could be ridiculously tiny, as small as four or five votes.[49] Fed up with such shenanigans, the pageant finally discontinued the award in 1974 after forty-six contestants voted for themselves.[50]

The lure of the scholarship money must have been great, because pageant watchers had long pegged the title of Miss Congeniality as a kiss of death. No recipient in the first forty-three years of the pageant's history went on to be crowned Miss America.

The Miss Congeniality who finally broke this jinx was perhaps the quintessential Miss America. Pert, pretty, pious, and still the only Miss America whose talent was ventriloquism, Vonda Kay Van Dyke was crowned on September 13, 1964, her reign balanced between the individualistic queens of the pretelevision era and the current crop of blandly interchangeable beauties. While she was neither the first nor the last Miss America to exploit the moneymaking potential that accompanied the winner's rhinestone tiara, she was perhaps the only Miss America to market herself extensively as a teen expert.

She was definitely not the sort of girl to cast a vote for herself. Born in Muskegon, Michigan, in 1943, Vonda was the only child of Dr. A. B. Van Dyke, an osteopath, and his homemaker wife. The deeply religious family later moved to Phoenix, Arizona, where Vonda attended the Phoenix Christian High School. There she exemplified the sort of clean teen behavior lauded by guidebooks of the era: she was on the staff of the school newspaper, captain of the cheerleader squad, and an active church member, regularly teaching a Sunday school class. She was attractive and well-groomed. No wonder she was later held up as a role model to teens hell-bent on carving out a small slice of independence by smoking, drinking, and wrestling with the opposite sex, or even by merely sassing back to Mom and Dad. She was a girl that even Pat Boone could respect. Indeed, she told reporters that the first thought to enter her mind after her name was announced as the contest's winner was "the awful big responsibilities I now had to my friends, my family, my country and to my God."[51]

Capitalizing no doubt on her parent-appeal and image as an irreproachable goody-goody, the Fleming H. Revell Company, a Christian publishing house, approached Vonda about writing an advice book for teens. The result was *That Girl in Your Mirror*, a slim volume incorporating advice, autobiography, and religious witnessing. By mid-March 1966, Revell reported that they had sold 60,000 copies nationwide out of the first printing of 100,000.[52] (On the other hand, Revell required stores to purchase a minimum of 100 books in order to participate in a special promotion, and these books were not returnable, so draw your own conclusions.) But the overall sales figures were respectable enough that Revell had Vonda do another book for teens, *Dear Vonda Kay*, which came out in 1967. *Dear Vonda Kay* was a compilation of letters received by Vonda Kay, and her (or her ghostwriter's) replies to them. These consisted of run-of-the-mill teen questions concerning smoking, drinking, cheating at school (all *verboten*, of course), make-up (OK if lightly applied), and so on. Because she and her publishing company were interested in proselytizing, she also answered questions like "What do you think of a girl who joined a certain church just because a boy she wants to impress goes there?" (Not much, Vonda replied, though in time the girl might sincerely become interested in the church.)

Why Not Ask a Celebrity?

Vonda Kay Van Dyke was far from the only celebrity to take pen in hand regarding teen behavior, appearance, and etiquette. Some, like Vonda Kay, had a direct tie to youth culture. Dick Clark was the clean-cut, affa-

"Betty Cornell's Glamour Guide for Teens"

by Betty Cornell (New York: Prentice-Hall, 1959)

Betty Cornell went Dick Clark and Pat Boone one better—she was a bona fide teenager. Although her name no longer rings a bell, she was a famous model in her day (it says so right here on the book jacket). Not that she didn't face hardship: "I found I did not have enough time between modeling jobs to keep up my college work. So I devoted myself exclusively to modeling." Yet she still managed to pen at least two guidebooks for teens.

When it came to handing out advice, however, Cornell channeled my mother along with countless others:

"If only she weren't so sloppy."
This remark uttered ruefully or indignantly has caused the downfall of many an attractive teen-ager. Girls whisper about it behind her back. Boys mutter about it in their locker rooms. The word gets around and dates come few and far between.

But of all teen guidebook authors, only Cornell revealed the awful truth of adult life in such a stark and unrelenting manner: "Jobs that bring in money steadily are jobs at which you must work steadily." Too true, alas, too true.

ble, youngish host of *American Bandstand*, as well as the author of *Your Happiest Years* (1959) and *To Goof or Not to Goof* (1965). Singer Pat Boone's bland cover versions made raucous black rhythm 'n' blues safe for middle-class white teens, and his books *Twixt Twelve and Twenty* (1958) and *Between You, Me and the Gatepost* (1960) offered the sort of wholesome, upstanding advice one would expect from him. And what teenaged fan of TV's *Partridge Family* could resist Susan Dey's *For Girls Only* (1972), with its cheery assertion that there were "thousands of things you can do" to catch a boy, "such as baking him a birthday cake or asking him to show you how to change a tire or sewing patches onto his jeans or letting him beat you just once at Scrabble"?

Other celebrities were less obvious choices (to modern eyes, at least) for the mantle of teen advice expert. In the early 1960s, Connie Francis was getting 5,000 letters a week—all, to hear her tell it, from troubled teens asking for advice. Actually, she wasn't the only celebrity author to cite a high volume of teenage mail as a reason they wrote an advice tome, but it's difficult to understand just why a teen would turn to Connie Francis in a time of trouble. Dick Clark—we still associate him with teens. But Connie Francis? Though she was only twenty-four when *For Every Young Heart* came out in 1962, Connie seemed less a teenager than a maiden aunt, and a square one at that. "Never wear slacks on a date," Francis advised, "unless it's to a rugged outdoor picnic or an evening at an amusement park. Otherwise, I think slacks are an insult to a boy." But, to be fair, Francis occasionally sounded like a real human being— fighting tears, for example, at age thirteen when her secret crush told her not to give up the accordion because "it hides your figure from the TV cameras," or getting into a shoving match with a boy at her high school over a place in line. And let's not forget the little spitfire's seventh-grade fistfight with Jenny Stanford:

> She grabbed my hair, I shoved her in the face, and then we really went at it. And though I was proud of it then, I hate to admit it now—I really gave it to her, but good.
>
> At the end, her friends were silent; mine were yelling, "Yea! Connie!" and there stood Jenny with the tears streaming down her dirt-smudged cheeks.
>
> "Let me know the next time you want to fight!" I gloated and flounced off, covered with dirt but feeling great, hair straggling down over my eyes, and a big rip in my dress. (Such a cute little dress, too— yellow organdy, all dainty and feminine.)

Yea! Connie! Otherwise, the advice here is pretty much the status quo: keep body and mind clean, obey authority figures and gender role rules. But strip away all that stuff (yes, that's most of the book), and Francis kinda sounds like fun.

Another celebrity who claimed letters from teens spurred her to write a guidebook was midcentury songbird Patti Page. *Once Upon a Dream* (1960) was subtitled "A Personal Chat with All Teenagers," though it was clearly aimed at girls. And chatty it was: "Let's take off our shoes, relax and let down our hair together . . . curl up in your bed and I'll just stretch out in an easy chair, and now—now we're ready to start dreaming-out-loud together." But readers shouldn't get too relaxed, for in Page's world, only the strong survived:

> You have to fight for the good things you want. You have to compete with other girls. What's more you have to make up your mind to win. Other-wise you'll not have your pick of the best boys. You'll have what's left over.

I'll give Page some credit, though. In the first chapter, "A Room of Your Own," she expounded upon the importance of independence and a private space. Alas, before you can say "Virginia Woolf," she's telling us about "charm—the magic wand"—and as for individuality, that ended after marriage:

> You are constantly being told, I know, that girls have to be "interesting." That's all right when you're trying to attract men, but now we're talking about your husband. And I think you'll find, when you're married, that it isn't nearly so important for you to be interesting as it is to make your husband feel that he's interesting.

Page's theory was that a husband wanted his wife to remain the same girl he fell in love with. "Being interesting" threatened him and the marriage.

Mostly, though, celebrity authors concentrated on generic informa-tion concerning pleasing one's parents and getting along with others.

They reassured readers that one day they would get married and have children. But while they gave tips on how to meet the opposite sex, as well as what to do on dates other than necking and petting, they didn't get into the mechanics of sexuality. To teach their adolescent daughters the facts of life, parents turned to a whole other set of guidebooks.

Chapter 3

I Am Curious Pink:
Teen Guides to Flinging the Woo

The vagina is a wonderful engineering job. Its tissues and muscles are not only tough but elastic, much more elastic and durable than any girdle ever produced.

Maxine Davis,
Sex and the Adolescent (1958)

hock-full of healthy, happy, obedient teens who exuded wholesome zest while engaged in parent-sanctioned activities, midcentury teen guides to sex and dating described a more innocent world, albeit one in which the lines of allowable behavior were firmly drawn according to gender, and "normalcy" was by definition white and heterosexual. Midcentury teenage dating manuals gave advice from a parent's point of view, and urged readers to respect adult authority while discouraging displays of adolescent sexuality. As writer John Marr succinctly put it in his *(Anti-) Sex Tips for Teens: The Teenage Advice Book 1897–1987,*

"These are not guides for being a happy teen—these are guides for having a happy parent."

Parents have always been squeamish about telling their children about the facts of life. Not surprisingly, most procrastinated—usually until their tiny tots had sprouted into teenagers. By the time puberty rolled around, however, the thought of facing down a surly adolescent who was more concerned with practical applications than theory when it came to sex ed was a greater challenge than many parents could handle. To fill the gap, a plethora of manuals discussed both the facts of life and the techniques of dating, to better help young people navigate the rocky shoals of romance, while at the same time channeling their hormones into the appropriate bywaters of legal marriage. Unfortunately, the facts of life could be a mixed bag—they prepared a teen for dating—which, ideally, led to marriage and reproductive sex (good) or, less ideally, to going steady and its risk of heavy petting (not so good)—or for premarital sex and a life in ruins (bad), whether or not you had a baby (very, very bad). To avoid the latter situations, pink think worked hard to make marital sex sound like fun—but not too much fun.

A cautionary tale was offered to moviegoers in 1959, in the campy classic *A Summer Place*. Gorgeous young Sandra Dee and studly Troy Donahue struggle against passion before "going all the way"—and who could blame them? In reality, the movie was little more than a soap opera in which two mismatched couples swap spouses during a vacation on Pine Island, Maine, while their teenage children busy themselves with falling in love.

Before Molly (Sandra Dee) is even off the boat that brings her family to the island, she and the innkeepers' son, Johnny (Troy Donahue), are making goo-goo eyes at each other. Moments after their introduction, the frisky twosome is down by the old goldfish pond getting better acquainted—or necking and groping, as Molly's sour pickle of a mother terms it, telling her hot-to-trot daughter that she "doesn't understand the value of a decent reputation." Mother Dear really shifts into high gear after Molly and Johnny spend a chaste night together when their boat capsizes during a sailing picnic, calling in an evil-looking doctor to ascertain her daughter's virginity. "I've been a good girl," Molly hysterically screams again and again before the examination. Soon thereafter, she is shipped off to an all-girls boarding school. Finally, despite her vile mother, her father's marriage to Johnny's mother, Johnny's father's spectacular descent into alcoholism, and several other unlikely plot twists (did I mention this was a soap opera?), Molly and Johnny find themselves alone in the abandoned lookout over the beach. "Are you bad, Johnny," Molly pouts, "have you been bad with girls?" Soon they sneak back to the house, neither his spotless white dinner jacket nor her crisp white party dress betraying the fact that, not only have they both been bad, but their romp has resulted in conception. After facing parental disapproval, they get married and head off to Pine Island—perhaps to live happily ever after.

Not surprisingly, *A Summer Place* garnered loads of teen press for its young stars. *Datebook* magazine featured a scene from the film on its cover, and declared Dee and Donahue "the perfect couple." Other reviews were less enthusiastic. *Newsweek* noted that "the best scenes of all are provided by . . . the Pacific Ocean" (standing in for the Atlantic Ocean, no less), while the *New York Times* called *A Summer Place* "one of the most laboriously and garishly sex-scented movies in years." *Time* magazine, however, sounded suspiciously like a teen advice manual when it excoriated the film for "having demonstrated the various values of adultery" and making clear "that sexual dalliance between unmarried adolescents is really quite all right provided they are in love and willing to confess all to their parents and stand up in church when the girl gets pregnant." Worse, the film's "adolescent love scenes [were] an inflammation to imitation."

You wouldn't guess from all this hubbub that 50 percent of married women born after 1900 were not virgins at the time of their marriage—according to Alfred Kinsey, whose landmark *Sexual Behavior in the Human Female* was published in 1953. What must have been just as shocking to the teen advice experts was Kinsey's statistic that 95 percent of American women petted before marriage.

Considering the risks, then, it was easier to let the so-called experts do the talking, especially if Mom and Dad weren't too willing to provide the details. Not that the experts were any less confused by the human body and its tricky reproductive habits. According to a 1962 article in *For Teens Only* magazine, human eggs were "formed inside the uterus." (They're actually formed in the ovaries—but you knew that, right?) Meanwhile, Lois Pemberton's *The Stork Didn't Bring You* (1948) characterized menstruation as one of "nature's way[s] of relieving sexual tension."

Sometimes the facts were reliable but the presentation was suspect. Frances Strain authored a series of sex ed manuals (*Being Born, Teen Days*), but she clearly considered herself an Artist. The following passage from *Love at the Threshold* (1952) bespoke the frustrated poet in her heart. The female reproductive system, she wrote, was a "symmetrical figure of great beauty. . . . [It] looks in outline for all the world like a Grecian urn." Even better, viewing sperm under a microscope reminded the imaginative Strain "of nothing so much as a huge crowd of traders milling about on the floor of the Stock Exchange."

Other writers got so wrapped up in presenting birds, bees, and para-

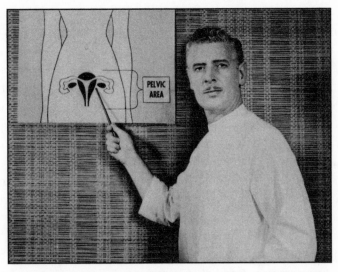

According to Frances Strain, the female reproductive system looked "in outline for all the world like a Grecian urn." You be the judge.

According to the Experts: A Glossary

hermaphrodite	"A female bisexual" (Pemberton)
homosexual	"A bad boy or bad man who wants to play with the penis of another boy just to get the pleasure out of doing it." (Fr. Filas)
masturbation	"A tyrant that robs its [female] victims of the incentives and radiant energy for worthy accomplishments. . . . Oftentimes the remedy for this situation consists of a minor surgical operation spoken of as *circumcision*." (Shryock)
orgasm (male)	"Takes place shortly after the penis enters the vagina" (Pemberton)
orgasm (female)	"No more essential for conception than a mink coat or a lipstick" (Davis)
penis	"The muscular organ through which [boys] urinate" (Pemberton)
sex	"Works only in marriage" (Fr. Filas)
testicles	"Hang in a pouchy sac . . . one slightly above the other for your comfort and convenience" (Pemberton)
vagina	"The female receptacle" (Fr. Filas)

mecia that they neglected to tell readers the physical details of human conception. Harold Shryock, M.A., M.D., was a "medical evangelist" (*shudder!*) who wrote a number of advice books aimed at teens and young adults. *On Becoming a Woman* (1951) was his book for teenage girls. He described how a new life began with "the union of two germ cells . . . the cell from the father having been implanted within the mother's body." Shryock was coy about how—short of abdominal surgery—such a "union" was to occur, but was quick to affirm that "the only proper time for a union to occur between a female germ cell and a male germ cell is after marriage." It wasn't until a later chapter ("Secrets About Boys") that Shryock let it slip that the penis ("an organ that is quite different from any of the female reproductive organs") was used for "introducing seminal fluid into the vagina of the wife."

By now, you should have noticed that in the teen advice genre even facts carried a certain bias. Nowhere was this more apparent than when it came to that "very special day" in every girl's life. Her first period marked an adolescent's entrance—at least physically—into Womanhood. It also provided the experts an excellent opportunity to combine body mechanics and pink think all in the same lesson.

The Joy of Becoming a Woman

It was a small booklet, its aqua cover brightened with splashes of feminine pink. My best friend Ruth's older sister kept it in her sock drawer, a hiding place that was no match for two prying ten-year-olds. Ruth was the one who found it. At first, I feigned polite interest in her discovery. Disinterest soon gave way to disbelief and then to outright foreboding as I listened to the information she imparted. For years afterward, even the booklet's title, *Very Personally Yours*, was guaranteed to give me the willies.

One day, everything was fine, and I ran around in my underwear, boxing and wrestling with my dad and my brother. The next day, a friend and I wormed our way through her sister's bureau and discovered that our future was filled with breasts, hips, pubic hair, and—blood! As if this weren't disconcerting enough, according to *Very Personally Yours*, one was actually supposed to be happy about these absurd bodily changes:

From your earliest chalk-and-blackboard days, you've looked forward to your graduation—dreamed of it, with stars in your eyes. It's as though all your young life, you've been waiting on tiptoe for the very special day that would mark the commencement of a wonderful adventure: your debut into the adult world.

So, too, your physical self has been preparing for another momentous adventure: your graduation from "little girl" to grown-up. This slow body process has been at work so quietly you were scarcely aware of it. Then, one day, you knew. You began to menstruate.

Very Personally Yours was a pamphlet published by Kimberly-Clark, manufacturers of Kotex, designed to teach girls all about menstruation. Relentlessly cheerful, it glorified the "miracle" that was about to befall our young bodies, and peddled a particular vision of womanhood along with a certain brand of sanitary napkin.

Very Personally Yours was only one prong of a Kimberly-Clark juggernaut aimed at instilling brand loyalty in soon-to-be-consumers of their sanitary products. If you are of a certain age, you remember the day in the fifth grade when the boys went out to play kickball, while the girls stayed in to watch a special film presentation. Segregated in a darkened classroom, the girls were treated to *The Story of Menstruation*, a Walt Disney Production originally released in the 1950s but still being shown at least as late as the early 1970s, when I saw it. My memory of the film is rather sketchy—I was much too overcome by guilt and shame to pay adequate attention. Thank goodness there wasn't a quiz afterward.

Luckily for us all, Janice Delany, Mary Jane Lupton, and Emily Toth provide the following synopsis in their wonderful book *The Curse: A Cultural History of Menstruation*:

> In the Disney world, the menstrual flow is not blood red, but snow white. The vaginal drawings look more like a cross section of kitchen sink than the outside and inside of a woman's body. There are no hymen, no clitoris, no labia; all focus is on the little nest and its potentially lush

lining. Although Disney and Kimberly-Clark advise exercise during the period, the exercising cartoon girls (who look like Disney's Cinderella) are drawn without feet; bicycles magically propel themselves down the street without any muscular or mental direction from the cyclist. The film ends happily ever after, with a shot of a lipsticked bride followed immediately by a shot of a lipsticked mother and baby.[1]

In fact, it was just this connection between menstruation, marriage, and motherhood that left me confused at best, and horrified at worst. I mean, I was ten years old! At that age, fed on a diet of *Bewitched* (where Darrin didn't let Samantha use her powers) and *I Love Lucy* (where Ricky treated Lucy like some sort of imbecile child), getting married didn't look like any fun at all, let alone having a baby.

According to most experts, such a lack of enthusiasm was problematic. Menstruation was to be met with the same sense of keen anticipation and wonderment generally reserved for Christmas morning. "So what's so joyful?" asked Mary McGee Williams and Irene Kane in their book *On Becoming a Woman* (1959). This was a good, sincere question, to be sure. But pity the poor girl who asked it and faced Williams and Kane's double-barreled onslaught of pink think ammo. "Well, let's stop and think about what menstruation . . . means," they began, oh so cozily, in a "just us girls" tone of voice. But the screws quickly tightened. "[F]or perhaps the first time in your active, tomboy life, you must accept that you are a girl":

> For most girls, this acceptance is an exciting, who-wouldn't-want-to-be kind of thing, something you've looked forward to since you saw your mother nursing a baby brother, or dreamed about a kitchen of your own, or imagined yourself a well-loved wife . . .

While any active tomboy worth the name was still reeling from this terrifying pastiche of impending domestic bliss, the authors zeroed in for the kill:

A frank, modern discussion
of everything a teen-age girl
<u>wants</u> and <u>needs</u> to know

**ON
BECOMING
A WOMAN**

DELL
F RST
EDITION
A179

25¢

Introduction by
LOUISE BATES AMES
of the Gesell Institute

"[F]or perhaps the first time in your active, tomboy life, you must accept that you are a girl." On Becoming a Woman, 1959.

The girls who resent menstruation, who talk about "the curse" and the bother of "being sick," who get all mixed up about this time in their lives, are those who may have emotional doubts about being a woman. . . . Here's a time for some real soul-searching, if you find yourself deeply disturbed about being "stuck with" the role of a woman. It's a time for re-evaluating the role of women in the world.

Not that this was a feminist reevaluation of women's role by a long shot:

When you know the deep, true love that a woman feels for a man, when you experience the tremendous joy of comforting, sustaining and understanding a man you love, when you know the happiness of childbirth—you will be acting the role you were created for. To know this fulfillment, you must want it, learn about it and be ready for it. The teen years are the perfect time for learning to be a woman . . . for turning from dolls and sandlot ball games to the feminine skills of cooking and sewing and prettying yourself (for this too is a feminine art).

Now, who could possibly feel "disturbed" about that, unless it was one of those female inverts Williams and Kane discussed in a later chapter ("if the crush translates itself into a desire for physical contact with a member of the same sex, it is time to ask guidance from a physician, minister or trained counselor")?

On the other hand, the "guidance" offered by at least one man of the cloth was truly disturbing. Mercifully, I'd forgotten what religion class at my Catholic high school was like, but it all came back in a flash the first time I listened to *Sex Education of Children*, a 1964 recording by Father Francis L. Filas. Mostly a lecture on how sex education is really "character education," interspersed with some holy humor (courtesy of that man in Des Moines who asked Fr. Filas, "if we practice rhythm, can our children sing in the choir?"), this album gets downright odd when the good father comes to the subject of menstruation. He tells the story of a junior high school bandleader whose first period arrived while she was on the football field during halftime. Completely unprepared when she felt the blood flowing down her legs, she spent a year in a mental institution. Then there was a motherless young girl endowed with what Fr. Filas refers to as "very prominent breast development," who wore a tight sweater to school one day. Harassed by the boys in her sixth-grade class, her teacher asked her to go home and change into something less form fitting. The "shock of being sent home in disgrace" brought on her first period. She thought she was dying so . . . she committed suicide! Fr. Filas wanted parents to know how important it was to prepare their daughters for the advent of menstruation, but such stories inadvertently imparted

In their early years, girls may enrich their lives and prepare for their future responsibilities as wives and mothers. There are indeed so many things that go to make up a full life!

The pamphlet How Life Goes On and On, *1933, 1940, taught the facts of life and menstruation, as well as the "feminine arts."*

the teller's own horror of the female body and its messy mechanics.

Such rhetoric made booklets like *Growing Up and Liking It*, a menstrual education pamphlet advertising Modess sanitary napkins, seem absolutely benign. "This is what you've been waiting for," cooed a mid-1960s edition. Menstruation was "part of being female . . . part of growing up . . . part of the wonderful process of changing from a child into a woman." And, in a fit of perkiness not matched before or since in menstrual education materials, it boldly declared that "the fun is just beginning!"—leading me to doubt that the author ever menstruated.

Biology, Destiny, and You

As Williams and Kane hinted in their paragraphs on the menstrual cycle, childbirth was integral to true femininity. Nor were they the only experts to feel this way. In an article that appeared in the October 1948 issue of *Calling All Girls* magazine, Dr. Marynia F. Farnham wrote that menstruation was "not the bane of your existence, the 'curse' as some girls call it, but a singular blessing." She concluded that "your menses . . . is the key to the crowning achievement of your marriage."

Biology, after all, was destiny. "What are little girls made for?" asked Lois Pemberton. Her answer? "The female of the species throughout all of nature is destined for motherhood." Giving birth is downright miraculous, of course, but remember that Pemberton's book purported to teach the facts of life to teens—a group notably more interested in the ins and outs of good old nonreproductive sexuality than in Pemberton's cheery assertion that "your obstetrician" could stop labor pains "with his choice of the many new drugs now available." According to Pemberton, a girl who loathed the physical changes of adolescence or was "shocked at the thought of motherhood and horrified at the idea of ever being beholden to a husband" was a pitiable object. Not only did she want to be a man, in Pemberton's opinion, but she and others like her were "well on their way to becoming social misfits and outcasts for life"—or at least until they discovered cosmetics. "Instead of deriding the wallflowers," Pemberton told her readers in a testimonial to the restorative powers of make-up, "drag 'em along to the powder room, dust on some glamour, and pass along some know-how for snaring a man."

Experts viewed a reluctance to socialize one-on-one with the opposite sex (in an appropriately wholesome manner, of course) as somewhat suspect, at best. Duvall's common-sense assertion, in her 1958 manual *The Art of Dating*, that the "late-maturing youngster need not feel 'queer'" was a breath of fresh air at a time when what many other authors suggested made "queer" seem mild by comparison.

While I didn't take the opportunity either to explore "the feminine role of the woman pursued by a man" or to practice my "newly discovered womanliness on boys [my] own age," as Williams and Kane counseled, I did experience what they referred to as "the emotion-testing experience called the *teen-age crush*." Heaven knows these august ladies—not to mention the whole preachy advice-spewing pack of their esteemed col-

Lewis Powell—a hottie in custody, 1865.

leagues—would have collectively keeled over from a collective bunching of panties if they had only known about the very first object of my preteen desire.

Even in his own day he was, without doubt, a boy with a bad reputation. In fact, he'd been dead over a hundred years by the time I found his picture in a history book. But what a picture! Leaning back against a scarred stone wall, he gazed off to his right—defiant, unrepentant, and bristling with sexuality. Ignoring the heavy irons circling the sitter's wrists, the photo might be one of those modern-day out-of-focus black and white high-fashion shots where it's impossible to tell what's really going on—are they selling perfume or that wallet carelessly tossed in the corner? My dream boy was Lewis Powell (aka Paine), a twenty-year-old co-conspirator in the plot to assassinate Abraham Lincoln, and the man who knifed the secretary of state nearly to death on the night of the president's murder. As if his succulent photo wasn't enough, the text further tantalized me by mention of his "bull-strong neck" and "incongruously charming dimples." I knew he was a criminal, but he made me feel so. . . . It wasn't until years later that I realized the word I was searching for was "horny." Look, it could have been worse: it was right around this time that a friend of mine confessed she thought Ernest Borgnine was cute. My crush on Lewis Powell eventually petered out. While he easily fit into my daydreams, I never quite got over the other picture in that history book— that of his body hanging silent after his execution.

Anyway, most of the experts firmly believed that once a girl attained puberty, she naturally wanted to start dating—but again, it all depended on how she felt about being a woman. Joost A. M. Meerloo, M.D., put it this way in a 1949 article in *Miss America* magazine:

> Naturally, your attitude towards boys will depend a lot on how you feel about *being female*. Girls who regard women as inferior to men don't really enjoy developing into womanhood, either physically or mentally. Many of them prove it by their positive genius for getting the male sex to dislike and ignore them. . . . Do they know *why* they're such poor date bait? Of course not. The reasons aren't visible to the naked eye.

The reasons may not have been visible to the naked eye, but they almost surely were the fault of the girl at hand. You see, despite what you may have learned playing the Mystery Date game, dating wasn't all trips to the beach and the bowling alley. Nope—going out with boys was serious business indeed. According to *Joyce Jackson's Guide to Dating* (1958):

> [T]he very existence of our democratic form of government depends upon happy family life, and we all know that happy family life starts with the marriage of a boy and a girl who are well-suited to each other. Why, you might even say that the future of our whole country rests right in the hands of us teen-age girls.[2]

Girls, Joyce said, did "most of the promoting of dates," and those who refused to participate threatened the nation's very stability. Then again, from its first sentence (the peppy admission "My name is Joyce Jackson—a teen ager") *Joyce Jackson's Guide to Dating* was more than a bit disingenuous. In reality, Helen Louise Crounse was over forty when she wrote this classic of the teen advice genre, which perhaps explained some of her alter ego's antiquated philosophy.

Dating was important because it led to what "Joyce" referred to as "probably the biggest decision of your life—the choice of a mate. A poor decision and the rest of your life can turn into a miserable existence." It was all or nothing. Joyce suggested that a girl who had gone through high school and college and still hadn't found "the one" might try graduate school, "especially one where the men students outnumber the women." A college education so gained never went to waste, she reassured readers, as housewives were "called on occasionally to give book reports in the P.T.A."

Part of the problem was that a girl couldn't simply ask a boy for a date. She had to wait for him to broach the subject, or risk going against Nature: "Let him be the aggressor. He's supposed to be. That's the way he heard it. And he's listening to instinct. He wants to capture, so don't go . . . asking him what he's doing tomorrow night or the next night or the next."[3] Boys, the experts stressed again and again, liked—and were therefore more likely to date—feminine girls. The first of "15 Ways to Make Boys Like You," listed in a 1962 teen magazine, was to "Be A Real Girl": "This just means adding to a boy's feeling that he's a male by being very female yourself. . . . Man-tailored clothes are smart in their place, but frills will flutter a man's heart faster."[4]

If your frills left him flutterless, however, there were plenty of ways to manipulate the poor sap into asking you out, most of which rather closely resembled the plot lines of canceled sitcoms. You could "temporarily 'lose' your locker key" and "ask if you can keep your sweater in his locker." Or you could " 'mistakenly on purpose' pick up one of his books in your stack, [and] leave one of yours with him. It'll take a phone call and a get together to straighten out the confusion." Both of these suggestions came from *The Ingenue Date Book* (1965), which, not thirty pages later, had the audacity to suggest that "directness and honesty are much admired by boys."[5]

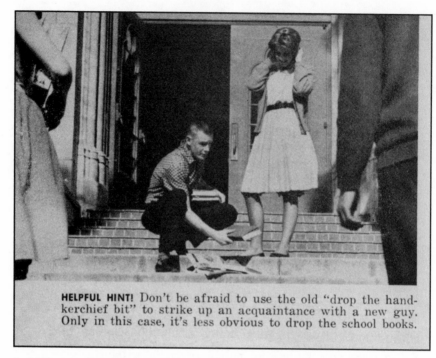

HELPFUL HINT! Don't be afraid to use the old "drop the hand-kerchief bit" to strike up an acquaintance with a new guy. Only in this case, it's less obvious to drop the school books.

In 1960, up-to-date girls dropped their books, not their hankies—it was "less obvious."

The leading strategy for "talking with boys" revolved around learning *his* interests:

> [To develop friendships with boys] you will probably need to know more about such things as outdoor sports and games, making model airplanes, working with "ham" radios, collecting stamps or records, or even repair-ing cars.[6]

Learning about these activities was not presented as being useful for self-enrichment or even being pleasurable; it was simply in order to meet boys. A home economics text discussed "Making conversation easy" using the example of "Debbie" and "Larry." Debbie initiated the conver-sation with Larry by asking him about his interests: "Do you like football?" Shyness, the same text asserted, could be alleviated by being able to *forget yourself* and *think of others* and their interests."[7]

Smart girls learned to "do things"—sports like swimming, skating, and golf were all certified man-traps, as were dancing and parties. Joining clubs, especially those "in which boys do a major in participation," was another sure bet for instant popularity. How about the debate team? "Don't debate whether you can debate or not. Get into that club and have a good time arguing. Let the man win the argument, and you'll win the man."[8]

Acting "as his companion—instead of his competitor" was another way for girls to display their femininity. Whether the activity involved was bowling, dancing, or simple conversation between a girl and her date, she did not compete. Instead, by taking "pride and interest in HIS accomplishments and HIS interests," she added to her feminine charms.[9]

What to Expect on a Date

The anatomy of a date followed a basic pattern that rarely changed from one guidebook to the next. According to Edith Heal's *Teen-Age Manual* (1948), the boy was expected to call for the girl at her house, where he met the family. "He expects to be looked over and is prepared to talk to your mother and dad for a reasonable interval, but . . . he expects your co-operation. . . . It is your solemn duty to be at the door when Jimmy rings." She introduced him according to the strictures of etiquette ("Mother, this is Jim. Jim, this is my Dad.") and told her parents (and, by proxy, her date) when to expect her home. Then it was off to the dance/movies/other sanctioned dating event. Girls tongue-tied by the close presence of a member of the opposite sex could draw upon the *Teen-Age Manual*'s list of conversation starters, as "a successful evening often depend[ed] upon [her] ability to get the conversation under way." The boy, meanwhile, took "the lead in spending his money" at dinner. A girl needed to be pleasant even if she had a bad time, because "no one

Evelyn Millis Duvall: The Queen of Teen Agony

Without question, Evelyn Millis Duvall was the grande dame of the teen advice genre. Besides the classic *Facts of Life and Love for Teenagers*, her books included *When You Marry*, *Why Wait 'Til Marriage*, *Sense and Nonsense About Sex*, and the high school texts *Family Living* and *Being Married*.

Compared to catty Joyce Jackson, Duvall was a loving mother figure, a little square maybe but clearly with your best inter-

Evelyn Millis Duvall, ca. 1947.

ests at heart. Born in 1906 in Oswego, New York, young Evelyn partook of the same types of activities she later advocated in her books: school drama productions, the debate team, glee club, and athletics. After graduation from Syracuse University (summa cum laude, no less), she married social counselor Sylvanus Duvall in 1927. She founded the Association for Family Living in 1943 and was involved with organizations dedicated to marriage, child development, and sex education for the rest of her life.

Duvall assured readers that young people liked members of the opposite sex who were careful of their personal appearance, courteous, and fun to be with, and emphasized what she termed "wholesome dating experiences." Pick-ups (meetings that occurred anywhere your parents, teachers, or religious leaders weren't) were too risky for girls or boys—church groups, community centers, and the YMCA were better places to meet potential dates. Nor was it a coincidence that Duvall boosted the "Y" at every turn: her publisher, Association Press, was a YMCA subsidiary.

feels comfortable in the presence of a girl who sulks or sneers, no matter what the provocation may be." Shy girls could avoid being wallflowers by knowing how to "dance a fox trot, one-step, waltz, and at least two of the newer favorites such as: samba, rumba, conga, and jitterbug steps in moderation." Equally undesirable as shyness was acting like what Heal called a "wildflower"—a girl whose behavior was beyond the pale of subdued femininity, one who powdered her nose "at the table and tried to powder [her] date's nose though he struggled against it." Barring an evening cut short by such brazen behavior, a girl's escort bid her a chaste farewell at the appointed hour. Petting or necking was a no-no. ("The plain truth," Heal told readers, "is necking is a bad imitation of serious grown-up love.") More or less, these were the basics of the ideal date proffered by teen dating guides for almost thirty years.[10]

Some books were even more detailed in their descriptions of dating behavior. *Datebook's Complete Guide to Dating* (1960) was dizzyingly comprehensive, giving tips on what to do, what to wear, and how to act (to name only a few examples) on first dates ("We've never known a boy worth dating twice who gave up on a girl simply because she had first-date scruples about kissing!"), blind dates ("Shoes are a special problem—unless you're so tiny that you have never yet met the boy *you* towered over"), car dates ("Sit down on the seat first, *then* swing your legs and *wraps* into the car"), study dates (*"Don't* set up shop in front of the TV set"), museum dates ("Wear a skirt and blouse, or a conservative date dress"), even church dates ("How much you participate is strictly a matter for your own conscience").[11] Even the generally sensible Evelyn Millis Duvall devoted three full pages of *Facts of Life and Love for Teenagers* to a "pattern" for an appropriate first date, beginning with "John calls for Mary at her home at the appointed time" and ending with "So Mary is careful not to linger at the door, which might make John wonder what she expects him to do."[12] No doubt one of the reasons the manuals went into such excruciating detail was because the more time dating teens spent on the minutiae of etiquette, the less time they had for sexual exploration—in theory, at least.

Petting, Parking, and Reputation

Suppose a girl threw caution (and her advice books) to the wind and found herself and her date in a parked car on Lover's Lane. It was her responsibility, the experts warned, to keep things from getting out of hand. "If the wolf-pack is getting larger and more ferocious," wrote Gladys Denny Shultz in *Letters to Jane* (1960), "I think we may lay much of the blame to such practices as parking and petting. To the average male mind, the girl has given a go-ahead signal in permitting these things." It certainly wasn't *his* fault: "Boys by nature, facts and statistics prove it, are a lot less aggressive than girls. They don't get 'fresh' unless a girl provokes a 'pass,' " wrote Lois Pemberton. They had "an inherent respect for womankind and motherhood," yet girls who indulged in petting ran the risk of unleashing "one of the most powerful forces in Nature"—evidently the hurricane in his pants. It didn't even have to be petting, as "the merest touch of a girl's hand, even a flirtatious glance" (*The Ingenue Date Book*) was enough to bring on a gale force wind.[13]

Girls, the experts agreed, were less easily excited by sex stimulation and more slowly moved to demand sexual contact. Besides, as Evelyn Millis Duvall stressed in *Facts of Life and Love,* "girls and boys alike, as well as almost everyone else, consider[ed] it the girl's responsibility" to keep the boy's sexuality (not to mention her own) under strict control. "You're darn right," said Jim, one of the boys consulted for a 1959 article

The Difference Between Necking and Petting

Alfred L. Murray was an ordained minister and author of several advice guides for young people, including *Youth's Courtship Problems: Youth's Problem No. 2* (1940). Even for a man of the cloth, Murray was extremely Victorian in his moral outlook. Young women who allowed themselves to be picked up ran the risk of being kidnapped by "professional white slave traffickers," while kissing, or "osculation," as Murray termed it, led to a raft of evils. Murray himself displayed a suspicious amount of enthusiasm when it came to adolescent sexuality, and devoted an entire chapter to the differences between necking ("includes caressing and embracing") and petting ("includes kissing, necking, and fondling, be it light or heavy"), as well as such arcane derivatives as "mugging" ("petting, on the heavy side"), "smooching" ("necking"), and "flinging the woo" ("just love play").

in *Teens Today*. "Any girl who thinks a guy's going to put on the brakes first is either naïve or just plain dumb."

A girl's virginal reputation was inextricably bound up with ideas of worthiness and commodity. "Just What Valuation Do You Put on Yourself, Miss Teener?" asked the subtitle of a 1940 article in *Better Homes and Gardens*, before explaining that "no 16-year-old girl is going to keep her shining immaculateness very long sitting around in a beer shack until 2 or 3 in the morning."[14] Young women who were too "eager" for dates, who were "boy crazy," or who stepped out of sexual bounds lacked self-worth. "[S]elling your own personality [was] like selling a 14 carat gold wristwatch," wrote Becky Lynne, in an article called "Are You Boy Crazy?"[15] A girl didn't want to get bested in the dating economy. Harold Shryock was even more specific:

A good reputation is what sells a given make of automobile, a certain kind of chinaware, a specific brand of hose, or a particular model camera. . . . Personal reputation is just as important to a person's success and happiness in life as is the reputation of a product to the success of the company who produced it.[16]

The "fast" girl who kissed and petted would be "shopworn and shoddy with a low value sign on her before she ever wakes up to the fact that life gave her an extra measure of good things," wrote Lois Pemberton.[17] Given the equation of virginity with value, it's not surprising that "cheap" was another synonym for girls who pushed the sexual envelope.

So what did the normal teen girl suffering (no matter what the experts said) normal teen girl urges do? Sublimation was the key. As previously mentioned, the guides provided many suggestions for wholesome dating activities, to help channel potentially sexual urges into harmless activities like sports. Joyce Jackson dated the equally fictitious former Winter Carnival Ice King, Mix Lawrence, and her secret for "keeping" him nicely illustrated this line of thinking: "When I am with Mix, I keep a conversation going. It reduces the time that might be given over in a weak moment to a sexual urge that knows no stopping." The *Ladies' Home Journal's* teen column urged girls to "anticipate the kiss to come" by squeezing her date's hand while cooing some variation of "Sorry, Bill, not just now. Good night," before disappearing inside the door.[18] But Ann Landers came up with the most novel solution in *Ann Landers Talks to Teen-Agers About Sex* (1963):

Housework, particularly floor-scrubbing is not only great for the female figure, but it's good for the soul. And it will help take the edge off your sex appetite. Cooking, baking and sewing will prepare you for homemaking. Energy siphoned into these constructive channels will leave less energy for erotic fantasies.[19]

Obviously, Ann had never heard of the Naughty French Maid.

Baking cookies or going bowling was all well and good, but what happened when you didn't want to say No? You certainly couldn't find any information about birth control in any of these books. Most experts barely mentioned the subject before they dropped it like a hot potato, as did Williams and Kane: "Birth control is a controversial subject. . . . But it is worth pointing out, as a practical caution, that there has not yet been devised a foolproof contraceptive." And even though *The Seventeen Book of Answers to What Your Parents Don't Talk About and Your Best Friends Can't Tell You* (1972) laudably hoped its readers were "responsible enough . . . never to have intercourse without the appropriate precautions," it didn't say just what those "precautions" were or how teens could get them.

Joyce Jackson had a theory (she did about most things) as to why some girls made the mistake of indulging in premarital sex: "I think that—believe it or not—the Santa Claus myth that they learn as children serves later to confuse them." Grace Talbot, a wrong-thinking teen of Joyce's acquaintance, wondered whether "pre-marital sex relations [were] really bad" or if one was "merely supposed to pretend she thinks they are bad," just as she was "supposed to have enough sense not to believe the [Santa Claus] prattle" her parents told her. Poor confused Grace! Jackson could have told her that premarital sex relations "destroy[ed] love instead of maintaining it" because:

> Sex is a part of Nature. All nature is not good. Polio, cancer, heart disease—think of the many ways in which we have to fight to control Nature. With regard to sex, Nature cares only about perpetuating the human race. It cares nothing whatsoever about your future happiness once it gets its work done. It says smugly, "That's not in my department."[20]

True enough—that's why Carl Djerassi invented those popular little pills to control wayward nature. But Jackson had a different solution in mind:

> We control certain aspects of Nature known as disease by fighting germs; we control certain aspects of Nature known as sex by a tiny slip of

"Sexual Conduct of the Teen-Ager"

by Dr. S. U. Lawton, M.D., F.A.C.P., and Jules Archer
(New York: Berkley Publishing Company, 1955)

As you may have guessed from its lurid cover, the book of this title wasn't a sensitive guide to teenage sexuality. Instead, it's a wonderful example of the teensploitation material that appeared beginning in the late 1940s. The public was fascinated by the juvenile delinquent—an antisocial teen terror packing a switchblade and a bad attitude. J.D.s sneered at the whole teen advice market while they drank, smoked, and petted to the tempestuous strains of rock and roll. *Sexual Conduct of the Teen-Ager* purported to be "a shocking, challenging study of youth today . . . based on personal interviews and scientific research." Was any of it true? Who cared? This was hot stuff, justified because "when the welfare of our youth is at stake, there can be no room for squeamishness." Undocumented stories of "beer spiked with benzedrine . . . marijuana

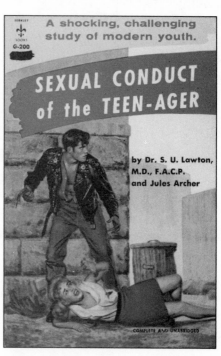

Black leather jackets and torn blouses. *Teensploitation, 1955.*

cigarettes, and complete sexual promiscuity and experimentation" vied with tales of "non-virgin clubs" and "summertime sex vacations." Then there was the unnamed "midwestern school" where "shocked authorities learned that the initiation fee for pledged boys consisted of cunnilingual activity with girl members." Now that's thinking, gals!

paper known as the marriage license. Just this little piece of paper gives the people who apply for it a chance for happiness, while others who practice marriage without it must often live out their lives in misery.[21]

But even for soon-to-be-married couples, premarital sex was a long-fused keg of dynamite:

Years later, maybe even twenty, guilty feelings for our sins may overtake us, causing severe nervous and psychological disorders . . . intense suffering, complete collapse—pain, shortness of breath, other physical torments, even insanity.[22]

Joyce Jackson wasn't the only one forecasting disaster. "The little black clouds of memory, the deep feeling of guilt, the feeling that sex is secret and wrong will rise up to plague you," was Williams and Kane's dire prediction. One of the advice-filled *Letters to Jane* (1960) related the tale of a husband who, instead of the usual wedding night banter, told his new wife that "if she had agreed to sex relations before their marriage—and he had suggested it—he would never have married her." Yet another guidebook (*Youth's Courtship Problems*) told the sad story of a girl who asked for a "divorce from her husband because she was unable to forget her premarital heavy petting experiences with other men." Clearly, hubby wasn't doing something right.

Of course, the connoisseur of prescriptive literature must always remain aware that the gap between reality and ideal can never be ade-

quately measured. Even in the golden days of yore, real life rarely mirrored either the saccharine do's or the horrific don'ts portrayed in the
advice books. For example, while guide writers pointed out again and
again that church was a good place to meet the sort of wholesome young
people one might like to date, reality could be a bit more complicated, as
one woman recalled in Brett Harvey's *The Fifties: A Women's Oral History*: "I started to go to this church group as a way to find a better group of
friends to relate to socially. But I found out they were just as horny in
church as they were outside of it! It was everywhere!"[23]

This discrepancy between flesh and blood and paper was what made
teen dating manuals so appealing—to adults, at least. Parents may have
hoped their children emulated the behavioral standards set forth in the
manuals, but a movie date described by a young woman in 1951 was
probably more representative: "Everybody sits in the balcony eating pop-
corn, whistling and shooting paper airplanes, and no one would think of
getting home before three."[24]

Just the sort of "disturbing behavior" Evelyn Millis Duvall had in
mind when she urged teens to "enjoy the show without annoying their
neighbors." But whether they met boys at a church group function, in the
balcony of the local movie palace, or at a record hop, sooner or later most
girls were faced with the question of marriage, and those who weren't
were still faced with its specter.

Chapter 4

Something Old, Something New, Something Borrowed, Something ... Pink: Weddings, Marriage, and, Heaven Forbid, the Single Girl

Love! Pelvic love! Carnal love! Love, rising like a salmon to the lure of an insignificant fly, took the hook from which there was to be no deliverance.
Richard H. Hoffman, M.D.,
"I Met the Wrong Man,"
Why Are You Single? *(1949)*

A 1944 Listerine ad featured a big-eyed little girl, her mouth rounded into an "oh" of excitement, her eyebrows raised in wonder. "Whew," the copy read, "Sis won't be an old maid after all!" Instead, the little spy observed her older sibling "kissing that wonderful Marine" and, thanks to the mouthwash that solved the problem that had stood in Sis's way until now, "gloating over the twinkling diamond on her

103

finger!" At a time when marriage and motherhood were such foregone conclusions for most women, *Women's Home Companion* magazine featured a series of articles for "Pre-married Women"—not "unmarried," with its scary connotation of impending spinsterhood, but "pre-married," with the assumption that a white wedding was just around the corner. Obviously, Sis and Susie weren't the only ones who worried when Cupid was late in calling.

Little sister hoped for a white wedding, too. Listerine ad, Ladies' Home Journal, 1944.

Spinster into Single Girl

This was a traditional fear. A nineteenth-century guidebook dedicated to "the Unmarried Gentlewomen of England," *The Afternoon of Unmarried Life,* suggested that "spinsters" follow the tenets of True Womanhood: purity, piety, submissiveness, and domesticity. Readers were admonished to "repress selfishness" by reading historical and religious works, and performing Christian service for others. The guide presented these inspirational lines in a poem called "Thirty-five": "Have we no charm when youth is flown / Midway to death left sad and lone?" Even eighty years later, the experts (in this case marriage counselor/psychologist Dr. Clifford R. Adams and writer Vance Packard) concurred that thirty-five was the age "when an unmarried woman can no longer consider herself a 'young maid.' "[1]

Living alone was "an abnormal state for a woman." "Psychiatrists agree," Adams and Packard explained, "that except in unusual cases women who live alone will become neurotic and frustrated." Other experts—such as those included in the 1949 collection of essays called *Why Are You Single?*—considered singleness "a form of social delinquency—a private betrayal of the greater needs of society as a whole." Perhaps the unmarried woman who lived across the hall suffered from coitophobia ("a morbid dread of marital relations") or worse:

> There may be a dread of the sight of a naked body (gymnophobia). . . .
> Apheophobia characterizes the behavior of those who dread to be touched. There may even be a morbid obsession against household duties, a dread or intense dislike for housekeeping.

"Small wonder," another expert mused, "that, in this chaotic world, human beings (especially women) reflect the need for supervision and guidance."[2]

The popular press speculated that the single girl either had a dread of marital relations or was insatiable. "Must Bachelor Girls Be Immoral?" asked a 1952 article in *Coronet* magazine. "Thousands" of single women romped "through one affair after another, feeling satisfied and adjusted in so doing, and psychiatrists frequently condone their habits," reported *Coronet* (obviously not consulting the authors of *Why Are You Single?*). But there was a price to pay for sexual satisfaction. "Promiscuous girls [were] cutting their own throats for marriage," reported a psychoanalyst. The happiest marriages, the article concluded, were those in which the bride was a virgin.

Faced with such complexities, it's not surprising a single gal might want to reach for an advice book. Such guides mostly fell into two categories: those giving advice on enjoying one's single status, and those devoted to ending said status ASAP. My favorite example of the former is Marjorie Hillis's witty and urbane (so much so that *Vanity Fair*'s Frank Crowninshield wrote the introduction) *Live Alone and Like It: A Guide for the Extra Woman* (1936), which now seems about forty years ahead of its time. "There is a technique," Ms. Hillis maintained, "about living alone successfully, as there is about doing anything well." Hillis characterized the single woman who persisted in picturing herself as "poor little me, all alone in the big bad world" as "an outstanding example of a superbore." That alone is enough to recommend it, but unlike later advice mavens who considered "single" and "celibate" synonyms, *Live Alone and Like It* actually provided a chapter about s-e-x entitled "Will You or Won't You?" Marjorie's down-to-earth advice is still valid: "Hold a little mental investigation of the case—and then do exactly as you please."

Finally, there is the collection of "case studies" with which Hillis illustrated each chapter's salient points. These instructive little vignettes featured a series of anonymous young women, either happily acting out Hillis's advice or suffering the consequences of not doing so. Ah, to be Miss R., spending a lazy Saturday evening at home, "taking a tub," then rubbing "herself down with a pet toilet water":

> After this she put on a brief step-in and a pair of maroon satin lounging pajamas and ensconced herself on the couch in the living room, armed with two or three of the latest magazines. Before dinner, the maid brought her a glass of sherry and some simple crackers.

"Why Are You Single?"

Pity the individuals who purchased a copy of this 1949 book, edited by Hilda Holland. Expecting useful information and perhaps a bit of succor for their single state, they were instead confronted with such accusatory chapters title as "The Chip on the Shoulder," "The Marriage Shyness of the Male," "Married Neuters," "Deserters from the Marriage Process," "I Met the Wrong Man," and "Are You Emotionally Mature?"

Find a copy of this book, follow Marjorie Hillis's excellent advice, and soon you will find yourself wrapped in white marabou and satin, living in the style to which we should all become accustomed—single or not.

But the book that, by its own admission, "torpedoed the myth that a girl must be married to enjoy a satisfying life" once and for all (well, almost) was Helen Gurley Brown's *Sex and the Single Girl* (1962). Brown found the typical single woman so driven to get married "by herself and her well-meaning but addlepated friends [and, one might add, the typical advice book] . . . that her whole existence seems to be an apology for *not* being married." She also declared that "being smart about money is sexy"—a far cry from the training for wifely consumerism provided by high-school home ec texts. However, her protofeminist sympathies didn't stop Brown from offering her readers advice on dress and interior design, or from including recipes for enchanting dinners for two and thoughts on entertaining—just like her guidebook peers. Similarly, when the self-proclaimed "health nut" Brown urged readers to investigate wheat germ and working out, it wasn't with increased physical strength and healthy body image in mind. The fact that fitness and diet could make her "fanny cute enough to be patted" was the Single Girl's payoff for all those hours in the gym.

What made *S&SG* so revolutionary was Helen Gurley Brown's belief

"The Bachelor Girl"

by Kay Martin (New York: Macfadden Publications, 1963)

"'Spinster' is an excellent name for a yacht; Old Maid is a kids' card game. Learn to reap the most fun and fulfillment from being a bachelor girl!" Clearly an attempt to cash in on *S&SG*'s popularity, *The Bachelor Girl* lacked Helen Gurley Brown's enthusiasm and wit, not to mention her originality. But the major philosophical difference between Bachelor Girl and Single Girl lay in their attitudes toward sex. The Bachelor Girl

> wisely recognize[d] that the sex act [was] only a partial fulfillment for the normal female; childbearing and rearing are a necessary part of the triumvirate which completes the female sex cycle.

What made the Single Girl so revolutionary, of course, was that she wholeheartedly rejected this "triumvirate." The Bachelor Girl eventually wanted marriage and motherhood, even though she knew that it was "mathematically impossible for every unmarried woman to find a husband," thanks to statistics that "proved" a shortage of eligible—unmarried—males. Martin refreshingly decried the "mantrap" mentality of other advice books ("Men are people . . . people are not 'snagged' "), but she nevertheless provided a list of states with low male populaces, and suggested that readers increase their marital odds by relocating.

By the way, like Helen Gurley Brown, Kay Martin neglected to provide her readers with information on protecting themselves against pregnancy or sexually transmitted diseases. Recipes for Lobster Thermidor, yes; why and where to get condoms, no.

that single women could experience "unadulterated, cliffhanging sex" without remorse. (And evidently without protection, as nowhere in its pages does she mention either contraception or the possibility or prevention of venereal disease. It was the pre-AIDS era, but nevertheless I'm sure many a Single Girl wound up sadder and wiser.) She urged her readers to "reconsider the idea that sex without marriage is dirty," and promoted her belief that marriage without premarital sex was an act of "complete lunacy." Married men, Brown maintained, were perfect partners for the no-strings sexuality she advocated, even though she herself was, in fact, married—which makes me wonder if she and her husband, like one of the couples she described in a later chapter, had "an 'understanding' that [the husband] may frisk around a bit." Of course, all of this was guaranteed to cause apoplectic fits in the hinterlands. As a result, S&SG shot to the top of the bestseller lists, spawning in its wake a film version, a record, at least three sequels, and a host of imitators.

Neither the advent of the Single Girl nor the dawn of the women's movement stemmed the flow of conservative advice books. Harriet LaBarre's A Life of Your Own (1972) was aimed at spunky "live-alone" gals à la Mary Richards (heroine of The Mary Tyler Moore Show), yet it was strangely reminiscent of an earlier era. In fact, overlooking the chapter on "Physical Security," you might think you were reading How to Be Happy While Single (1949), which assumed that single women led empty lives that needed to be filled with good works. The chapters on money, clothing, home decorating, and food could almost have been lifted directly from its pages. Regarding sex, LaBarre suggested that her readers "consider making an emotional commitment" before proceeding with what she termed "an affair," but once again, she offered no information regarding contraception or disease prevention. A Life of Your Own may have promoted self-esteem, but it made single life sound about as exciting as crocheting a potholder. Similarly, reading Audrey Gellis's How to Meet Men . . . Now That You're Liberated (1978) while wearing a New Freedom maxi pad did not a member of NOW make. Instead, Gellis suggested that her presumably liberated gal readers consider becoming cocktail waitresses, receptionists, or—heaven forbid—"crafts peddlers"

"After Sex with the Single Girl"

by Richard Bernstein and William Storm Hale
(Los Angeles: Marvin Miller Enterprises, 1965),

"Swingers Guide for the Single Girl: Key to the New Morality"

by Marie and Hector Roget
(Los Angeles: Holloway House Publishing Co., 1966)

Both of these are examples of how the "adult" books market cleverly took advantage of the media hoopla surrounding the publication of *Sex and the Single Girl*. The cleverly titled *After Sex . . .* was not, of course, the serious work of social criticism revealing "startling facts on the rocketing rate of illegitimate motherhood in America today" that its cover led readers to think. Instead, its "scores of authentic case histories" catered to one-handed readers interested in "Wilma" and her "erotic dreams of Ross and his organ."

The *Swingers Guide* was a less racy but nevertheless fascinating artifact of the mid-1960s sexual revolution. Its purpose was "to help modern women . . . live happily and contentedly . . . in the Age of the Pills," of which the authors were enthusiastic proponents. This is the sort of book that men bought for girlfriends reluctant to engage in premarital sex. Here, for example, is what they had to say about "The Female Pills":

> A touchy bit of indecision that bothers many girls, when first entering into a sexual relationship with a man, is about which one of them should be insuring that conception does not occur.

Don't let the question fill your pretty head. The average man prefers not to be annoyed with remembering such details, regarding conception in the Age of the Pill to be the women's responsibility.

The Rogets advocated so-called Instant Sex—which entirely did away with foreplay and female sexual arousal. Good thing they told their readers not to "expect complete sexual satisfaction from every sexual encounter"!

in order to increase their chances of meeting a mate. She was in the vanguard, though, when it came to exploiting the technological wonder called CB radio for dating purposes:

CB radio has swept the country and is definitely here to stay. Most CBers seem to be men, probably because [it] appeals to macho fantasies . . . of a rugged loner traveling the open road. . . . If you own a car, install a CB radio. Learn the lingo and adopt a colorful CB name for yourself.

That's a big 10-4, L'il Hustler.

Baiting the Wolf Trap

Many women were less interested in the Single Girl lifestyle than in how to meet and marry Mr. Right as soon as possible—and once again the guide writers were there to serve her needs. Zsa Zsa Gabor got right to the point in her pink-paged *How to Catch a Man/How to Keep a Man/How to Get Rid of a Man* (1971): "The best way to attract a man immediately is to have a magnificent bosom and a half-size brain and let both of them show." Others went into more detail, but the rules for attracting a man were nicely summarized in this selection from "Must Bachelor Girls Be Immoral?":

The lonely mademoiselle had best improve her personality, her looks, her cooking, her dancing—make herself into the most capable, likeable and captivating female possible. She should join clubs, take up sports, go where mixed crowds gather and, in due time, she should lure herself a couple of nice beaux.[3]

It may have taken 200 or 300 pages, but this was more or less the standard advice given out by all the guidebooks. Charles Contreras presented a more baroque variation in his 1953 booklet *How to Fascinate Men*. Contreras suggested that lonely mademoiselles adopt the principles of successful businessmen when trying to land a marriage prospect—and there was no question that matrimony was the outcome his readers desired. The cover illustration featured a blonde bombshell winking over her man's shoulder, a blazing engagement ring on prominent display as she cradles his head. Just as a salesman "would not attempt to sell a product without first looking over the potential market, analyzing the competition, preparing himself with all the knowledge possible on the subject" before presenting his product in "the best possible manner," neither should the bachelor gal enter the dating pool without taking similar precautions. Femininity was the key to capturing a man, according to Contreras. Take Jane, for example. She "is just an average girl, not beautiful by accepted standards," but "she has learned to make herself attractive":

> Wherever there is a chance of meeting men Jane makes a point to be present and is always very careful to appear at her very feminine best. . . . Jane's attire is of the most feminine design and unless there is some special occasion, she avoids "jeans," "slacks," "peddle [*sic*] pushers" and "shorts" like the plague, for she knows that such apparel accentuates the worst features of the female form, in addition to which she is aware, only too well, that there is nothing cuddly about a woman wearing pants. Bare feet, even at the beach, and sandals that show the toes are taboo, for this girl is smart enough to realize that there is decidedly nothing attractive about a bare foot. She wears sheer stockings as much as possible.[4]

I can almost hear him drooling over those stockings, can't you? But appearance was only part of the conniving—that is, "enchanting"—woman's arsenal. The "proper mental attitude" was essential. Men simply couldn't resist a simpering idiot—a woman who showed "an attitude of frailty" and appealed "to a man's chivalry by being gentle, timid and cuddlesome" (which she couldn't do in pants, of course).

If you can't imagine yourself living up to that description, maybe you just need a little practice. Luckily, Contreras included a number of exercises to help gals develop femininity. All you need is a mirror and a few simple props. First of all, however, put on your "most effeminate apparel." Then, visualize yourself as "a demure girl who knows very little, if anything, about worldly ways":

EXERCISE A

Stand before a mirror, with a piece of adhesive tape placed horizontal across the glass about the height of the average man's head from the floor.

Imagine that you have just met an attractive man upon whom you want to make an impression and start by opening your eyes as wide as possible, looking directly into the eyes of the man and bring[ing] forth a smile that has all the innocence and trustfulness of a five-year-old child . . .

Start an audible conversation, in a well-modulated voice, by asking this imaginary man how long he has been in town and where he lives, etc., after allowing sufficient time for his answers, while looking at him with the eyes wide open. When the conversation has been in progress for a few minutes drop your eyes and produce the biggest blush possible—if a blush will not come easily draw a mental picture of yourself alone upon a stage before an auditorium full of people and you have just had some very embarrassing situation arise.[5]

That's right, you're standing there talking to a freaking piece of adhesive tape stuck on the mirror (not to mention pretending it's answering back), and you *need help* to imagine an embarrassing situation. Maybe it's best we progress to:

How to Fascinate Men,
1953.

EXERCISE E

Arrange a coat on a hanger about the height of a man and imagine you have known him for a few weeks or more and have done something to make him very angry. Stand in front of the coat, take a lapel in each hand, open the eyes wide . . . if a few tears can be produced, so much the better—look directly into the eyes of this imaginary man and say: "You're not really and truly going to be angry with me," and at the same time give him your best childish confiding, trustful look. Practice this exercise until it can be put over without a flaw, for there are few men when the stage is properly set for this act, who can refrain from gathering a woman in their arms and kissing her.[6]

Perhaps, but how many women are there who would respect the dope that fell for this?

Personally, I'm glad I didn't read the Franks' *How to Be a Woman* before I got married. According to them, a relationship involves "at least 12 persons, not counting in-laws":

> As a woman, you bring to marriage first your image of yourself as a female-feminine person. Secondly, there is your conception of what a wife should be and, thirdly, of your role as a mother . . .
>
> Four, five, and six are your images of the masculine roles. They are a blend of all you have observed and felt about men, but nonetheless real for existing only in your mind.

Your husband brought a similar six "persons" with him to the altar. Had I known all this, I think I might have given up on the whole idea of marriage. I'm not even sure what a "female-feminine person" is—nor did the Franks explain it.

Neither my husband nor I knew there was anyone besides the two of us standing at the altar on our wedding day. Surprisingly enough, without help from the Franks or any of the experts, I had found the right guy. In fact, not long after I leaned over the table and asked him if he'd ever heard of the tonsured sixties band The Monks, it was obvious to us both that this was The Big Romance. Two years later, it was just as apparent that The Subject of Marriage must be broached, yet week after week went by as both of us daintily circumvented any serious discussion of the same. Then I attended a wedding shower for a friend.

Rice, Satin, and Silverware

According to Penelope Worth, whose "Girl Talk" column appeared monthly in the fifties romance magazine *Exciting Love* ("Combined with Thrilling Love and Popular Love"), a wedding shower is an event where "everyone,

How Not to Catch a Man

In any given situation, knowing what NOT to do is often more instructive than knowing what to do. Therefore, single or married, every gal needs to know which of her charming little idiosyncrasies causes the opposite sex to flee in the opposite direction. Here's a verbatim list of what Alma (*Your Power as a Woman*) Archer calls "male grievances" to avoid.

1. Don't wear styles that men consider queer. (*How to Pick a Mate*)

2. Very few of them like all red hats. (*She Knows How*)

3. Men are disillusioned by such things as hair curlers, awkward positions and postures, unattractive sounds in the throat, making up in public. (*How to Pick a Mate*) They've noticed the way we yank down our girdles. (*She Knows How*)

4. [Avoid] wearing a ring on your long center finger. (*Your Power as a Woman*)

5. Men instinctively writhe at the sight of ugly, chipped fingernails. (*Your Power as a Woman*)

6. Don't fail to answer a man, and promptly, when he addresses you; he may feel slighted by the inattention. (*How to Pick a Mate*) Inattention hurts a man's ego. (*She Knows How*)

7. Don't show too much INdependence; it can be irritating but DEpendence can be used to cater to a man's ego. (*How to Fascinate Men*)

8. Unless you are the pixy type—but definitely—or under sixteen, call a Manhattan a Manhattan, and leave a Pink Lady alone. (*She Knows How*)

9. Never forget that men do not like women to know more than themselves and always remember the quotation: "Brains do not handicap a girl if she keeps them well hidden." (*How to Fascinate Men*)

10. Men have an aversion for girls who play with shredded lettuce. (*She Knows How*)

not just the bride-to-be, is excited." True enough, but where Miss Worth suggested "light refreshments" such as "platters of tiny fancy sandwiches . . . petit fours and fancy cookies, coffee and tea," my set tends to prefer fancy alcohol and slutty lingerie. My friend's shower was no exception. Returning home with romantic visions of connubial bliss floating in my head, not to mention half a bottle of Champagne in my bloodstream, I realized that this was the golden moment to bring up The Subject. My boyfriend lay comfortably on the couch, lost in reverie (well, maybe watching *Hard Copy*). This was just as well, as the element of surprise probably worked in my favor. As it turned out, any planned speeches I may have had fell by the wayside, as I fell on top of My Beloved and slurred, "When are you going to ask me to marry you?" (It may have been a bit forward of me, but no less august a personage than Zsa Zsa Gabor herself concurred with my technique: "I proposed to every one of my husbands . . . it is wonderful for his ego.") Being the fearless kind of guy that he is, he merely laughed and said he didn't think that now was the time to discuss it, but that he'd figured all along that we'd get married. Satisfied with this, I joyfully extricated myself from him and passed out on the other couch.

In the past, such a scene was unlikely to have occurred. Prior to the seventies, couples who roomed together without benefit of matrimony were "likely to find themselves isolated from their community and [given] a wide berth socially," as *Why Are You Single?* described it. Even as late as the early 1970s, the much-married Zsa Zsa Gabor was leery of shacking up: "To me, if you are a young girl and you find a boy 'groovy' and you go off and move into his 'pad' with him, you are definitely making a terribly bad mistake."

Living at home up until the time of one's marriage made gifts brought to the showers and the wedding itself an important source of appliances and kitchen tools. That's where a wedding planner like *To the Bride* (1956) came in handy. Distributed by merchants who wanted brides-to-be to sign on at their gift registries, *To the Bride* was part cookbook and part hardbound advertisement for china, silverware, glassware, and stainless steel, all wrapped up in prose that is either cloying ("Soon you will reach that day for which you have planned and dreamed since you were a little girl . . . Your Wedding Day!!"), prone to exaggeration ("Undoubtedly the greatest invention since the discovery of electricity is the marvelous new Sunbeam Automatic Electric Controlled Heat Frypan"), or both. Filled with suggestions that the wedding was an excellent occasion for unbridled consumerism, the book included handy lists of name-brand appliances, bed linens, etc., for the bride to distribute to her friends and family. Couples who commenced cohabitation after the wedding ceremony actually needed these items to set up housekeeping for the first time, but I still wonder if brides who received utilitarian gifts were as thrilled about it as the one who appeared in a 1955 ad for the "Rid-Jid Knee Room Adjustable All-Steel Ironing Table," holding an iron and surrounded by "seldom used luxury gifts" the rest of the copy assured us she didn't want.

One of those luxury gifts was sterling silver flatware. If the manufacturers of sterling silver advertised heavily in teen magazines, they went into overdrive in publications like *Bride's* and *House Beautiful's Guide for the Bride*. Perhaps because no one really *needed* sterling flatware, its advertising scaled heights of emotionalism seldom seen outside that for products like mouthwash and acne medications. Owning your own silver was a "thrilling, heart-filling thing," according to one 1947 ad. "Inferior quality, like false pride, will trip you up sooner or later," editorialized *Bride's* magazine. But the master of thrilling, heart-filling melodrama was International Sterling. "Aunt Beth, do you remember the day I told Tom I'd marry him?" began one 1947 ad, which featured a white-gowned bride grasping the hand of an attractive older woman: "Oh, I was in the stars about it. I guess I didn't come down to earth till we had the family talk, and Mother and Dad told me they could swing the wedding, but not much in the way of 'worldly goods.'"

Thank God for Aunt Beth, who understood that weddings were exactly the time for worldly goods, and lots of 'em. "*Have* your International Sterling, honey . . . even if it's just two place settings!" Soon all her friends have sent place settings as wedding gifts, leading to a happy end.

In 1957, another International Sterling ad gently chastised women who didn't follow Aunt Beth's shining example. A pensive woman looks past her nicely set table, while her young daughter peruses the flatware. The caption reads, "They tried to tell me, but I wouldn't listen . . . "

"*Most brides would prefer a deluxe ironing table to . . . seldom-used luxury gifts," 1955.*

I'll never forget how we furnished our first apartment! I made lists like mad and we dashed around in a starry-eyed daze buying all sorts of impractical things.

Oh, Mother and Aunt Charlotte tried to talk some sense into me, but I was too young to appreciate . . . or even listen to advice.

But now, with Suzy growing up, I wish I hadn't been so independent.

Luckily, to celebrate their sixth wedding anniversary, they purchased a set of International Sterling—"one of the most satisfying possessions a woman can own." Advertisements like these suggested that there was nothing consumerism couldn't solve, as if the only thing between heartbreak and happiness was the proper stemware or a set of monogrammed towels.

From Dining Room to Bedroom: The Wedding Night

Couples who didn't cohabit before the wedding ceremony faced another potential problem, this one not so easily solved as the need for household appliances. In the early 1950s, half of all brides were virgins at the time of their weddings.[7] Virgin or not, the public's smirking assumption was that a honeymoon couple was on their way to a conjugal bed for the first time. "Who would choose the fish-bowl of a large resort?" asked an advertisement for "The Farm on the Hill," a honeymooners-only resort in Swiftwater, Pennsylvania.[8] At the Farm, honeymooners enjoyed "charming seclusion" away from prying eyes. Even a guide for men, *Esquire Etiquette,* noted that a groom might register and get the key in advance, "so that you can spare [your bride] the possible embarrassment of standing around in the lobby thinking she looks like a newlywed."[9]

Wedding night woes were understandable. Given that teen girls were told again and again to sublimate their sexual desires and keep those of their boyfriends in check, it's not surprising that midcentury marriage manuals frequently mentioned the problem of frigidity or "female impotence." "Few women enter marriage sexually awakened and ready for complete response in the sex act. Many American girls are brought up to be 'nice,' to repulse the advances of men, and to refrain from any genital stimulation. Marriage demands a completely different pattern of behavior, and it is extremely difficult to remake oneself overnight," wrote Evelyn Millis Duvall in *Being Married,* a few chapters after listing eighteen ways in which girls could "repulse the advances" of dates (which

For the ideal honeymoon, if a trip is planned, it is better not to make it too strenuous, too long or too expensive.

The ideal honeymoon. From The Age of Romance, 1933, 1940.

included "ask for a cigarette" and "pass off attempts as a joke"). The authors of *How to Be a Woman* warned young brides they might find their first sexual experiences to be disappointing. "If so, don't despair. You are not frigid or abnormal. There is nothing 'wrong' with you." Other experts were less understanding. Women who didn't make the transition from self-controlled virgins to sexually uninhibited lovers were "not only imperfect wives" but "bad mothers unsuited for the task of bringing up children." Further, a husband suffering "a discordant married life as a result" of his wife's frigidity might be "impeded and injured in [his] professional progress."[10]

Compared to the above, another guide's recommendation that brides-to-be practice stretching the hymen "a little each day for about ten days, until three fingers can be admitted"[11] presumed a high degree of familiarity with one's genitalia, highly unlikely at a time (1943) when tampon manufacturers regularly reminded consumers that their product could be safely used by virgins.

The Mysterious and Slightly Scary World
of Feminine Hygiene

The vague knowledge many women had about the region below their waists contributed to the mystifying nature of an early 1970s television commercial: a woman dressed in an elegant evening gown puttered around her dining room, lighting candles, setting the table and in general getting ready for a swanky meal at home. A voiceover extolled the virtues of a wonderful product called FDS Feminine Hygiene Deodorant Spray. The last scene featured the woman seated alone at the beautifully set table. She hears the door open and leaps up, moaning, "He's home!" in a nasal voice so obnoxious that to this day it is perversely wedged in my brain right between "Watching Scotty Grow" and "The Night Chicago Died."

As a nine-year-old watching the commercial, I was confused. What was a "feminine deodorant" anyway? Did you spray it under your arms? Around the room? I was shocked several years later when I discovered just how and where the product was meant to be applied.

I didn't think too much about feminine hygiene beyond that—after all, as far as I could tell, that part of my body never smelled bad. Several semesters in the women's studies department acquainted me with the feminist viewpoint, as well as the biological fact—nobody really needed deodorizing sprays, douches, or scented tampons.

But it wasn't until I started to collect old magazines that I realized just how, well, disturbing, the world of feminine hygiene could be. There were those Lysol ads, for one thing. That's right, Lysol—the same foul-smelling liquid, originally developed as a substitute for carbolic acid, used to scrub bathroom floors—was for years promoted for use as a douche. And if that concept wasn't frightening enough in itself, there was the ad copy. "Forgotten anniversary?" began one 1952 advertisement. "Could be your fault!"

> If your husband's neglect is making you miserable, the reason may be so simple that you haven't realized it could be so serious. Carelessness about intimate feminine hygiene can bring doubt, uncertainty—even

Fake Marriage Manuals

It wasn't trash, it was social science! After all, these were just the "facts as told to the doctor," and what the reader's filthy mind made of them was something else entirely. *Sex and Marriage Problems (From the Intimate Records of a Psychoanalyst)* (1948) is an example of this type of book. "Case studies" with titles like "The Girl Who Couldn't Say No," or "The Strange Love Triangle," made the somewhat racy material within seem more acceptable to individuals who otherwise wouldn't be caught dead reading it. Meanwhile, marketers knew that sleaze sells. The cover of *What Today's Woman Should Know About Marriage and Sex* put the last three words in large type over a picture that would have been right at home on a romance novel, but the material inside included articles such as "How Much Insurance Does the Young Family Need?"

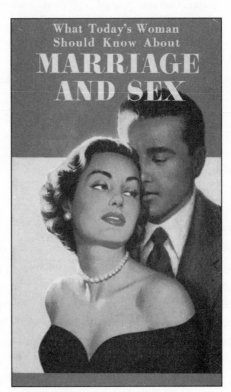

Marriage, sex—and insurance, 1949.

definite "coolness"—into an otherwise happy marriage, and what a shame to let this happen to you . . . when effective precaution is as simple as douching with "Lysol." It couldn't be easier!

Or more terrifying! But this prose was stuffily academic compared to one of Lysol's 1930s ads:

Women are sensitive—shy. Down deep in their hearts they know what's the matter. But something keeps them from telling—even their doctor—and from listening to her advice when she has guessed the truth. Such a case came to my notice recently. I could see my patient thought it "wasn't nice" to face the problem of marriage hygiene frankly. So I sent for her husband. "I'm sorry I had to send for you," I told him. "But your wife won't listen. Now you must teach her what to do." [!!!!] I explained about Lysol—the antiseptic that can always be trusted. I told him how safe it is—how gentle. I told him that the whole medical world approves, uses, recommends it. He went away comforted. And when I next saw his wife, her fears had vanished like dew in the sun. They had both grown young again.[12]

Lysol wasn't the only manufacturer of feminine hygiene products whose advertising campaign equated marital happiness with frequent douching. Norforms vaginal suppositories promised "easier, surer protection for your most intimate marriage problem," while Zonite, Lysol's biggest competitor, warned, "Don't Let False Modesty and Ignorance Ruin Married Happiness!" Another Zonite ad turned the heat up a notch and tugged at a mother's heartstrings: "Don't let your daughter risk married happiness . . . even her health and womanly charm!"

Be sure your daughter knows how important the practice of complete hygiene (including intimate internal cleanliness) is to married happiness, her health, after her periods and to combat an odor even graver than bad breath or body odor.

As for bad breath, that could be combated with a simple swig of

The vital first step to "continual marital congeniality," 1948.

Zonite, too—twenty years before its appearance as a douche, it had been marketed as a mouthwash ("The Taste Tells You Zonite Gets Real Results"). But these were only two of Zonite's multiple personalities: In the mid-1920s, it had been promoted as an enema. That's three orifices, one product—talk about value for your money![13]

While marital scare tactics were a staple of feminine hygiene advertising, manufacturers explored other avenues as well. In the 1930s, McKesson & Roberts made the rather original claim that feminine hygiene played "an important part in the maintenance of a good personality." Conversely, a poor personality resulted "from a lack of attention to the intimate toilet." This was remedied, of course, by the proper use of their "safe and non-poisonous" douche powder, Odorfin.

In the early 1960s, Norcliff played the femininity angle. Its V.A. brand douche powder was "a cosmetic for daintiness and cleanliness" that "no woman who value[d] her femininity" could afford to be without. According to the accompanying pamphlet, really feminine women just couldn't get enough of the stuff: V.A.'s "flower freshness" was "so delightful that many women tuck tiny packettes [sic] in their lingerie drawers—just like sachets." These, presumably, were the same gals who found douching to be "relaxing and pleasant as your daily bath or shower." They probably enjoyed pelvic exams, too.

Beginning in the 1970s, feminists understandably decried the way in which these ads linked female anatomy with germs, odor, and dirt, not to mention sold female consumers an unnecessary product. But they missed an important point: in the dark days before the pill, many women read the ads as coded messages regarding contraceptive potential. Certainly this was why the ads were addressed to married women, itself a code word for "sexually active." Sexually active women didn't want to "be troubled with uncertainty," as one Lysol ad read. They wanted a product to "kill every germ it touches," because they understood that "germs" meant "sperm." During the 1930s, Lysol even ran a series of ads in popular women's magazines featuring "frank talks by eminent women physicians." As reported by two muckraking female journalists, Rachel Lynn Palmer and Sarah K. Greenberg, M.D., the campaign was based on the inference that "women could free themselves of the fear of unwanted pregnancies by using Lysol douches."

Furthermore, a leaflet inside the package noted that "[t]he douche should follow married relations as a cleansing and antiseptic agent."[14]

Douching with Lysol or Zonite was certainly no more disgusting (or effective) than drinking gunpowder or eating dried chicken gizzards, both of which were considered contraceptives according to nineteenth-century frontier folk medicine. It was, however, more dangerous. While Lysol assured consumers in its 1930 booklet, "The Facts About Feminine Hygiene," that "the only possible harm in the use of 'Lysol' is through your own carelessness," Palmer and Greenberg begged to differ. They verified that Lysol was implicated in the deaths of at least six women (most likely "through their own carelessness" and a failure to sufficiently dilute the Lysol with water).[15]

Zonite wasn't all that safe, either. Its leaflets included the following "caution": "Do not let Zonite come in contact with dyed fabrics; the active principle is a powerful bleaching agent."[16] That active agent was sodium hypochlorite—we use it today as laundry bleach.

And, of course, as Palmer and Greenberg took pains to point out, Lysol, Zonite, and other douches were ineffective as contraceptives.

The rise of the pill and FDA regulations in the sixties drove Lysol back into the household cleaning products aisle and greatly curtailed Zonite's advertising. As late as 1963, however, Norcliff still advised women to douche after marital relations, even though it noted that V.A. powder was "not a means to avoid pregnancy."

A quick trip to the local supermarket reveals that the feminine hygiene scam is as popular as ever. These days, however, manufacturers restrain themselves to the "internal cleanliness" line of advertising. Alas—you'll never find a product as versatile as Zonite.

When the Honeymoon's Over: The Total Woman versus Fascinating Womanhood

So you've landed the man of your dreams, packed your wedding veil away, and combed the rice out of your hair. Everything's A-OK on the feminine hygiene front. You're smoothly on the road to happily ever after, right? Well, real life has a nasty way of intruding upon starry-eyed brides. Before you know it, you're suffering from waxy yellow buildup, Junior and Little Sister are at each other's throats, hubby's staying at work late an awful lot lately, and your sex life is practically nonexistent.

Betty Friedan called it the "problem with no name," but what did she know? Marabel Morgan and Helen Anderlin knew that the housewife's dilemma sprang from a lack of femininity. *Real* femininity—the kind that happily took no for an answer, especially if hubby was the naysayer.

Helen Andelin majored in home economics at Brigham Young University. Her aspirations, according to the bio handed out by her publishers, "were to prepare herself to be a competent and successful wife and mother." Allegedly other young wives were soon asking for her advice. The result was *Fascinating Womanhood*, originally published in 1963 but—I was shocked to discover—*still in print* as of the turn of the twenty-first century. The core of Fascinating Womanhood can be extracted from Chapter 10's title—"Make Him No. 1." According to Andelin, your husband "wants to be the king-pin around which all other activities of your life revolve." Nothing gives him "a more enjoyable sense of power and manliness" than such supremacy. Wives need to remember, however, that "from a practical standpoint it is impossible [for hubby] to place her first, and she has no right to expect it." As a matter of fact, the Fascinating Woman avoids "a lot of preconceived ideas which may clash with your husband's manly dreams or masculine responsibilities—such as where you want to live, plans for children . . . "

If she disagreed with hubby's dictates, the FW practiced "childlike anger . . . the charming and showy anger, spunk and sauciness of a little girl." She stamped her foot, tossed her curls, and said, "Well, so this is the way you treat your poor little wife who works and slaves for you all day." Of course, Andelin realized that some men severely mistreated their wives, but "often men's ugly and cruel actions are the woman's fault." Likewise, if hubby spends "unnecessary time away from home, you have probably driven him to it by your unsympathetic attitude."

In 1970, *Time* magazine noted Andelin's attempts to inaugurate September 30 as National Celebration of Womanhood Day, on which each wife would "wear her most frilly, feminine dress . . . serve her husband breakfast in bed and 'tell him how great he is.' "

If you take a tincture of the Fascinating Woman and add a soupçon of Helen Gurley Brown, you'll end up with *The Total Woman* (1975). Prior to her wedding, Marabel Morgan thought marriage meant "ruffly curtains at the kitchen window, strawberries for breakfast, and lovin' all the time." Six years later, when husband Charlie called her "uptight" right there at the breakfast table, Marabel realized that the berries had gone bad. The stage was set for the birth of the Total Woman. Like the Fascinating Woman, the Total Woman believed in wifely submission. Because submission was heavenly ordained, there was "no way you can alter or improve this arrangement." In turn, hubby would gratefully respond—maybe with new furniture for the family room. Like the Fascinating Woman, the Total Woman was organized around the house, some Total Women going so far as to set "the table for her already completed dinner at 9:00 a.m." (The Total Woman didn't work outside the home, either.) This gave her plenty of time for her daily 5:00 p.m. bubble bath and personal grooming period. It was her goal to emerge "feminine, soft and touchable" when hubby came back from work an hour or so later.

This is where Morgan and Andelin came to a major parting of the ways. Andelin had eight children, so she evidently engaged in sex, but there's no indication that she liked it, lambasting as she did "jesting among married couples that would imply immoral acts." In the Morgan household, sex was "as clean and pure as eating cottage cheese," though decidedly more fun. Observing her husband's grim face as he left the house one morning for a busy day at the office, Morgan "wondered how I could revive him when he came home." That evening, she performed an experiment:

I put on pink baby-doll pajamas and white boots after my bubble bath. . . . When I opened the door that night to greet Charlie, I was unprepared for his reaction. . . . [he] dropped his briefcase on the doorstep, and chased me around the dining room table.

I, on the other hand, was unprepared to read that their two little girls "stood flat against the wall watching . . . giggling with delight" during this romp. Morgan defended frolicking in front of the kids: "But the children will love your costumes. It makes life exciting. Can't you imagine Junior on the sandlot telling his friends, 'I've got to go now, guys. Got to see mom's outfit for tonight.' " Morgan should have imagined what Junior later told his psychoanalyst.

The lessons Junior took away from Morgan's performances were not necessarily any less provocative than those provided by the experts. Boys and men faced the threat of sissyhood and the danger of masturbation, among other things. Pink think told women and girls to act in very specific ways around men—but how were men supposed to act around women? As always, there were plenty of experts to provide the answers.

"How to Be a Successful Widow"

by R. Louis Zalk (New York: Fleet Publishing Corporation, 1957)

Books for widows usually focused on monetary matters, but newspaper columnist R. Louis Zalk plunged boldly into the world of social advice—including the subject of widows who "played the field." Zalk quoted at length from a letter he received from the daughter of "one such woman":

My mother is disgracing us. I am so ashamed of her, I can hardly face my family and friends.

Father wasn't buried a month before she started having dates with men. And what men! Old, young, married, single, any kind.

She drinks and smokes, which are things she never did before, and she spends all her time in liquor places. . . . One night my husband found her in a cheap night spot with a young hoodlum. He had to fight them both to get her out of the place. . . .

Sometimes she has dates with travelling men and stays away all night. . . . She is 47. What a way for a woman of that age to act!

Zalk's advice? "Perhaps the best solution to the problem . . . is to have her confined to a sanatorium until she regains her better sense." Why? Because "she is ill. Illness requires treatment . . . " Zalk also explained that the "sudden cessation" of sexual relations caused "restlessness." No, no, not that kind of restlessness. Zalk meant insomnia. To cure women "suddenly denied the sedative effect of satisfactory sexual intercourse," he suggested the following alternatives: counting sheep, warm milk taken at bedtime, or reading oneself to sleep.

Chapter 5

A Manly Shade of Pink:
A Brief Guide to the Other Side

*He is courage personified, born protector of the
weaker sex. He will take the initiative, be the aggressor. He is expected to succeed. As the ultimate sign of
male superiority, he alone has the right to carry on the
family name. A son is the symbol of family continuity,
high success and national security.*

Clarence G. Moser,
Understanding Boys (1954)

So far, we've confined ourselves to the female of the species and the
many insidious ways pink think oozed into her life. From "big boys
don't cry" to "take it like a man," males have been subject to a kind
of "blue think" all their own. Let's take another look at "Girlish Boys and
Boyish Girls." Dr. Hohman devoted a great deal of attention to the case
of a boy who was sent to him for "retraining" at twelve years of age. The
problem? "Girlishness . . . so evident that even a doting mother could no
longer fail to be alarmed." Thank goodness, Dr. Hohman was there to

step in and ship the offending tyke off to military school as part of a "general plan to enforce more manly appearance, interests and behavior":

> He is being graduated from an Eastern college this year; a popular, well-adjusted, normally manly youth. If he had been allowed to continue in the course he was following at twelve, open homosexuality in adulthood would have been practically forced upon him by his looks, his dress and his manner.[1]

A close call, to be sure, but what caused things to come to such a desperate pass in the first place? In this case, it was the boy's mother's "admiring notice at eighteen months when he stroked with apparent delight a pink satin dress she wore."

You see, while a touch of tomboyishness in girls was what Dr. Hohman called "piquant," sissyishness was not a positive male personality trait in any way, shape, or form. A tomboy might grow up to be like the *Beverly Hillbillies'* Elly May Clampett, whose boyish attire only accentuated her feminine curves and manner—and, boy, did she know how to wear a dress when necessary! On the other hand, a sissy grew up to be Liberace—or worse. Maybe that's why the experts wanted to establish masculinity—that is, heterosexuality—as soon as possible.

Such attempts could be ludicrous. According to gynecologist and author Fritz Kahn, M.D., it was "usually possible to classify the baby in reference to his sexual type during the first few days of his life" by the way he reacted to his mother's breast:

> The strongly sexed child attacks lustily, with genuine carnal desire, while the undersexed child must be skillfully persuaded to suck. The ardent baby is unhappy if he loses the nipple. He grows furious, seeks it, and, when he finds it, nurses again with doubled pleasure. The phlegmatic baby simply acquiesces; if he loses the nipple, he forgets to go on drinking.[2]

His parents might as well have run out and bought him a feather boa right then, "strongly sexed" being a code word for "heterosexual," after all.

Of course, it depended on a boy's mother's "sexual type" as well. Kahn recalled the case of a male infant who refused to nurse. The problem was his mother, a "sexually infantile type, unattractive as a wet nurse from a biological point of view." She was probably still having clitoral orgasms (which the experts, in a now discredited theory, deemed less "mature" than those originating in the vagina), for goodness sake. Luckily fate, built just like Jayne Mansfield, stepped into the breach:

> After trying unsuccessfully for days to make him nurse, I placed the baby at the breast of a completely erotic woman who was lying near by. He immediately began to feed, and for days afterward he continued to protest if he was placed at his own mother's breast.[3]

By the age of fifteen, this baby was writing love letters "comparable to those of Abelard and of the young Bonaparte," his "masculinity" assured—at least according to Dr. Kahn.

One reason masculinity was important, Alfred Murray explained, was because "a woman likes a manly man":

> His strength, resourcefulness, mental ability, and character will be attractive to her. If he was weak in these, he will be a "weak sister" to his feminine friends. Women have a way of admiring the man they fear— fear because of his greatness.[4]

Murray apparently was unconcerned about the implications of such a surfeit of masculinity, but other experts worried about overly manly boys. Former FBI agent W. Cleon Skousen was concerned about boys and delinquency—so much so that he expressed his "special appreciation" to that paragon of masculinity, J. Edgar Hoover, and his "interest in youth problems," in the opening pages of his *So You Want to Raise a Boy?* (1962). "Rejection" was the root of the problem, according to Skousen. A boy who felt rejected during childhood would likely grow into a social outcast, a "'slum-bum,' or a juke-joint rock 'n' roll artist who require[d] all-night sessions and a 'barby' to keep the gang awake." Rejection "distilled anarchy in

It's Not Sissy Food!

In a world where the fear of homosexuality hung like a pall over everything, even breakfast cereals proved their manhood. A 1951 ad for Nabisco Shredded Wheat boldly proclaimed: "Give him a breakfast that's a good honest meal not 'sissy' food! . . . it's America's great body-building breakfast!" There was nothing "fancy-sounding or faddy" about the cereal, so it was OK for He-Men. If there was any doubt, the last line of the ad noted that Shredded Wheat was "the breakfast full of *power* from Niagara Falls," home of the Nabisco plant.

the minds of men like Rousseau, Nietzsche, Engels and Marx" and created "ne'er-do-well Bohemians, criminal psychopaths and . . . Beatniks."

The opposite of rejection was problematic as well. A mother who "smothered" her son by trying "too hard, constantly protecting him, continuously reminding him, lavishing him with love whether he reciprocates it or not, fighting all his battles, making all his decisions, doing all his work" ran the risk of turning out a son who was unprepared for adult life, "timid, dependent, afraid." In fact, as Skousen observed, the damage had already been done: "Studies of American boys who were captured in Korea showed that we had raised a soft, pampered generation. Many were easily discouraged and easily brain-washed." And no wonder Skousen was so concerned. In a section titled "What About Military Service?" he noted that "the Communists have set up a timetable of conquest which contemplates destroying American freedom by 1973."

Growing Up Manly

Little boys bent on averting this takeover could begin training for future military service with toys from the Montgomery Wards catalogue. Here they could find toy soldiers and miniature camouflage outfits aplenty. In its Christmas catalogue of 1966 (the year in which the United States bombed Hanoi for the first time), Wards devoted four pages to G.I. Joe, his buddies, uniforms and accessories. Each doll assumed "all poses necessary for rugged military action: charging, running, firing." Only they weren't "dolls," they were "action figures"—the better to conquer such parental objections as, "No son of mine is going to play with a doll!" There was even a Green Beret action set that featured child-sized grenades, machine and hand guns, and the titular headgear. If a full day's combat play wasn't enough, at bedtime Mommy could dress her little soldier in his martial pajamas— available in both Union and Confederate styles.

My favorite Wards war toy, though, was a G.I. Joe knock-off line of action figures called the Fighting Tigers. These were "for the red-blooded boy who likes his soldiers tough." Just how tough was somewhat open to debate, considering one of the dolls was Pretty Boy, whose salutes were "snappier than anyone [sic] in the whole Tiger squad." Lest that taint the rest of the outfit, there were members like the Combat Kid, who threw Molotov cocktails and "single-handedly knocked out 37 enemy tanks!" or "Tex . . . When he raises his rifle . . . the enemy is really in trouble. Down in Texas boys learn to shoot almost before they learn to walk!" Then again, there was "Rock . . . he's hard as a rock." Quite the macho brigade!

And of course, there were toy guns. From old west–style six shooters to M1 rifles (with "soft plastic bayonet") to outer space "guns of tomor-row," the well-armed little boy had access to firepower galore. Oh, there were some namby-pamby parents who questioned the wisdom behind trading snips and snails for tiny replicas of death-dealing hardware, but they were in the wrong. In a 1967 *Ladies' Home Journal* article called "What Makes Boys Masculine," child psychologist Bruno Bettelheim pointed at early childhood inhibition of masculine behaviors, such as

"Peacetime Pals," Sears Catalogue, 1960.

"play-shooting and killing," as the roots of "passivity and femininity in boys—and drug addiction and homosexuality" in adult males.

   Play shooting and killing was all very well and good, but unless a boy was planning on making the military his lifelong career, the need for a wage-earning job was inevitable. So, while Sis was working her way

"The Great Drop Game"

In 1957, *Boys' Life* published a story called "The Great Drop Game," in which "pigtail pandemonium breaks out when Sissy Wyatt tries out her secret pitch on the North End Nuggets." The story, by Earl Chapin, featured a scrappy female pitcher who winds up pitching in the big game against the Nuggets, even though her home team, the Scrappers, "wouldn't let her play regular games." With two men out and bases loaded, Sissy's fast ball saves the day. (Yes, in a somewhat subtle equation of sissyhood and girliness, the heroine is a tomboy named "Sissy.") But when the newly admiring Scrappers beg her to be their starting pitcher next year, Sissy, clearly under the influence of too much pink think, announces she has decided that "it's unladylike to play baseball."

though *I Want to Be a Beauty Operator* and *I Want to Be a Homemaker*, her brother had his choice of a wide range of "I Want to Be . . ." career books. There were, of course, the standard professions—doctor, dentist, and architect—which were all overwhelmingly male at the time these books were written. But not everybody would graduate high school, let alone make it through years of professional training. Truck driver, bus driver, and service station attendant were all possible future occupations. For those boys who marched to a different drum, there was the rather esoteric *I Want to Be an Orange Grower*.

Older brothers turned to *Boys' Life* ("The Official Magazine of the Boy Scouts of America"), where they read tales like "Yankee Doodle Commando" ("Unpublished stories of Valley Forge"), "The Manly Art" ("Learn about the basic techniques of boxing offense and defense from a ring expert"), "The Boy Who Saved the World" ("A Roastie-toastie space-ace man meets Captain Mex-On from Mars"), and "The Big Boss of Africa's

Night Life" ("A man-eating lion looking for a bedtime snack is proud, sure, and powerful").

As you can tell from the above, *Boys' Life* offered its teen and preteen readers something extremely different from what *Calling All Girls* or *Seventeen* offered theirs. Where were the articles about how to date a girl, or how to dress for his big first date, or how to act at the senior prom? Where were the articles about his changing body and its oh-so-fascinating fluids? Where were the advertisements for grooming supplies, wedding silver, and hope chests? True, late-1940s issues of *Boys' Life* had the occasional ad or two for Wildroot Cream-Oil Hair Tonic (a name that wouldn't make it past the focus groups these days) or rival hair dressings Vitalis and Kreml (ditto), but that didn't compare to the pages and pages of ads for shampoos, lipsticks, powders and other make-up that graced the girls' mags, not to mention all the editorial copy devoted to how to use these products. Instead, *Boys' Life* focused on sports, hobbies, nature, and, of course, scouting skills. Advertisers included Goodyear (no doubt figuring that the bike tire sales of today would turn into the car tire sales of tomorrow), Ford ("There's a Ford in your future"), and Gillette—all angling for early brand allegiance.

The future loomed equally large in other advertisements. Full page ads by Martin Aircraft gave readers "facts on the air age," the better to entice would-be pilots and/or factory workers. *Boys' Life* was a logical choice for the U.S. Army Recruiting Publicity Bureau's advertising dollar. Editorially, too, the magazine urged its readers to plan for future careers. "You're Old Enough," proclaimed an article in the February 1946 issue devoted to three overachieving youngsters who had gone on to great success in the highly technical fields of chemistry and electronics. Writer Darrell Huff was sure to point out that his subjects contradicted "the old picture of the young genius" as a slightly effeminate slide-rule-toting nerd by their involvement in such rugged arenas as the armed forces and college football.

Not that *Boys' Life* and its advertisers ignored all romance. Even Wildroot Cream-Oil Hair Tonic played the sex appeal card once in a while. "What Do Girls Say About Your Hair?" began one ad, which ended with a drawing of a well-groomed Wildroot user receiving a kiss on the cheek. But what girls said and thought about boys' behavior and grooming was never held over them as a must-reach standard. More to the point was a Kreml ad in which business success took precedence over sex appeal. Caricatures of three boys having bad hair days were captioned "Watered Stock," "Loan Shark," and "Scalper." The fourth drawing, of the boy who used Kreml, was labeled "High Grade Security." "'Liability Hair' Held Him Back" was the headline over all. There was barely a reference to girls or sex appeal—just the well-groomed look of the successful businessman.

Birds, Bees, and Boys

In their own way, sex education materials for boys were just as strict about gender roles as those for girls. Take, for example, *In Training* (1946), by Thurman B. Rice, M.D. Rice, a professor of

For boys, good hair was a sound business practice, 1940s.

bacteriology and public health at the Indiana University School of Medicine, meanders all over the place, reminiscing about the two-hour, all-weather nature walks of his boyhood days, the necessity of good health, and sports—always sports—in the dime-novel terminology of his youth. For example, more than good health was necessary "to push the old ball over the goal line. It takes punch, and that is what comes from the bounding bursting kind of health that breaks right through." Rice occasionally had his lucid moments, as when he correctly intuited that his readers might be "wondering what all this has to do with sex":

> Many persons suppose that sex is something that has only to do with the way in which children are created. . . . That is not true. Sex is influencing you every minute of your life. It is changing your voice . . . it is putting hair on your body; it is making you grow tall and strong and making you want to do things; it gives you courage. The fellows who are afraid are called "sissies" for the reason that they are like the girls when they are in danger or have hard things to do. To be able to fight it out according to the rules of the game and not whine when you are beaten or hurt is to be a man instead of a "baby."[5]

Real manhood was no job for "mollycoddles and softies." After all, "Lindy wasn't putting his personal safety first when he struck out across that ocean alone, and a half-back really going places around right end isn't thinking of his personal welfare."

Rice counseled boys to "save yourself until you have found your mate. This thing called sex is the most wonderful thing in the world. Don't spoil it. Don't be the father of bastards. Don't get venereal disease and have to see pus running from you." *Gulp*—no, sir. Did *anyone* have sex after reading that?

As with material aimed at girls, here, too, the emphasis was on premarital chastity. *A Boy Today, A Man Tomorrow* (1961) was written for the ten- to fourteen-year-old crowd, and concentrated on bodily changes as opposed to reproduction—or the "wonderful privilege" God gave to married adults. Its author nevertheless managed to make intercourse sound like some kind of midair refueling operation: "At the time of the union, the penis of the father

IN TRAINING

Believe it or not, In Training was about the facts of life, not football, 1946.

fits into the vagina (opening in the body, between the legs) of the mother. Then the sperm cells pass from his body into hers."[6] Nor were the boys' manuals any more likely to contain information about contraception. Roy E. Dickerson, the author of *Into Manhood* (1954), simply left it at "There is no need to take the time here to explain why the various things you may hear about that boys are using or doing are not reliable."[7]

The Solitary Vice and How to Handle It

While adolescent girls dealt with the "singular blessing" of menstruation and its attendant regalia, young men had their own cross to bear. Whether one called it self-abuse, self-pollution, or onanism, by midcentury the connection between insanity and masturbation was mostly a creaky relic of the nineteenth century. But that didn't stop some experts from preaching against the wages of the "secret sin," as did evangelist Oscar Lowry in his 1940 sex education book, *The Way of a Man with a Maid*:

> It takes the glow from the cheek, the brightness from the eye and life-blood from the veins. . . . Under its influence the habits become slovenly, the appetites morbid and perverted, the muscles flabby and weak, the disposition insipid, the spirits melancholic, and the whole demeanor sheepish, reclusive and embarrassed.[8]

Masturbation was a "soul-destroying" vice; young men were "entrapped by the devil of lust and concupiscence." Most of the authorities Lowry quoted had been in their graves for years and their theories long since discounted, but he still came up with some doozies on his own. There was, for example, the "young man . . . preparing for the ministry" who was plagued by this "baneful habit." He visited Lowry's office for advice:

> After making inquiry concerning his physical condition, I suggested he be circumcised at once. The result was a complete victory, and his recovery from seminal weakness was amazingly rapid. Instead of being mentally depressed, he went about his work with a new-found joy and hope. He graduated with honors, and was married shortly after his graduation and is today a successful pastor.[9]

And of course he never, ever did it again.

Despite holdouts like Mr. Lowry, by the 1940s it was generally agreed that masturbation was not a harmful activity. But that didn't make it all right. In the first place, masturbation was an "inferior substitute for the process which Nature can do better herself" (*In High at Sex-Teen* [1963].) Even Ann Landers agreed that "real fulfillment" could not be "found in a solitary physical pleasure." There was also the concern that frequent masturbation kept boys from more wholesome activities. In 1938, Dr. George W. Corner wrote:

The Facts of Life—"For Boys Only: The Doctor Discusses the Mysteries of Manhood"

by Frank Howard Richardson, M.D. (David McKay Company, 1959)

Author Frank Howard tells the story of Jack, his pals, and "Doc," the wise general practitioner. "We're going to call things by their real names here," he tells them, "for you lads are big enough now to discuss things like men, and not like kids that have to have baby names for the parts of your body, or the functions that they perform." So there's this "mystery juice" made by the testicles that makes "you begin to feel the way a man feels and have some of the thoughts and wishes that a man has," things like "courage and backbone and guts." This process is called adolescence. Pretty soon you get more and more interested in girls. Luckily, Doc is there to answer your burning questions:

> I say, doctor, just what is the fun in what the older fellows are always beating their gums about—petting, or necking, or boodling? Is it the same as what the older people used to call spooning?

There are three ways "the male elements" can leave the man's body, Howard explains: The first happens because "whenever the storage tanks get too full, they empty themselves," usually at night while the tanks' owners are asleep. Secondly, there's masturbation, which, according to Doc, isn't "much more serious than thumb sucking"—certainly an interesting choice of metaphor given the subject. Finally, there's intercourse, which can take place in one of two ways. Only in marriage is sex "natural, normal, and right. The other way is wrong, and always brings trouble of some sort or other as the result."

[P]eople who expect to do well in study and on the playing field, and ultimately to do hard and useful work in the world, cannot permit themselves to yield to every mood of self-indulgence. The mind and body
must be kept under reasonable discipline. For this reason sensible boys
and men will avoid as far as possible unnecessary sexual stimulations,
especially those which tend to cheapen and degrade one's ideas of sex.[10]

Dr. Thurman Rice agreed that masturbation sapped some of a young
man's strength "and that that little may be just what is needed to win."
He also warned boys against unnecessary sex stimulation, particularly
"trashy novels and stories that keep them stirred up about sex":

Love stories may be all right for some persons, but they are too "sissy" for
the real scout who wants to be out skating instead of sitting by the fire
and reading a sentimental story. It is all right to be with a really nice girl
occasionally, but who wants to be one of the simpletons who won't get
out on the gridiron because he can't leave a bunch of giggling girls long
enough and has to chase after them all the time?[11]

Conversely, the boy who went in for "athletics, scouting, hikes and all
that sort of thing" was "too busy to give much thought to sex . . . the best
way of keeping from getting into the habit of masturbation" in the first
place. After all, "when one has a beautiful book, a valuable watch or a
favorite tennis racket, one takes good care of it, and does not allow one-
self or any one else to misuse or abuse it," if you catch Dr. Rice's drift. Or,
according to W. Cleon Skousen, "Every boy should know that masturbation may be the first step toward homosexuality."[12]

Business Etiquette for Boys

So how did a nice, masculine boy go about meeting girls, anyway? Several experts listed "manners" as the number one quality girls looked for in
boys they liked to date. In fact, etiquette books are the blue think inverse

of the charm/beauty/dating guides aimed at girls. There were far fewer of
them, of course, but they filled an otherwise empty slot on a young man's
bookshelf. Books like *He-Manners* (1954) and *Stand Up, Shake Hands,
Say "How Do You Do"* (1977) gave readers the basics of letter writing (or
"He-Mail Made Easy"), table manners, telephone etiquette, and how to
tie ties and other clothing considerations. They also contained some
information on how to get, how to dress for, and what to do on dates. But
while boys were treated to a chapter or so on dating (or, in the case of
Stand Up, Shake Hands, "what girls and women expect of you"), there
simply wasn't a book for boys equivalent to Ellen Peck's highly detailed
and ever so Machiavellian *How to Get a Teenage Boy And What to Do
with Him When You Get Him* (1969). On the other hand, a book like
David McKay's *Male Manners: The Young Man's Guide to Dating, Good
Looks, Making Friends, Getting Into Schools, Etc.* (1969) spanned a
greater array of topics in its title alone than many girls-only books did in
their entirety.

At least one book more
closely mirrored its pink think
cousins when it came to dating
advice. *Blondes Prefer Gentlemen*
(1949) was written by Sheila
John Daly, whose columns ("On
the Solid Side" and "Tops Among
Teens") were syndicated in news-
papers through the country. Daly
devoted a full third of her book to
what she called "Big Dame Hunting" and sprinkled further rules
for dealing with the opposite sex
throughout the rest of its pages.
When it came to the chapters on
datetiquette, she wrote with a
precision usually reserved for
girls' dating guides. Daly also
included a "brief run-down on

Note the business meeting at lower right.

"Boys Beware"

Ten of the most harrowing minutes in the educational film canon, *Boys Beware* (1961) warned of the dangers of homosexuality. One day Jimmy hitchhikes home from the park. He is picked up by Ralph. During the drive, they engage in pleasant conversation, and Ralph gives Jimmy "a friendly pat" as he gets out of the car. Ralph tells Jimmy he'll see him again, as he always drives past the park on his way home from work. Sure enough, the next day Ralph picks Jimmy up again. This time they stop for a coke, and Ralph tells some "off color stories." Jimmy's heard stories like these before, so he doesn't think too much about it. They go fishing the next Saturday. Jimmy has a great time, and when Ralph shows him some pornographic pictures, he's curious, even though he knows he shouldn't look. At this point, our narrator chimes in: "Ralph was sick, with a sickness that was not visible like smallpox, but was no less dangerous and contagious, a sickness of the mind. . . . Ralph was a homosexual, a person that demands an intimate relationship with members of the same sex." The naïvely trustful Jimmy keeps seeing Ralph, even when Ralph demands "payment." Presumably this means coercion, and we see them climbing the motel stairs together. Jimmy tells his parents, Ralph is arrested, and Jimmy is given probation and released to the custody of his parents. Incredible. Think about it—first we are told that homosexuals are predatory and then we find out that Jimmy is given *probation* after he is molested! The moral, boys? Homosexuality is contagious.

the types of girls you're likely to come across in your date life." There was the gold digger, the wolfess, and the catty character, but worst of all was the bad sport:

> Nothing is fun for her—she won't go bowling because she "doesn't know how," she won't go out skating or tobogganing because it's just "too cold."

Pink is a very special mood

...and pink Serena by Modess is a very special napkin. New Serena, the luxury sanitary napkin, is softly pink to please you. Gossamer-soft, to pamper you. Contains a deodorant, for daintiness.

And new pink Serena is a very special kind of protection: one comfortable size, super absorbent to give you complete confidence.

Serena
by Modess®

Because "pink is a very special mood"—Serena sanitary napkins, 1958.

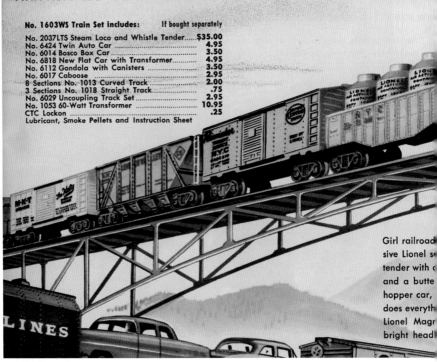

LOCOS HAVE ALL IT TAK

CLIMBER" 5-CAR STEAM FREIGHT $49.95

TWIN AUTO and NEW TRANSFORMER CARS

No. 1603WS Train Set includes:	If bought separately
No. 2037LTS Steam Loco and Whistle Tender.....	$35.00
No. 6424 Twin Auto Car	4.95
No. 6014 Bosco Box Car	3.50
No. 6818 New Flat Car with Transformer	4.95
No. 6112 Gondola with Canisters	3.50
No. 6017 Caboose	2.95
8 Sections No. 1013 Curved Track	2.00
3 Sections No. 1018 Straight Track	.75
No. 6029 Uncoupling Track Set	2.95
No. 1053 60-Watt Transformer	10.95
CTC Lockon	.25
Lubricant, Smoke Pellets and Instruction Sheet	

Girl railroad
sive Lionel s
tender with
and a butte
hopper car,
does everyth
Lionel Magr
bright head

The Lady Lionel train set featured "fashion-right" colors for "girl railroaders." From Lionel's 1958 catalog.

OUTFIT
No. 1587S

587S "027" "LADY LIONEL" TRAIN SET FOR GIRLS . . . $49.95

OKE! HEADLIGHT! MAGNE-TRACTION! FASHION-RIGHT COLORS!

ntry are in love with this exclu-
ul pink frosted locomotive and
car, a robin's egg blue box car
box car to go with it, a lilac
inated caboose. And her train
. . climbs grades with exclusive
llowy white smoke, beams a
s 5 ft., 11 ins. long.

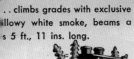

Lionel's No. 1587S 5-Car Train Set includes:	If bought separately
No. 2037-500LT Steam Loco and Tender in Pink Frosting	$29.95
No. 6462-500 Gondola in Pink Frosting	5.50
No. 6464-510 Box Car in Robin's Egg Blue	6.50
No. 6436-500 Hopper in Lilac	5.50
No. 6464-515 Box Car in Buttercup Yellow	6.50
No. 6427-500 Illuminated Caboose in Sky Blue	6.50
8 Sections No. 1013 Curved Track	2.00
5 Sections No. 1018 Straight Track	1.25
No. 6029 Uncoupling Track Set	2.95
No. 1043-500 60-Watt Transformer	8.95
CTC Lockon	.25
Lubricant, Smoke Pellets and Instruction Sheet	

*Thirty-nine cents' worth of glamour. Modess pink
sanitary belt, 1960s.*

The best-selling girls' game of the 1960s.

He's bold, he's bad—he's "the Dud" from the Mystery Date game, 1965.

"Your gown is beautiful! Spin again!" Campus Queen lunchbox, 1967.

A ladylike outlet for aggressive behavior. Wow! Pillow Fight Game, 1964.

She won't try to dance the rhumba; she won't help to clean up the gym after a school dance; she won't volunteer to act as prompter for the class play— and the very mention of a walk around the block is enough to throw her in a dead faint. Usually such girls just get too boring and are left out of every-thing. But if you happen to find one who is so attractive to you that you sim-ply must date her, try to show her how much fun she's missing. Help her learn how to do things, help her to relax and she'll love you for it.[13]

Don't be too sure of that, boys. You also might want to think twice before following Daly's advice regarding that frightful frump called Mom:

"[P]erhaps your mother has simply grown so used to being taken for granted and to being loved by your father as she is, that she has lost inter-est in clothes. You can help her revive the interest, help her to *want* to look pretty again. . . . Flatter her as you would a super date, not quite as often or as ardently perhaps . . . but just to make her feel "loved."[14]

If you wanted to send the old bag a bouquet, there was a whole section on choosing and sending flowers—a dead art by the time *Stand Up, Shake Hands* was reprinted in 1977, "as OUT as bowing to her when you ask her to dance."[15] I have to wonder who was buying these books—teen-age boys or their well-meaning (and probably female) relations? I can't imagine the average teen purchased his own copy of *Blondes Prefer Gentlemen* or *He-Manners*, but *Stand Up, Shake Hands* and a pack of BVDs was just the sort of Christmas-killing gift that moms and maiden aunts loved to give.

In general, where girls' guides focused on its applications in social sit-uations and entertaining, etiquette was presented to boys as a road map to future career success. According to Robert Loeb, etiquette's "big pay-off" was the ability to sell yourself "in person, or by mail and via the phone, for salary or wages." Tips on how to get a job interview ("Do not start off by trying to exhibit how clever and witty you are"), how to act at said interview ("Don't allow your talk to consume too much time"), and the niceties of on-the-job behavior ("Don't be a servile reptile . . . ") were necessary for future heads of family. According to *Smarter and Smoother*, a 1944 guidebook for both sexes, meeting a girl's father for the first time was "excellent practice for future interviewing and job-seeking, for no employer will give you a closer scrutiny than your date's father."[16]

Even *Stand Up, Shake Hands*, a book aimed at the Cub Scout set, included a chapter called "Conducting a Meeting," "because even billion-dollar mergers are based on the same rules you'll use to decide how the club house should be built and who'll be allowed to use it." Yes, some girls' guides offered hints on getting a job, but the title Loeb chose for *She-Manners*'s chapter on workplace etiquette made the differences crystal clear: "The Boss's Lap Is Not a Chair."

Proper manners for climbing the corporate ladder were more important than how to catch a woman because, among other things, the prospect of lifelong bachelorhood simply wasn't as terrifying as impending spinsterhood. "Crusty old bachelor" doesn't carry the cultural wallop of "old maid." Think about it—crusty old bachelors are sweetly curmudgeonly and only need a good (younger) woman to liberate them from their solitary ways, whereas old maids are dried up, bitter, and hopeless. Almost every Shirley Temple movie featured a crusty old bachelor, and the virginal little vixen always brought love and happiness into the old bugger's life.

In fact, the majority of men were "marriage-shy" by nature. According to psychoanalyst Theodore Reik, marriage was "natural for a woman; she takes to it as a duck to water," but as long as men were "young and vigorous and filled with the spirit of masculinity, marriage [went] against the biological grain."[17] There were few books for men about *how to be* happy while single because men, by definition, *were* happy while single.

That's why you didn't see too many ads like the one for Van Heusen shirts that appeared in the August 1944 issue of *Ladies' Home Journal*. In a twist on the more familiar female anxieties about singlehood, its protagonist was a worried young man: "I lost my head over Betty! Treated her like a queen . . . candy, flowers . . . everything! Popped the question a dozen times. But she couldn't see past my wilted shirt collar . . . 'How could I love and honor *that*?' she said." But then little miss smarty-pants Betty gave him a Van Heusen shirt, "And now she's collared me . . . for life." For once in the world of advertising, a man needed the product to make *him* more marriageable. Unusual, to be sure, but not quite revolutionary when you remember it appeared in a *women's* magazine.

"And now she's collared me . . . for life!" 1944

The Man in the Kitchen

Although the little woman was expected to do all the cooking after the wedding, while he was single, a man could use the kitchen to enhance his masculinity. While women's magazines and cookbooks were filled with ads and recipes for "husband-pleasing man-food" (for example, the Chocolate Nut Sundae cake that Calumet Baking Powder termed a

Pink for Men

In the mid-1950s, pink was for everybody. It was even marketed as a color for red-blooded he-men who formerly would have recoiled from its delicate and decidedly feminine associations. Of course, men had been able to purchase pink Brooks Brothers shirts since the 1920s, but never before had such a wide array of items in that shade been available to the male consumer. From pink-and-black saddle shoes to socks, shirt, and dinner jacket, a would-be Beau Brummell could swath himself in menswear's newest color, and few, if any, aspersions were cast upon his masculinity. It's not surprising that a rock 'n' roller like young Elvis Presley made stage appearances in pink pants and black jacket, or, on one memorable occasion, red pants and green coat with pink shirt and matching socks.[*] But in 1955, even the usually staid menswear pages of department store catalogues were filled with pink clothing for men and boys. Author Karal Ann Marling suggests that the masculine embrace of pink was merely "part of the general fascination with chromatic variety" that gripped mid-1950s America and represented a way for men to revolt against the decade's charcoal-gray conformity.[†] Like all fads, this one was relatively short-lived—by the early sixties, pink had faded from the fashionable man's closet.

[*] Peter Guralnick, *Last Train to Memphis: The Rise of Elvis Presley* (Boston: Little, Brown & Company, 1994), 182.
[†] Karal Ann Marling, *As Seen on TV: The Visual Culture of Everyday Life in the 1950s* (Cambridge, Mass., and London: Harvard University Press, 1996), 40–41.

"masculine dream-cake"), men's cookbooks emphasized food's erotic qualities, as well as the cook's machismo.

Men, as *Esquire's Handbook for Hosts* (1953) took pleasure in pointing out, were the "world's greatest" cooks. A woman cooked because she had to, but a man took "to the stove because he is interested in cooking, therefore he has long been interested in eating and therefore he starts six lengths in front of the average female," apparently stymied by her lack of interest in food. As you might have surmised, the *Handbook* was a guide not to seduction—though that may have been a pleasant corollary—but to sophisticated good living, *Esquire*-style: proper carving techniques, how to store wines, what to do with drunken guests, and how to play gin rummy. The prose was clever (albeit occasionally prone to a breathless, run-on style), the illustrations amusing, and the result rather charming.

These books made it clear that their recipes were special—"of, for and by men" was the disclaimer carried by the *Handbook for Hosts*. In the case of *Trader Vic's Helluva Man's Cookbook* (1976), the title alone exuded so much machismo that the jacket flap's assertion that this was "a MAN'S cookbook" was practically superfluous. And the recipe for "Sonofabitch Stew" in *Trader Vic's Kitchen Kibitzer* (1952) separated the men from the boys right off the bat. "Kill a sheep or a lamb or a goat," it began, "slit its throat and hang so the blood will drain into a pan."

More frequently, however, men's cookbooks emphasized the suavity required for successful big dame hunting, as opposed to the sort of blood sport espoused by Trader Vic. *Chef in Wolf's Clothing* (1950) included a chapter on "breakfasts for two," and its pages were graced with a charming cartoon wolf whose skill with both ladies and ladles encouraged would-be cooks in the bedroom and the kitchen.

The Single Man's Playbook

Just as men's cookbooks emphasized food's seductive qualities, so, too, did advice books for single guys generally offer pointers of a stiff-collared, bare-chested, nature—all about getting laid, not how to decorate one's apartment or spend a Saturday night alone. Psychoanalyst and sex counselor Dr. Albert Ellis's *Sex and the Single Man* (1963) paid tribute to Helen Gurley Brown's bestseller of the previous year. One of the first prolific pop psychologists, Ellis preached sex without guilt for both men and women. This basically meant that as long as you didn't lie to your

partner (a rather elastic concept in this book) or take advantage of a
minor or someone who was mentally defective, you could do what you
liked—unless you practiced "fixed homosexuality," in which case you
were an "emotionally disturbed" individual. He came up with some good
stuff—that a man's main sex organ was rarely his "sacred penis" (rather, it
was the hand with which he massaged his girlfriend's clitoris), and that
"oral stimulation" of the female genitalia was "not only permissible but
highly desirable."

What I liked best about *Sex and the Single Man*, however, were the
bits that made me feel like I'd found the other team's playbook. Who
knew the boys were getting this kind of information—*in writing*:

> On the whole, even from the very first night you make any passes at your
> girlfriend—which may well be the first time you meet her—you should
> try to go as far as you can possibly go with her sexually: since, much to
> your surprise, you may even be able to go all the way right at the start;
> and usually the further you get with her this time, the further you are
> likely to get with her the next time.[18]

No wonder the teen girls' guides devoted all those pages to keeping
Bobby or Billy at bay in the backseat—boys were organized! Pity the gal
whose beau practiced the "deftness and speed" Ellis recommended when
removing her clothing during a makeout session:

> . . . once you have fully bared a woman's breasts, or taken off her skirt, or
> removed her undergarments, it is unlikely that she is immediately going
> to get up and cover herself again. Feeling that she has been sort of
> unmasked, and that you are still continuing passionately to kiss and
> caress her, she frequently accepts the inevitable at this point . . .[19]

Apparently, real men never asked a lady to take her clothes off: "Do it
for her! And do it firmly, vigorously, in spite of some resistance on her
part"—the old "no" means "yes" strategy in action.

Ellis enthusiastically quoted from an unpublished manuscript by
N. D. Mallary, Jr., of Atlanta, Georgia. Written as "a long epistle" to his

son, "On Sex and Making Love" left *nothing* to chance when it came to stealing a kiss:

> *The car exit approach.* No woman expects a man in his right mind to kiss on a public thoroughfare. Fine! Do just that! You are taking her to supper on the second night. You park. You go around to open the door. As she puts her feet on the ground her head is down. Judge the distance accurately and arrange to have your lips poised when she looks up. Then kiss her. Do it gracefully and be careful not to bump mouths. Do it gently and don't hold it. Don't hug her. Dart in and out but make it good while you are there. This gives you the opportunity to verbalize the "goodness" of the kiss (at the right time and place) and simply proceed to kiss her again.[20]

Was this true? Did men really go through all this—for a *kiss*? How many of Ellis's readers actually practiced the "Happy Warrior" technique?

> Here you share a joke and both laugh. Reach out and cradle her against your shoulder in a spirit of camaraderie. At the split second the laughter stops she will inhale a deep breath. Place your hand under her chin, make it coincide with the inhaling, and kiss her in one motion.[21]

Ellis's technique must not have been foolproof, however, since he included a chapter on "Surviving Disappointment in Love"—the type of relationship info that women had been reading about since they were teens. For once, Ellis's advice differed not a whit from that given to women—ultimately, he noted, time was a great healer.

Dating Tips for Men

Even if he planned to use Ellis's techniques later in the evening, it behooved a man to spend time with his date out of the sack. Dating helped a man divine a potential wife's disposition and abilities—the knowledge of which could help him overcome any residual marriage shy-ness. A young woman who knew "how to prepare a tasty lunch" pos-sessed "the feminine qualities that would help a husband to appreciate his wife and home."[22] Similarly,

> What a girl does on a hike when she becomes tired or gets a blister on her heel, or how she acts when her dress is ruined by spattered mud, may give her companion a liberal education in feminine psychology! It is also revealing to see what she does about her share of cooking and clean-ing up at a weekend house party . . .[23]

Be it to attend a house party or enjoy a night on the town, it was up to the man to ask for—and plan—the date. Whether he was a teenager or a septuagenarian, there were certain rules to be followed. No book laid them out with greater attention to detail than *Esquire Etiquette: A Guide to Business, Sports, and Social Conduct* (1953), written with professional men in mind. Its 441 pages covered a wide array of topics, from how much to tip a cab driver to how to treat one's secretary (". . . her biggest legitimate gripe is being used as a nursemaid, shopper, personal book-keeper, errand-girl, maid, and social secretary . . . "). The man who fol-lowed its dating advice left nothing to chance.

When he telephoned the woman of his choice, the thoughtful male always offered an explicit invitation to a particular event or activity at a specified time and place. This gave the woman an opportunity to invent a previous engagement (thus sparing him "the double jeopardy of spending [his] money on the wrong thing") or a chance to pretend she was free, if she was "so unscrupulous as to break a date" for him.[24] On the other hand, an indefinite plan of action was a recipe for disaster:

> Anyone who knew so little of the feminine mind as to ask, "What are you doing tonight?" would be sure to show up in unexpected clothes, carrying too many unplanned-for flowers, expecting the girl to arrange the enter-tainment and all but guaranteeing a miserable evening.[25]

It was all right to consult the woman on minor details, of course, "but she wants you to remember that she is consultant, not engineer."

When the evening arrived, she also wanted "to be called for and delivered." Sitting in the car and honking the horn to alert her to his presence at the curb was not acceptable.

At the restaurant, the man was the intermediary between his date and the restaurant's staff. He asked what she wanted to eat and delivered the information to the waiter. "Etiquette render[ed] her helpless" by the tacit agreement of all. "She's in your power," the *Esquire* editors helpfully noted. A gentleman did not take this responsibility lightly. It was up to him to treat his date as "Someone, and preferably Lady Someone" throughout the evening, to "anticipate her every whim." He made sure she had "everything she wants before she even knows she wants it"—and he paid for it all:

> You handle the finances without comment. She, of course, is allowed to pay for nothing . . . not even tips to ladies' room attendants, if she lets you know she has forgotten her mad money. You come up with dimes for the phone calls she makes. . . . Automatically and without a doubt . . . everything's on you from door to door.[26]

The woman had some control over the proceedings, however—she was the only one who could declare the date over. No matter how obviously tired or bored either or both of them were, once dinner ended, the man had to suggest going someplace else, whether it was to a preplanned activity like a dance or a spontaneous trip to a night spot. Wherever they went, it was up to the woman to indicate it was time for her to be getting home. Even if her date was "about to drop . . . the only thing [he] could do (within convention) [was] to stall"—at least until she got the drift, and asked him to take her home.

At her door, the man thanked the woman ("even at these prices, *you* thank *her!*") and tried not to say anything "so infuriatingly vague as 'let's do it again sometime,' unless you really have no desire to see her again." Instead, "the complimentary thing" to do was to ask her if she was free on a specific

"25 Good Reasons for Men to Marry"

by Ira Lunan Ferguson, Ph.D., LL.B.
(San Francisco: Lunan-Ferguson Library, 1976)

Ira Lunan Ferguson sold his self-published books from the 1950s to the 1970s. His *25 Good Reasons for Men to Marry* (1976) was a guide "for all intelligent men aged 21 to 100." At first Mr. Ferguson's commentary seems normal, even wise. Then he starts telling you things that are a little too personal. Suddenly, he slips from near rationality into cuckoo-land. While this can be disconcerting with a stranger on public transportation, in print it's delightful! For example: "When a man is sick, his resistance is low . . . designing women will take advantage of this lowered resistance to get him to promise to marry her." Or how about this entry from his list of qualifications of "The Girl I Am Going to Marry When I Am Thirty": "She must have passable legs and hips, and definitely and obviously adequate bust. Breasts need not be as big as watermelons, but almost." Space doesn't permit me to list all of Ferguson's 25 good reasons that men should marry, but a couple will should suffice:

5. A Wife Is a Built-In Chef Cook: And of course along with being the cook, a wife is a man's waitress de luxe. She not only cooks and prepares his favorite dishes, but she serves them to him in style, treating him like the King-Emperor in his home that he is.

19. A Wife Is a Built-In Secretary: Of necessity the more educated man needs a wife who can act as his secretary at home when occasion demands. Not only does she have to take messages, parry questions, protect his privacy, run his

errands, but often she has to do a lot of his paper work, some typing and even taking dictation.

Ferguson's advice even extended to instructions on "How and When Should a Man Beat His Wife": "A man should never let his children see him spanking their mother, his wife. That's bad for morale." His belief that the word "pussy-whipped" would "be considered good English usage by the end of the century" seems almost prescient, though he was wrong when last I checked.

date in the future and let her "be the vague one with her 'call me' routine." Then he said goodnight—and that was it, as far as etiquette went.[27]

While *Esquire Etiquette*'s date plan was certainly no less regimented than those described by guidebooks for women and teenage girls, there was at least one glaring difference. Nowhere does it suggest that the man display appropriately masculine behavior to impress his date and remind her of her femininity. According to the women's guides, dating was an excellent opportunity for women to display feminine dependency while reinforcing male egos:

> A dinner date is your big chance to be *feminine*, to lean on your escort and make him feel like a man of the world.
>   It's still standard procedure for you to tell him what you want, and for him to pass it on to the waiter . . . Before you make up your mind, ask your date what he recommends, or what he's ordering himself. It not only flatters him—it tells you what's he's planning to spend . . .
>   Most of all, *enjoy* your food and make sure your date knows it. He'll take as much pride in your pleasure as if he'd cooked it himself![28]

In case of a gender-role emergency, the woman sprang into action: "[I]f the waiter asks you directly for your order, there's not much you can do but give it to him—but some girls report that they look at their dates as they do so, and the fellows then repeat the order, till the waiter catches on."[29]

Quick-thinking damage control like this allowed a couple to fall back into appropriately masculine and feminine behavior for the rest of the evening.

This isn't to suggest that the date described by *Esquire Etiquette* was free from gender expectations and restrictions. But where guidebooks for single gals spent pages and pages telling their readers how to dress and act so a man knew they were feminine, as well as how this reinforced his masculinity, etc., *Esquire Etiquette* cut to the chase: on a date, women were helpless, men had power, and that's just the way it was.

Even the most manipulative book for teen girls suggested that there were many things the reader could change about herself in order to meet boys. Men's guides like *How to Make Love to a Single Woman* (1975) told readers merely to *present* themselves as the sort of men women wanted to meet. A girl's personality was malleable; a man's was fixed, but he could always put on an act.

Furthermore, while pink think provided unceasing recommendations for every phase of a woman's courting life (and beyond), men occasionally got a break. For example, once a man asked a woman to marry him, all he had to do was sit back—at least until the ceremony. Wedding planning was a strictly female undertaking, during which "the groom-to-be is more or less of a shnook" who was consulted only on occasion.[30] The bride and her mother ran the show, so all a man had to know was "how to say, 'Tell me what I'm supposed to do and I'll do it.' "[31]

The Old Maid versus The Second-Time Single Man

Sometimes, married men had singlehood unexpectedly thrust upon them again. There were no smooth seduction techniques in *The Second-Time Single Man's Survival Handbook* (1975), just tips for pathetic Lonely Guys whose ex-wives took care of everything but the car and the money.

With chapters on how to find and decorate an apartment and shopping and cooking skills, it could almost have been a guide for single women. There were a few distinguishing characteristics, however: the section on clothing was written with the "chaps whose mothers or wives took care of replenishing their haberdashery" in mind, and started with the basics: "To learn your size, check the label of a comfortable pair of undershorts . . . " While the authors adopted a hearty, positive attitude (Chapter 1 was called "Yes You Can"), the stench of desperation and hang-dog pathos hung heavy over *Second-Time Single*'s pages.

The second-time single man was pathetic, sure, but this was only a passing phase: it was "just a matter of time before [the divorced man was] in love, or 'in like,' or even just 'in,'" with its connotation of no-strings-attached sexuality. Compare this to the stereotypical Old Maid, who never had her "first time." She had been "passed by" in the marriage market for a reason—she was "cold" or "masculine" or "highbrow," and nothing could rescue her from her predicament.

For women to avoid the Old Maid's fate, it was important to attract, woo, and win a man. Once she married him, it was important she hold on to him. The proper application of cosmetics and the cultivation of the ethereal quality called charm could help her in all departments.

Chapter 6

Pink 'n' Pretty:
The World of Charm and Beauty

 *Beauty and charm are feminine prerogatives. No matter what demands your daily life and work make on you or how much responsibility you carry, you deserve a part in the gay drama of feminine allure: the fun of dressing up and smelling sweet and looking good enough to eat; the pleasure of feeling treasured and adored.*

Mary Milo and Jean King Marshall,
Family Circle's Complete Book
of Charm and Beauty *(1951)*

We are about to embark upon a thrilling expedition to the Land of Loveliness—to swipe a few words from Paralee Nichols's *How to Achieve Inner Beauty and Outer Charm* (1961). I mean, let's face it, no matter what our physical appearance is, we hate it. We're too fat/too skinny/too short/too tall/too hairy/not hairy enough or have a bland personality. Therein lies the tremendous appeal of beauty culture.

With a few quick strokes of the mascara wand, we can liberate our inner glamourpuss, that calm, cool, and collected creature forever surrounded by adoring members of the opposite sex. A new shade of eye shadow, and move over, Miss Monroe, a new girl's in town. A touch of cosmetic hoodoo and a wonderful, if short-lived, personality change takes place. Show me a gal with blood-red nails and toes to match, and I'll show you a woman ready to take on whatever the world has to offer.

I'm not immune to this line of reasoning. I can't decide which ten records I'll take to that proverbial desert island, but I do know that when I'm sitting on its sandy beach you'd better give me lipstick or give me death. You see, I'm convinced that the right lipstick not only makes me look taller and thinner but imparts the devastating wit of a latter-day Dorothy Parker the moment I apply it. So what if I leave most of it on glasses, napkins and my husband's mouth—there's always the joy of pulling out lipstick and mirror, and performing that wonderfully satisfying reapplication. Predictably, a gal having this much fun by herself in public made some folks nervous. "It dismays a man when you become so preoccupied tracing your lip curve that you forget his existence," warned *Good Housekeeping* magazine in 1940. "As one victim reported, 'A girl gets that rapt look, and I know she wouldn't hear me if I asked her to marry me.'"[1] Jealous, if you ask me, but he wasn't the only one to imbue the mighty little cylinder with such mesmerizing abilities. According to Dr. Bernard Appel, author of *Skin Beauty and Health* (1948), lipstick spoke "more loudly and clearly than any other cosmetic. It can be made to say harshly, 'I don't care.' Naively, 'What's it all about?' Sophisticatedly, 'I know everything.'" I'll take three of that shade, please. After all, with so much power packed into an easy-to-carry package, one lipstick is seldom enough—though even I was embarrassed the day I found eight different tubes in the bottom of my purse.

The Importance of Being Charming

But I was one of the lucky ones. A cavalier attitude toward make-up application could lead straight to disaster. The following cautionary tale appeared in Viola and Alexander Swan's *Beauty's Question and Answer Dictionary* (1931). Don't let it happen to you:

> "Grace" had been sent to jail on a bad check charge. She had been a ste-nographer and although more than ordinarily competent she was forced to drift from one job to another and finally to make ends meet she resorted to writing "bad" checks. Her skill as a stenographer and typist were made use of in the offices of Mrs. Vada C. Sullivan, Matron of the Los Angeles County Jail. With characteristic interest Mrs. Sullivan soon discovered the underlying cause of "Grace's" downfall. It was her appear-ance. No employer could accept unkept [*sic*] nails, muddy complexion and shoddy clothes, no matter how closely associated with efficiency.[2]

With a few semesters of charm school under her belt, Grace never would have fallen so low. Then again, she shouldn't be blamed for her ignorance, as charm was an esoteric quality that wasn't easily described to the neophyte. "You cannot define charm in a word," said beauty czar John Robert Powers and co-writer Mary Sue Miller in their *Secrets of Charm* (1954)—it took them almost 400 pages. All that, and the best they could do was "we know when we are in its presence." Posture, speech, dress, make-up, personality—all were elements of charm. According to Paralee Nichols, the charming woman had a special glow imparted by "a healthy mental attitude." Like an overage Girl Scout, she was "unfailing in her service to others," and thus always engaged in "some form of constructive activity." Her voice was "like music, or the still ripple of a stream." She did not speak unkindly of others, gossip, or "delight in lurid newspaper accounts of the latest murder." Nor was she found with "questionable people" in "questionable places." Above all, she was cheerful and did not "complain about her life, no matter how difficult, or perhaps tragic, it may have been." Finally, she had "the respect of all who meet her, the esteem of co-workers and bosses and the love of all who know her," possibly because she never did "ANYTHING THAT IS AWKWARD AND GROTESQUE JUST FOR THE SAKE OF A LAUGH," as Margery Wilson thundered out in capital letters.[3]

Charm and beauty went together like French and poodles—or so the experts wanted you to think. In reality, however, the pairing was imperfect. A beautiful woman without charm was an empty shell. A charming woman without beauty—well, if she were charming, she'd be well-groomed as a matter of course. Beauty guides, cosmetics manufacturers, and charm schools blithely promised women such lofty rewards as happiness and greater self-confidence if they developed face, figure, *and* personality to the experts' exacting specifications. Only then might they attain what Mary Milo and Jean King Marshall, the authors of *Family Circle's Complete Book of Beauty and Charm*, termed "feminine success."

It didn't matter how accomplished a woman was, personally or professionally—she needed the gloss of charm. Syndicated beauty columnist and author (*Lady, Be Lovely* [1955]) Edyth Thornton McLeod conceded that women could accomplish great things in the world. But if they lost "their charm and good manners" in the process, they could "not be real successes and they will not be happy." Milo and Marshall warned readers to make the connection between beauty and happiness before it was too late:

> If you don't put forth the effort to make the best of your looks and to give yourself the personal care you require, you are likely to be left out of the big, important things in life, such as love and personal success, and to miss out on many daily pleasures of happy human activities and relationships.[4]

The *Charm Teachers Manual* (1965) was even more direct when it came to the importance of beauty, charm, and personality training. You see, women wanted "to fulfill their innermost urge to procreate," which required "the attention of the opposite sex, the acquisition of a husband and the establishment of a home." Thus, personal appearance was crucial, "a matter of putting herself on display at the best possible advantage to make the man she likes notice her and make the initial moves toward getting to know her," according to Milo and Marshall. Paralee Nichols concurred. It was not selfish "to desire loveliness in order to attract a husband who will father the children you will guide into the world of tomorrow"; this was "probably the greatest undertaking any woman will ever know."[5]

According to Alma Archer's *Your Power as a Woman* (1957), it wasn't just a woman's "right and duty" to look and be her best, it was an "obligation to take pride in [her] womanliness." A woman's "vitality . . . and good looks" reflected her "kindness to the world," according to *The Cosmo Girl's Guide to the New Etiquette* (1971). Her shining example lit a path for others to follow; her good manners and charm made men "instinctively *want* to remove their hats in elevators, to help us with bundles, as well as with budgets," Edyth Thornton McLeod assured readers. In turn, if a woman forgot "to say 'thank you' for some act of courtesy," it was up to the man performing it to "verbally remind her of her bad manners, or lack of good ones, whichever you prefer!"[6]

A gal's responsibility went much deeper than looking good at the occasional PTA meeting. Indeed, attractiveness had international implications. Writing during some of the Second World War's darkest hours, Margery Wilson urged readers to become *The Woman You Want to Be* (1942) because it was their task "to keep the world from despond, to keep the prettier gestures of good living going" during wartime. It was women's task to "preserve civilization" with their "ideal femininity." I don't feel so bad about those eight lipsticks after all.

"Win a Special Victory—for him!" began a patriotic 1944 ad for Diana Deering Cosmetics:

> Out there . . . he cherishes a mental picture of you, which, etched by time and memory, has reached perfection. Plan now to be as lovely as he dreams you are. Diana Deering will help you. Begin with the Diana Deering Personal Analysis of your beauty problems and follow faithfully

(as regularly as *he* answers reveille) every step of your specially advised routine. Work toward . . . radiant beauty for the day of his return.

If that didn't tug on your heartstrings strongly enough, "Remember, *only the fair deserve the brave!*" Sure, the ad pictured a lady Marine, but that was probably because after such wanton manipulation, Christy, Inc. (the manufacturer of Diana Deering cosmetics) felt compelled to include the following public service announcement in a lower corner: *"So proudly they serve! Marines of song and story are playing their part in victory today. You, too, can be a Marine."* Semper fi!

"Only the fair deserve the brave"—beauty as patriotism, 1944.

The Road to Happiness Is Paved with Beauty Products

Cosmetics companies were quick to back up the experts' claims linking personal appearance and happiness. Facial cleansing, for example, was a sure route to matrimony if one believed the slew of soap ads featuring happy, freshly scrubbed young brides. During the mid-1940s, a successful advertising campaign for Pond's Cold Cream used photographs of young society women and the slogan, "She's Engaged! She's Lovely! She Uses Pond's!" Prominently displayed in each ad was a picture of a huge engagement ring, alongside an equally breathless description of a "sparkling diamond, dew-drop clear, with a small diamond set on either side" or a "handsome 2½ carat diamond in an unusual platinum setting." The message was clear: romance and social success came to the woman who creamed her face with Pond's (and rather erotically, at that, "sending her white-covered finger tips over her forehead and cheeks, around her nose and mouth in little spiral whirls"). Woodbury's Facial Soap used "candid" photos from a variety of weddings. The bride's "velvety complexion" was always "a tribute to Woodbury—the soap with a beauty cream ingredient." Cuticura made the connection between their product and matrimonial success even more directly: "He fell in love with her clear, smooth, naturally radiant complexion— that unmistakable Cuticura look." According to the ad, "hundreds of doctors" as well as "clinical tests" proved Cuticura was the "best" soap, but what was science when the "joy of thousands of happy brides prove[d] it beyond question"?

It's as if personality and appearance were the first two links in a long and complex chain that ended in success and happiness if a woman applied herself properly, or in ignominy and loneliness if she didn't. We've already seen how Listerine played on women's fears of lonely spinsterhood. But their advertising brought other anxieties into the picture as well. "You can lose him quick when your Charm starts slipping," began one 1955 ad.

Smart Girl!
SHE USES CUTICURA!

Hateful blemishes are cleared up— her skin is baby-soft, alluring!

GOWN AND VEIL BY BONWIT TELLER. COMPLEXION BY CUTICURA.

He fell in love with her clear, smooth, naturally radiant complexion—that unmistakable Cuticura look!

Unlike most medicated skin preparations, Cuticura does far more than help clear up externally caused pimples. It also helps counteract blackheads, flaky dryness, oily shine. Helps repair damage from washing incorrectly or using preparations that starve and dry the skin. Wakes up your complexion tone.

It's a medically-tested fact! When you start using Cuticura Soap and Ointment regularly, your skin begins to glow again—often in just 7 days!

A two-way treatment—that's what most skin needs. And Cuticura gives you: An exquisite soap that *alone of all leading soaps is superfatted and mildly medicated* to help maintain the natural moisture and normal, healthy acidity of your skin. An effective ointment that contains a precious blend of softening and medicated ingredients that work while you sleep.

Cuticura is best! Hundreds of doctors say it. Clinical tests, use by certain leading hospitals, and the joy of thousands of happy brides prove it beyond question! Do get Cuticura Soap and Ointment today and see for yourself.

Cuticura

Available in Canada   Proved Way to Lovelier Skin

The joy of thousands of happy brides, 1955.

Take Mary Ann's case . . . the very first day she arrived at the attractive little seaside hotel the best-looking man in the place latched on to her. And, before she knew it, she was in the middle of a gay whirl. . . . Then, all of a sudden, his interest turned to indifference.

That's right—after all those gay times dancing cheek to cheek, he finally noticed her reeking breath. A 1940 ad for Mum, an underarm deodorant, reminded wives and "girls in love" that it wasn't "enough to be pretty and smart. A girl must be *dainty*, too . . . nice to be around at *any minute of the day or evening*" when hubby or a potential beau might leap out unannounced. Mum guaranteed "*lasting* charm . . . if you want to be popular," and who didn't? Mum even guarded against "unpleasantness" on sanitary napkins—though I can't think of anything more unpleasant than a crotchful of cream-style deodorant (except douching with Lysol).

Other products had no cosmetic usage whatsoever, but that didn't stop their manufacturers from marketing them as prophylactics against emotional disappointment. Another wartime ad, for Lux dishwashing soap, showed an upset husband (in uniform, for extra pathos)

"It could happen to any girl... it could happen to you" (1955).

watching as another man (perhaps a superior officer) looked disgustedly at the hand his wife has offered him, despair written on her face. Her crime? "I hurt Bob's pride by my dishpan hands." That wasn't keeping the world safe for democracy, now was it? If only she used Jergen's Lotion, to "keep the feminine Softness that enslaves a Man," as a 1940 advertisement promised (though hubby might not have been too pleased by that, either).

"But, Honey, I Never Wear Make-Up"

Perhaps the reason the ads focused on the man-trap qualities of clean skin and soft hands was the generally accepted belief that men didn't like make-up. They didn't like their girlfriends wearing it or, more understandably, the streaks of foundation and lipstick occasionally left on their coats and faces. This left most gals in a quandary. Men allegedly didn't like a made-up face but, as Helen Gurley Brown sensibly pointed out, "if you listened to *them*, your lashes would be flaxen, your lips waxen . . . and then—bing!—they'd be off chasing the first beautifully made-up girl who came along."

In theory, this meant making up with a light hand, unless you were going out for a night on the town. In practice, however, it often meant making sure you didn't get caught with a naked face—ever! For working girls, this meant stashing what Eve Nelson called "a first-aid beauty kit in her bottom desk drawer or in the back of the filing cabinet" (though a charming woman wouldn't dream of touching up anyplace other than the restroom, of course). And in a 1964 article reassuringly titled "How Do You Compete With the Girls He Meets?" *Good Housekeeping* magazine told homebound housewives to stow a purse-size mirror and lipstick near the front door ("lifesavers when the bell rings unexpectedly") and in the car ("mighty handy when you have to rush to meet the 6:10").

Cosmetics manufacturers were happy to help this little deception along. "Why tell him it's make-up . . . he's convinced it's you!" read a 1960 ad for Revlon's Touch-and-Glow foundation, in which an elegantly made up woman and her date touched foreheads over a candlelit table. The chic young woman who advertised Max Factor's Hi-Fi Fluid make-up a few years later noted conspiratorially, "when he calls me a born beauty I don't argue. I just keep the Hi-Fi close by!" And who can forget Miss Clairol's famous "Does she or doesn't she?" campaign: "Hair color so natural only her hairdresser knows for sure!"

But the undisputed queen of undercover maquillage was writer Laura Cunningham. Her contribution to *The Cosmo Girl's Guide to the New*

Etiquette was a chapter detailing how to keep one's make-up on under difficult conditions—say, while water skiing in false eyelashes, eyeliner, and a twenty-four-inch fall. The first two were easy; they came in waterproof varieties. Not surprisingly, keeping the wig on was a somewhat trickier proposition:

> I fastened it to my head with extra combs sewn into the matting. Then I glided gracefully along, relaxed my hold on the rope in peaceful waters, and gently slid into the depths at exactly a 45-degree angle. Once underwater, I clasped my hands over the fall and then surfaced. There I was, long tresses swirling romantically, when my date came zooming back.[7]

Only a woman who proudly claimed that her husband hadn't seen her face *au naturel* in three years would be willing to go through this rigmarole. Likewise, Cunningham urged all good Cosmo girls to keep "a magnifying mirror and her *essentials*"—foundation, shadow, lipstick, and brown contour make-up—"hidden under the bed." That way she could rise at dawn, "survey the damage," and make repairs before loverboy awoke, none the wiser.

Considering all the work you did to make sure he thought the roses in your cheeks bloomed naturally, it wasn't surprising that "one of the biggest shocks" many new husbands got was "the discovery of how much apparatus" it took for their wives to be beautiful. "Let your beauty care be as much of a mystery as you comfortably can," *Family Circle's Complete Book of Beauty and Charm* said, "but don't try to hide your beauty practices. Let your husband find out about them naturally, without having them forced upon him unpleasantly." Thoughtful wives kept their grooming aids in a special chest in the bathroom, or at the very least as separate from his as possible, lest he "pick up your dusting powder instead of his talc" because, as we all know, those are two *completely different* products! Of course, sometimes a woman couldn't keep all that gear out of sight even if she wanted to. In such cases, she was supposed to endow her beauty tools with "an aura of mystery and charm" that would "attract, not repel" her husband.[8]

Few were as obsessed with hiding all traces of physical existence as English writer and "expert in happiness" Veronica Dengel, author of *Can I Hold My Beauty?* Ms. Dengel went so far as to suggest readers actually remove the chapter on feminine hygiene from her book "so that your husband need not know just what we have talked about." Ms. Dengel's concerns went far beyond the usual exhortation to hide all traces of one's beauty products. She begged readers to "Never, never leave a [sanitary] napkin in a wastebasket or any receptacle where your husband might possibly find it." Heaven forbid you purchased your monthly supplies in his presence. Instead, you were to "Order them by 'phone from your department store in the large containers so you will not have the embarrassment of rushing to the corner chemist's where you may be well known"—and no one suspected that you, um, you know . . . menstruated. Charm restrains me from going into further detail, but I trust you realize that "modesty in matters of the bathroom is essential if you wish to preserve that certain quality of fastidiousness which is precious to women of refinement." And while we're on that subject, no beer in public, ladies, as "it makes a woman seem rather ordinary."[9]

As you may have noticed, anxiety about a woman's appearance ratcheted up several notches the moment she married. Oh, sure, snagging a man to father your children was an important reason for cultivating charm, but once you landed the sucker—that's where your job really began. "A happy, satisfying marriage" was the "key to feminine beauty," according to Milo and Marshall, but the smart wife planned ahead. Taking care of her looks gave her "self-assurance and pride that at some time [might] enable her to keep her marriage intact . . . "—perhaps when that gal in accounting, the one who kept a copy of *Sex and the Single Girl* in her desk drawer, came around. Most experts warned wives not to "let themselves go" after the marriage ceremony. Women who did "slip backward into drab facelessness" could rarely stop the landslide-like "downward trek to oblivion," as Eve Nelson so comfortingly put in *Take It from Eve.*[10]

Of course, finding time away from her household tasks to carry out her beauty routine "without annoying her husband" presented a problem, as did trying to please him with her dress and make-up. For, as *Family*

Circle's Complete Book of Charm and Beauty pointed out, "men who before marriage found certain mannerisms and make-up attractive" occasionally objected to them after the knot was tied. If this was the case, it was the wife's duty to help her husband outgrow the jealousy underlying such objections:

> First of all, make a super effort to appear extremely attractive to him. Be sure your boudoir and nightwear are becoming, dainty, and extra-special. Dress up for your evenings alone together and flirt with him in private. Make as much or more out of going with him to a movie as of going to a party or a dance where you will have the company of other men.[11]

She could never let her cosmetics guard down, even for an instant. To do so administered "a powerful blow to her husband's ego."

Pride in his wife's appearance was "a powerful aid and spur to a man," one that might lead to "greater pride in his own appearance" and resultant "economic asset." Your good grooming at the breakfast table might inspire hubby to wear a clean suit to the office, a detail the boss would take into account when raise time came around. In the meantime, skimping on beauty products was not the way for a financially struggling couple to save money:

> No wife should spend too little on her appearance. Her clothes and attitudes toward them reflect to the outside world how well she and her husband are managing, how happy her marriage is, as well as revealing her social potentials. And a wife should keep up in her appearance with changes in her husband's business status. . . . This does not mean foolish spending or wasting of money on clothes—it merely means that in the business world a man is often partly judged by his wife's ability as a hostess and as a friend. . . . The wife who deprives herself also often deprives her husband.[12]

Just as financial insecurity was no reason to lose one's "beauty standards," neither was minor illness—in the words of John Robert Powers, "the pretty patient has the necessary morale to recover quickly"—or even pregnancy. All a gal needed to do was cinch up one of the many special pregnancy girdles available and ride out her time until delivery (though she might don a "perky" hat for "added courage"). After all, motherhood actually made women more beautiful, according to the "many physicians" cited by *Family Circle's Complete Book of Beauty and Charm*. Childless women were the ones who needed to worry, as they were "more likely to have nervous and emotional troubles, poorer bodily function, and generally more precarious health than the mother." In fact, a woman without children was little more than a sexual neuter; "to be beautiful, one must first be a woman—and being a mother is being a woman in the true sense of the word."

But, as Eleanore King pointed out, while a lucky few were born with charm, others (presumably the childless and others lacking in feminine success) could *earn* it. Indeed, more than one career was made on this observation. Every two-bit actress from L.A. to Dubuque and beyond had her say, not to mention a slew of self-styled experts in beauty culture. According to them, any woman could achieve charm and beauty. All she needed was self-discipline, and the proper guidebook.

Measuring Your Charm Quotient

To aid in the quest, most guides started out with a self-evaluation section. I'm not sure anybody "passed" these grueling tests, though I'm reasonably sure those who could weren't reading these books. Taking stock was "not an amusing chore," as former strongman Joe Bonomo noted in his 1947 *Hollywood Success Course*, but critical self-appraisal gave "a genuine and invaluable insight" into a woman's weaknesses.

Height, weight, wrist circumference—evaluations often began with a tape measure, but quickly progressed to more subjective qualities. *Your Power as a Woman* rated one's "womanly aptitude" with the following questions among others on a list that analyzed "how familiar you are with the basic principles of smartness, proper grooming and clever shopping":

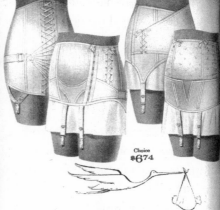

Choice $6⁷⁴

Await the Stork in

Extra firm, boned support

Our firmest back support helps prevent or relieve backache due to pregnancy. Adjustable cluster-lacer and long, well-boned back give you excellent support. Sidelaces adjust easily for a comfortable, expanding fit. Easy-care cotton and Dacron* polyester with rayon, rubber elastic front panel. Reinforced at bottom to provide stay-in-place support, front panel is shaped to lift and hold. 4 garters adjust. 10 in. long at front. 17 in. long in back over-all. (14 inches waist down). White.

Waist sizes 26, 28, 30, 32, 34, 36, 38, 40-in. *State waist size before pregnancy.*
18 K 1166—Shpg. wt. 1 lb. 4 oz.......**$6.74**

Belt support comfortably lifts the abdomen, then crosses in back to distribute extra weight and help relieve fatigue. Lightly boned for support. Side laces adjust easily for proper figure expansion. Soft, Arnel triacetate jersey at upper front, adjusts up and down for coverage . . is prettily embroidered with rosebuds. Soft flannel backing cushion the full-length side hooks. 4 garters are adjustable. White rayon and cotton batiste.

Waist size 24, 26, 28, 30, 32, 34, 36, 38 inches. *Please state waist size before pregnancy.*
18 K 1223—Shipping weight 1 lb.......**$6.74**

Two-purpose Supports

. . one front to wear BEFORE

. . and one front to wear

AFTER the baby comes

$7.74 girdle	$8.74 panty	$12.72
A **free booklet** to help choose your baby's name included with this garment! Separate fronts are of acetate, rubber, nylon leno elastic. Prenatal front, reinforced to cradle and support, laces-in for fit and expansion. Firm, flat, post-natal front hooks-in. Power net (nylon, acetate, rubber) back panel. Down-stretch satin elastic (acetate, cotton, rubber) back panel. Nylon tricot panty crotch detaches. 4 garters, detach on panty.	Exceptional support! Two separate cotton fronts. Adjustable sides and let-out darts in pre-natal front expand for a perfect fit. Contour-shaped, it cradles comfortably, helps eliminate strain with proper support. Post-natal front hooks in, is lightly boned to help restore your figure. Knit rayon jersey back has inner-bands for support without boning. Detachable shoulder straps help distribute extra weight during pregnancy. Side hooks. Crotch hooks on; extra crotch included. Front is 10 in. long; back 13 in. long. 4 garters. White.	

State waist size before pregnancy.
Small (24–26); **Medium** (27–28); **Large** (29–30); **Extra-Large** (31–33) in. Shipping weight 1 lb.
18 K 1250—White Girdle.......**$7.74**
18 K 1251—White Panty.......**8.74**
18 K 1153—Extra crotch. Wt. 2 oz..46c

State waist size before pregnancy.
24, 25, 26, 27, 28, 29, 30, 31, 32; 34 in.
18 K 1120—Shpg. wt. 1 lb. 4 oz...**$12.72**

266 SEARS PCBKMN AMDSLG   *Reg. DuPont. T.M.

Two-way Stretch

Knit-in contour fits with flexibility, and elastic innershield gives you firm abdominal support. All cotton, nylon, rubber, rayon. Side lacers adjust as figure changes; are lined with cotton flannel. 4 garters and Nylon tricot crotch detach.

State waist size before pregnancy. **Sizes** small (24–26); Medium (27–28); Large (29–30); Extra Large (31–33) in. Shpg. wt. each 12 oz.
18 K 1211—White
$5.54.........**2** for **$10.00**
Extra crotch for panty.
18 K 1209—Shpg. wt. 2 oz...46c

Lightweight Garter Panties

Wash this cloud-soft garter panty in the machine—it stays like new! Made of cool, porous Helanca® nylon yarn, it's shaped in front to give you comfortable expansion. 4 garters are detachable.

State waist size before pregnancy. Small (24–26); Medium (27–28); Large (29–30); Extra Large (31–33) in. Shpg. wt. each 4 oz.
18 K 1110—White
$2.83...**2** for **$5.50**

Wonderfully soft Helanca® nylon yarn panty has knit-in reinforcements for body comfort and wear. 4 garters are detachable. Take advantage of this thrifty price—buy 2 for real savings!

State waist size before pregnancy. Small (24–26); Medium (28–30; 27); Medium (28–30); Large (31–33) inches. Shipping weight each 4 ounces.
18 K 1105—White
$2.44...**2** for **$4.5**

Maternity girdles, Sears Catalogue, 1960.

1. Are you always sure when to offer your hand in an introduction?

2. Are you always sure whether your accessories should match or contrast with your gown; and do you know what shoes, bags, and glove materials are suitable for all hours of the day?

3. Have you kept pace with your husband's position as well as his interests?[13]

By Archer's own admission, "very few" women could answer these questions (and others like them) to their "complete satisfaction." Indeed, she and other beauty experts often named a lack of self-confidence as "the biggest single obstacle" between a woman and attainment of "her ultimate power."

Sometimes a good imagination was more useful than a small waist measurement when answering the questionnaires. *Family Circle's Complete Book of Beauty and Charm* asked readers what animal and bird they most resembled, as well as what kind of parts one would play "on the stage, in the movies, or working in radio or television." In such cases, there were no "wrong" answers, though the fact the you were reading the book in the first place generally indicated there was room for improvement.

Still other quizzes were detailed beyond belief. The following multipart lesson in peeping-tomism appeared on a "Candid Mirror Analysis Chart" in *Can I Hold My Beauty?*:

21. DRESS—and as you get yourself into your clothes, watch yourself. Pretend you are observing a stranger:

    a. Are you amusing as you pull on your girdle?

    b. Are you engaging as you put on your bra?

    c. Is it interesting to watch you draw on your stockings, adjust the garters, and step into your shoes?

    d. Are you diverting as you reach into your slip?

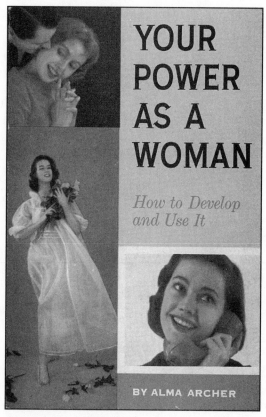

Your Power as a Woman *depended on charm and beauty.*

    e. Is your appearance wholly delightful as you emerge from the neckline of your dress?[14]

    Thank goodness Dengel told readers not to "waste time on regrets about the past negligences which have wrought havoc with your appearance." This after all was the "hook" that kept the experts in business: the reader's naïve faith in a better future. No matter if your ankles were too thick, your shoes didn't match your gloves, and there was nothing remotely amusing about the way you put on your panties—given a couple of months, the guides promised to make a sparkling new silk-purse you out of your old sow's ear self.

Under such a system, body parts became lodestones for character flaws. Hands, in particular, were "pointers to the personality," according to Milo and Marshall: "What do yours tell about you? . . . [C]an you use them for specific communicative gestures to express tenderness, to do useful work and otherwise keep them relaxed and appealing? Controlling your hands helps you to control yourself."[15]

Luckily, "hand poise" wasn't too difficult to acquire. "Lead from the wrist!" ordered Veronica Dengel, while Margery Wilson encouraged readers to "sit down in front of a mirror and invent five different positions in which to place your hands," lest they—and, by extension, you—appear "monotonously phlegmatic." Even *The Cosmo Girl's Guide to the New Etiquette* contained a two-page list of "Things to Do with Your Hands That Men Like," though these included such surprisingly tame (for *Cosmo*) suggestions as "Do needlepoint," or "Take a letter (like his secretary)."[16]

Another necessary attribute of the charming woman, the experts agreed, was a pleasant manner of speaking. After all, as Alma Archer pointed out, no "million-dollar sable" could hide "the tawdriness of an ashcan voice and vocabulary." On the other hand, a good voice was "warm, sincere" (McLeod) with "tones of emotion in it" (Wilson). Convinced your own pipes squeak like Olive Oyl on helium? Here's an exercise in vocal modulation from Margery Wilson:

> Take the word "love" and say it until the meaning of it trembles in your voice. Then in that same manner say "Good-morning"; "How interesting"; "Do come again soon." Let your face reflect what you have put into your voice and witness the miracle of Charm in yourself.[17]

Like a bad chemical spill, the miracle of charm seeped everywhere. There simply wasn't any part of the anatomy that couldn't do without some small improvement. "She's a thirty-year-old gal with fifty-year-old elbows," sighed Eleanore King before imparting words of wisdom on "how to have feminine elbows." One began by "de-caking" them with an emery board, then applied a lubricant (King recommended "hormone cream" for those past thirty), before covering them overnight with special homemade cotton and muslin "elbow patches" held in place with adhesive tape. "This method really glamorizes your elbows fast for that Saturday night date," noted King.[18] Meanwhile, *Family Circle's Complete Book of Beauty and Charm* recommended "nasal massage, starting with your fingers at the outer hollows of the nostrils and moving upward in tiny pats to the eyebrows" to "help maintain the shape and condition of the nose."

The charm guides micro-managed readers' lives with an attention to minutiae middle managers only dream about. There were proper ways to write letters ("you should have a 'wardrobe' of stationery, with at least six different styles and sizes of paper, with matching envelopes") and carry your purse ("slide your wrist under the handle and bend your elbow so that the bag rests on your hipbone in a position that slashes diagonally across the girth of the hip").[19] There was even a prescribed number of bowel movements (two per day, according to Veronica Dengel). Guidebooks devoted pages and pages of detailed instructions to maneuvering up and down stairways gracefully, sitting, standing, and exiting a car like a lady. The latter I can understand. In fact, my best high-school friend and I once spent a whole afternoon in the late 1970s practicing getting out of her mother's TR-7 while wearing our skyscraper heels (I think hers were Charles Jourdan and mine were Maud Frizon). I'm concerned, however, that we may have botched the whole deal by ignoring how we got *into* the car. Simply reversing the exit procedure wasn't good enough. No, entering the car was "governed by a set of modern regulations" requiring four paragraphs of description from Powers and company.

A Higher Education in Charm

As we've seen, with so many rules to learn, the experts recommended getting an early start. But what about those adult women whose mothers hadn't the foresight to instill good beauty habits during infancy, and who found the guidebooks and home study courses unsatisfactory? These misguided souls needed the sort of personal instruction in grooming, dress, diction, poise, and popularity only a charm school could provide— for a price, of course. The previously mentioned John Robert Powers was but one of many entrepreneurs of charm. A former silent-screen actor, Powers founded one of the first modeling agencies back in the 1920s. Thirty years later, his franchises throughout the United States offered classes in "poise, personality and appearance" to housewives and teenagers alike. "Let experts study your makeup, hair, clothes; improve your voice, your figure, your walk," read an ad in the back of *Glamour* magazine. In 1960, a basic ten-week Powers course consisted of three fifty-minute weekly classes spread over a ten-week period. Attendance was restricted to eight women per class at an average cost of $192 per student, a rather substantial investment equivalent to slightly over $1,000 today. No matter the cost, the chance to "become perfectly groomed [and] shiningly self-confident the 'Powers way'" has enticed enough women to keep the company in business to this day.

Plenty of other organizations promised to introduce students to new vistas of charm. There was the Dorothy Carnegie Course, advertised as the first step toward "a more stimulating, meaningful life," which purportedly taught students how to "get along with men" and "help your husband get ahead" in addition to becoming "a better conversationalist." The Nancy Taylor Schools, a franchise located in over 300 cities in the United States and Canada, offered a charm and finishing course for which I have the four-volume set of textbooks. Nancy Taylor also offered secretarial and stenographic courses, and it was a point of pride that graduates of the Taylor office work programs attended classes "in proper Make-up, Fashion, Poise, Appearance and Manners," special training that gave them the "'always right' look" that future employers "preferred" at a time when secretaries were hired as much for their looks as for their skill. Graduates were also entitled to "FREE JOB PLACEMENT FOR THE REST OF YOUR LIFE" if they mailed in a special form. A Nancy Taylor graduate had only to present her full set of books plus a validated International Registration Certificate to receive these lifelong privileges.

Since I currently own her textbooks, I hope that Judy Bishop (who wrote her name on the flyleaf and carefully detached the "International Registration Certificate" along the perforated line) has risen above the steno pool by now. Judging by her school-girl scrawl, I imagine Judy was less concerned with future office work than wowing the boys in her high school homeroom with newly learned make-up tips. It's impossible to know if Judy profited by the Nancy Taylor Course, but she dutifully noted the shrinking measurements of her waist, abdomen, lower hip, thigh, knee, calf, and ankle over a three-month period in 1968.

Women who couldn't afford charm school had the option of purchasing phonograph records that promised lessons in charm and/or beauty. The *Lady Look Charm Course* (1968), for example, was a recorded synopsis of model Dee Stocks's nine-hour course in charm and beauty, which promised to help "women of every size, shape, and age become more attractive and gracious companions." Hair stylist George Masters discussed the do's and don'ts of hair care as well as "coiffure personality" on *The Masters Touch* (undated, but probably from the mid-1960s). *Bazaar's Secret Formula for a Beautiful New You* (ca. 1963–64) provided a nine-day diet along with nine "Wonder Exercises" and nine "Relaxing Exercises" all set to music. The exercises were designed for *Bazaar* by the "famous fitness authority" Nicholas Kounovsky, who narrated the records in his gentle Russian accent. The exercises themselves were decidedly nonstrenuous: more like stretches than aerobics. The editors at *Bazaar* obviously held no illusions as to their effectiveness: one of the fashion tips included in the printed material suggests that you "make a friend of your corsetiere . . . let her suggest a wardrobe of girdles and bras that do the most for your figure."

From Pointed Cup to Natural Look:
A Brief History of Bras in the 1940s to 1970s

As anyone who has looked at an old fashion magazine knows, the shape of the bosom changes almost as quickly as hemlines rise and fall. The corsets of the 1890s created an imposing "mono-bosom" look, while

1920s-era flappers bought special flattening bras to hide their natural assets. The 1940s and 1950s were a veritable Rococo era of brassiere design, when fashion focused on the bosom, and the lingerie industry did everything it could to support (eek!) the national fetish.

A harbinger of the shape of things to come crested the horizon in 1943. During filming of *The Outlaw*, director Howard Hughes had a problem on his hands. The seams of starlet Jane Russell's lingerie showed through her skimpy top in one scene, and the full-breasted actress refused to go braless. So Hughes designed a special cantilevered brassiere. But when Russell tried the garment on, she found it "uncomfortable and ridiculous." Instead, she wore her own bra, after she "covered the seams with tissue [and] pulled the straps over to the side." According to Russell, Hughes "could design planes, but a Mr. Playtex he wasn't."[20] The long-time spokeswoman for the Playtex's line of "18-Hour" bras and girdles, she was, after all, in a position to know.

But the New Look of postwar fashion really brought the bosom into prominence. Introduced by designer Christian Dior in 1947, New Look suits and dresses incorporated voluminous skirts springing from sylph-like waists, unpadded shoulders, and peplumed hips. To carry off the look successfully, serious foundation garments were required—in particular an item known as a waist-cincher. Once the waist was tightly bound, the bust was thrust up and out with a highly structured bra.

Or maybe it was all Frederick Mellinger's fault. In 1946, Mellinger was working as a buyer at a New York mail-order firm when he told his managers to consider stocking some satin and lace nightgowns—the sort that went with "every mental picture [he] had of girls who turned [him] on" when he was in the army. The bosses sneered at his suggestion, so Frederick moved to Hollywood and opened his own mail-order business. The rest, of course, is history.

Frederick's of Hollywood specialized, then as now, in provocative lingerie and clothing sold via its mail order catalogue and through ads placed in magazines devoted to feminine pulchritude or Hollywood scandal. The emphasis was on glamour—towering heels, rhinestones, and lamé. Perky little drawings of pneumatically perfect women modeled bras, girdles, swimsuits, and peignoirs with names like "Twin Stars," "Ridin' High," "Shock Wave," and "Curves Adrift." The "Hollywood Profile" bra was "introduced to the public for the first time" in 1957:

> For you who have dreamed of heaven-sent cleavage and youthful pointed uplift—but never found it—Frederick spent two years designing the bra that will do both! Any bust obeys the gentle persuasion of the magic "in-up" angle pad, built in from the side. Lower bust in slipper satin, upper bust, peek-a-boo nylon, exquisitely stitched.

The Hollywood Profile was so highly engineered that ads included an arrow helpfully pointing out "you" to potential purchasers. It was, the copy asserted, "a never before sensation at [the] never again price" of $5.00.

Mellinger was inspired, he later wrote, by the desire to "help make ANY woman her most feminine. . . . I knew there had to be ways to reproportion women and give every loveable one of them equal opportunity in the eyes of men!" These, ah—stirring—words recently appeared on the Frederick's web site. But when Frederick Mellinger got down to brass tacks in a 1971 interview in the upstart fashion digest, *Rags*, the lingerie king's much-vaunted "love of women" disintegrated like so much old foam rubber.

> You ought to see what we can do. Our switchboard girl is a 21-year-old tomboy and we turned her into a 26-year-old hooker, and I mean that in the best way possible. . . . When a woman comes to us and she's got a spare tire, we put her in something to compress it, or call the attention somewhere else. If her boobs are full but they're saggers, we give her something to lift them up, give her the cleavage she wants. It's sort of like being in the meat packing business.[21]

Speaking of "meat," Mellinger also recounted the fabled day when Russ Meyer brought 43D pin-up model June Wilkinson in for a fitting, a day chronicled by men's magazines *Adam* and *Modern Man*: "I couldn't believe it, but Russ swore they were real. He told me I could hit 'em with a baseball bat and I wouldn't dent 'em."[22]

But it wasn't just the back-of-the-men's-magazines manufacturers who were selling these amazing garments. Circular-stitched, cone-shaped "bullet bras" designed by the major lingerie companies sold like hotcakes. Between 1949 and 1978, Maidenform sold roughly 90 million torpedo-cupped "Chansonette" bras throughout the world. The Holly-wood-Maxwell Company advertised four different whirlpool bra styles—"Glamour Whirls for Glamour Girls"—in *Seventeen* magazine. (They also offered consumers a "free illustrated brochure, 'The Full Dimension Story.'") Peter Pan Foundations promoted its "Merry-Go-Round cup" ("the secret's in the circle").

Deep in the back of my lingerie drawer, unworn but far from unloved, resides a pointed relic of this era. She originally hailed from Montgomery Wards, but I purchased her at a vintage clothing shop. This whirlpool-stitched, foam-rubbery beauty thrusts my anatomy into such stratospheric proportions that I simply can't wear it with a straight face (or out of the house, for that matter). How on earth did women wear these on a daily basis? Certainly, this brassiere pushes the wearer into such a ludicrous caricature of femininity that it actually impedes arm movement. She maintains the same stiffly conical shape simply lying on my desk as she does when she's being worn. One wrong move and she'll put your eye out.

Of course, the beauty authorities had something to say about bras like this one. A guide for teen girls called *Put Your Best Look Forward* (1960) advised readers never to "buy a bra with pointed cups to wear under a sweater" because "the effect was nearly always cheap." According to writer Genevieve Antoine Dariaux, bras that were "too rigid, too padded or too provocative" were "deadly enemies to a woman's elegance." As was a large bosom:

> The current collective adoration for the big bust and the publicity given to the monstrous measurements of certain movie stars is a phenomenon perhaps worthy of the attention of a psychiatrist, or the jury at a live-stock exhibition—but it certainly has nothing to do with either fashion or elegance.[23]

"Instant Beauty"

by Robert Alan Franklyn, M.D., with Marcia Borie
(New York: Frederick Fell, Inc., 1967)

Robert Alan Franklyn, M.D., was a Hollywood plastic surgeon who advocated what he called "Cleopatra's Needle"—the direct subcutaneous injection of silicone. It was safe—the Dow-Corning Center for Aid to Medical Research noted that when "medical-grade 100 per cent pure silicones are used, the body is said to be unaware that they are present." According to Franklyn, visible aging began when "bags" appeared under the eyes of twenty-six- or twenty-seven-year-old women. These could be reversed with a minor eye lift, but it was still all downhill from there. Women who reached their late forties without taking advantage of the preventative nature of Cleopatra's Needle or a minor face lift risked major work later on.

Franklyn also advocated breast implants made of "a polyether sponge called 'Surgifoam.'" Sheathed in Teflon, they were so indestructible that the good doctor predicted "a hundred years from today the only trace left of some patients will be two plastic foam sponges."

Cleopatra's Needle was also a boon to those "desiring only normal improvement" in cup size: "Imagine popping into the surgeon's office at 5 p.m. for the antidote not to what to wear but how to wear that now low-cut gown to tonight's dinner party!" Super!

Franklyn had only the best intentions. He had "seen everything from broken marriages to attempted suicides because of the lack of what is considered today the prime female endowment." Thank goodness for the thoughtful husbands who "repeatedly [brought] their wives . . . to become endowed."

Of course, by the time Dariaux wrote these words, in a guide called *Elegance* (1964), bullet bras and voluptuous figures were on the way out.

Maybe it was fashion's new emphasis on youthful naturalness, but by the late 1960s, no self-respecting hipster gal would be caught dead in a whirlpool cup—or a bra at all. In 1965, avant-garde designer Rudi Gernreich followed up his topless bathing suit (the "Monokini") with the "No Bra" bra. Offering a modicum of coverage for the modest, but little support for the well-endowed, the "No Bra" seemed to be little more than another of Gernreich's publicity-garnering shock fashions. Then again, as fashion columnist Eugenia Sheppard remarked upon viewing Gernreich's transparent blouse in 1964, "It's very square to wear a bra with Rudi's clothes."

By the end of the decade, a certain amount of fashionable nudity had filtered down to the woman in the street. Of course, not everyone felt comfortable parading down Main Street with nothing between her maidenly charms and the cold cruel world but a thin layer of see-through blouse. Some reached for band-aids, and others turned to a new generation of undergarments designed to provide the "natural" look to those too modest to go nude. Warner offered a transparent body stocking to the public in 1965 but, except for the young and supple, most women continued to wear more traditional brassieres.

To some, going braless was a fashion statement; to others, it was an act imbued with political symbolism. On September 7, 1968, the Miss America Pageant in Atlantic City, New Jersey, was the site of a major demonstration by proponents of the women's liberation movement. Initiated by the New York Radical Women, the action protested the pageant's exploitation of women. The demonstrators crowned a sheep "Miss America" and tossed "instruments of torture to women" into a "Freedom Trash Can." These items included high-heeled shoes, curlers, false eyelashes, and copies of *Playboy, Cosmopolitan,* and *Ladies' Home Journal,* as well as those deviant servants of male supremacy, the bra and girdle. The demonstrators had every intention of burning the contents of the Freedom Trash Can but were prevented from doing so by the city. Nonethe-

The Wonderbra

Ironically, 1968 also saw the birth, in Britain, of that scourge of feminists and savior of the flat-chested, the one and only Wonderbra. For those unacquainted with them, Wonderbras are quite simply heavily padded underwire brassieres that push the wearer's natural attributes up and out, creating cleavage, cleavage, cleavage (unless, like some of us, you are merely pushed up and out of the cup altogether). The antithesis of the natural look, the Wonderbra was an immediate hit in the U.K.

Almost thirty years later, the Wonderbra was introduced to the U.S. market. It was an unqualified success: in the first two months after its initial appearance in 1994, Saks Fifth Avenue's flagship New York store sold 20,000 Wonderbras. To some women, the bras were a cheap alternative to surgery, a boost to self-esteem in more ways than one. For others, fashion's return to the push-up bra and consequent emphasis on the bust (not to mention the sudden ubiquity of breast implants) signaled a disturbing return to pre-feminist ideals.

less, the media had a field day reporting that the feisty gals had, in fact, horror of titillating horrors, burned a brassiere. Some feminists claimed that the press invented the bra-burning story to discredit the movement, but historian Alice Echols maintained that the demonstration's organizers actually spread the rumor to stimulate media interest.[24]

The Miss America action generated significant national reporting on the nascent women's movement. But no matter how lofty the demonstrators' original goals, there was one long-lasting and immediate outcome: women's lib and bra-burning became inextricably intertwined in the public mind. Countless sitcoms and stand-up comics chortled salaciously about those wacky feminists and their unloosed bosoms, parents and daughters argued fiercely about a girl's right to go braless, and Ann Landers (perhaps apocryphally) warned readers contemplating throwing their brassieres into the freedom trash can to first take the "pencil test."[25]

The lingerie industry's reaction to all this was rather predictable: in the early 1970s, brassiere manufacturers began offering new styles to meet the "no-bra" fashion look. The natural yet supported bustline quickly became the new standard. "Can you possibly still be wearing a . . . hard-line bra?" *Cosmopolitan's Hangup Handbook* asked with disbelief in 1971. A year later, the *New York Times* noted that "brassieres [were] staging a comeback, particularly soft-look ones . . . notwithstanding the women's liberation movement." Older, more conservative women hadn't become "libbers" overnight, but they knew a good thing when they saw it. They moved out of their heavy, old-fashioned foundation garments and into the lighter bras and girdles in unprecedented numbers.

When all was said and done, the big question about beauty remained: how many women actually had the time, energy, or inclination for the complex ablutions prescribed by the guidebooks? Even the experts recognized they were locked in a losing battle for what little free time remained to readers engaged in a combination of housework, career, and the demands of motherhood. "Don't you ever take time out from your household chores to read about what wonderful advances have been made in the retarding of advancing age?" the Rev. Samuel H. Lowther excoriated a white-haired woman in her late forties who wrote that she feared her husband was "attracted by some of our more glamorous friends." Any successes Rev. Lowther may have claimed for his "Beauty Through Prayer" column in bodybuilder Joe Weider's *American Beauty* magazine were more likely due to his brow-beating drill sergeant's manner than divine intervention. "Now listen to me!" he barked:

> I suppose your white hair is drab and lifeless because of neglect, when actually it should be your glory. Certainly you can't retain your beauty and charm if you spend all your time pushing a vacuum cleaner and washing dishes. A little effort at least is needed. God never intended that a woman's spirit should be old at fifty.[26]

Secular humanists were perhaps better motivated by Paralee Nichols's stories in *How to Achieve Inner Beauty and Outer Charm* (1961) of "an ever-faithful servant" she called "'Mr. Subconscious,' a pugilistic little guy" who was "always ready to listen to any demands you make upon him and to deliver the very thing you order." But whether you enlisted God or Mr. Subconscious for help, one thing was clear: the experts' ideals of charm and beauty were all but impossible to meet.

Chapter 7

Working Girl's Pink

The career girl is characterized by the firm step and bold eye of the male executive—to which, however, she often adds chic and such feminine wiles (when needed) as the pleading smile and pretended helplessness.

Oliver Jensen,
The Revolt of American Women (1952)

I
f you're reading this book, chances are very strong that you have a job. Whether it's a career you really love or a day job that supports your real work as an artist or writer, forty hours (or more) a week pays for your home, food, and fun. Chances are also good that you've never worried that working comprised your femininity.

For many years, women did worry about the effects of working on their femininity. In 1939, *Ladies' Home Journal* published the results of a survey that asked, "What Do the Women of America Think About Careers?" The results varied. Sixty-four percent of respondents said a woman holding "an important position in business" did not lose any of her "feminine qualities." But when it came to traditionally "masculine" careers, women were conflicted. Asked if they would "have as much confidence in a woman physician as a male physician," 53 percent said yes. But when the question was, "Would you have as much confidence in a woman surgeon as a man surgeon?" the numbers were reversed: 62 percent said they would not. Likewise, women engineers came in for condemnation—only 17 percent said they'd trust the women as much as the men. One of the respondents, a schoolteacher, even joked, "A woman builds a more comfortable and convenient home—but deliver me from her bridges and engines!"

This was precisely the assumption behind a 1950 International Harvester ad campaign that announced a line of newly "femineered" refrigerators. "Femineering" combined the best of both feminine and masculine ingenuity. The refrigerators were "woman-planned" by home economists "for new at-a-glance food-finding" but designed and built by presumably male engineers.

According to this strategy, woman instinctively understood home, family, and refrigerators because her "real character" sprang from "the fact that nature . . . made her what scientists call 'womb-centered.'" In a 1960 article called "How to Know When You're Really Feminine," Leonard Wallace Robinson observed that women's "husband-centered and family-centered" nature sprang from the "unique psychological trait" that lay at the very core of their femininity:

> Psychiatrists call this characteristic "essential feminine altruism." Simply stated, it means that the hallmark of real femininity is . . . regard for and devotion to the interests of others. . . . For the true woman, then, children and husband come first, *way before self*, for that is how her altruism expresses itself.

While this didn't necessarily preclude women from working, particularly "for the good of the family," such "altruism" helped make marriage woman's "real" career.[1]

Who knew more about refrigerators than women? 1950.

This idea was nothing new. Of course, from the mill girls at Lowell to the shop girls at Macy's, women have long earned wages outside the home. In the aftermath of World War II, however, naysaying commentators were increasingly vocal about the phenomenon. In 1949, psychotherapist Beatrice M. Hinkle, M.D., wrote that "few normal women [chose] a career as a substitute for marriage." One wonders if Dr. Hinkle was one of the few professional women to maintain normalcy despite her

"Am I a Career Woman?"

"Should you consider a career—or a husband?" Test yourself with this quiz from the November 1947 issue of *Ladies' Home Journal*. Give yourself a check for each *Yes* answer.

1. Do you like *either* public speaking *or* horseback riding?

2. Have you ever wanted a business of your own?

3. Would you rather work with men than with women?

4. Did you attend college two years or longer?

5. Have you earned as much as $150 a month?

6. Do you dislike housework, especially cooking or sewing?

7. Can you usually make your points in an argument?

8. Are you either over 26 or above average height?

9. Do you have one or more special talents?

10. Are your clothes practical rather than frilly?

11. Do you like to guide or supervise others?

12. Were you an honor student in school?

13. Have you worked 5 years or longer?

14. Do you friends think you an independent person?

15. Are you relatively inactive in church work?

16. If married, would you want your own bank account?

17. Were you an athlete while in school?

18. Have you been trained for a business job?

19. Are you either a pronounced introvert or extrovert?

20. Do you dress for men rather than for women?

If you 16 checked or more, it is doubtful that marriage alone will satisfy you. In fact, you may prefer remaining single. A score of 10 or less suggests that you are not a career woman.

career. Alas, the contributor's note at the back of *Why Are You Single?* doesn't specify Dr. Hinkle's marital status. Married or not, she maintained that despite "the many avenues open to women for interesting work and financial independence . . . the innate desire for a home with husband and children" was still woman's "strongest and deepest longing."

All this made the working mother a suspicious character. The October 1958 installment of *Ladies' Home Journal*'s popular monthly column "How Young America Lives" featured the story of Sally Shannon, a working mother of two young children. The Shannons seemed like a happy family, and Sally emphasized she worked as a secretary at United States Information Agency because she liked to, not because she had to. "Does that mean I'm not a good mother?" she asked. Her attitude was no less defensive than the article's title: "I Work and I'm Not Hurting Anybody."

Of course, the very next month, the *Journal* ran a series of essays asking "Should Mothers of Young Children Work?" The titular article featured a roundtable discussion between business and community leaders (including the U.S. Secretary of Labor, a senator, and Billy Graham), members of the psychiatric community, and six mothers (three who worked, three who didn't). Not that one needed to read the roundtable discussion that followed—the subtitle said it all: "Unless a woman understands her role, she creates havoc among those she loves."

One of the roundtable participants was Mrs. (not Dr.) Florida Scott-Maxwell, a Jungian analyst with twenty years' experience, who worried that working before marriage brought out women's "impersonal," masculine side. After the wedding, this made them "restless and bored in their homes." The root of the problem? Those evil twins—self-awareness and education:

> When a woman begins to understand herself, she understands she has a masculine side as well as a feminine side and that masculine side is in constant danger of getting out of hand in our industrial, emancipated society. When a girl is in college and cultivates her mind, this may stimulate, even inflate, the masculine side, and she can become aridly intellectual, with a strong power drive, and then it is easy to become a doctor or a lawyer who is hardly feminine at all.[2]

Then again, Scott-Maxwell noted a few paragraphs later that "America has grown great by stressing the masculine," and cooed over "the very thrust of your marvelous skyscrapers!"

Fellow panelist Dr. Mirra Komarovsky, a sociologist, told of a student who "spoke very movingly about how proud she was that her mother was a teacher—that it made her proud to help her mother in the home care of her brother, and that it was awfully exciting when her mother came home and had fascinating things to say about what happened to her that day." The student expressed how close she felt to her mother at such times, and how her ideal in life was to be like her mother. Without missing a beat, Scott-Maxwell replied, "This is the type of woman who is very valiant, but I would say is perhaps distorted by having her children and her career. She creates an atmosphere of activity, of achievement, but I think it very doubtful if she could teach her daughter any deep feminine wisdom this way."

According to Scott-Maxwell, "love" was what women had to give the world. "As long as the house is there—no matter what age the people in it—it can't really be a home unless the woman is there representing the feeling quality." Working women were thinking women. The act of thinking "impoverished" a woman's ability to feel, which to Maxwell-Scott was woman's chief value.

Academics or Home Economics?

The belief that women were innately home-oriented led to the question of just what sort of college education they should receive. In 1947, Dorothy D. Lee, associate professor of anthropology at Vassar and mother of four, wondered "What shall we teach women?" Should colleges be filled with courses "on baby tending and dressmaking" or simply the traditional academic subjects? Both were important, Lee affirmed. Women should be taught the traditional subjects, but with a difference: "We should present, as we have always done, our erudite facts and theories, but along with directives which have specific reference to women in our culture." No, this wasn't an early call for women's studies:

> Our courses in psychology, for example, should be a realistic introduction to the human situations with which women deal. It is not enough to teach a student how an individual is expected to react when sitting alone in a control room with the black shades down and the sounds muted; we should also give her some idea of how a man will act in the confusion of living: celebrating in a night club, or when his car stalls in traffic, or when he loses his job, or when his son wins a prize.[3]

The assumption was that no matter how much education she received, a woman would eventually leave the work force to become a housewife. One woman, identified only as a Former Coed, answered an early 1950s *Time* magazine survey of college graduates with a comment on what she felt was a need for more homemaking education:

> Many college women, like myself, make the mistake of not training for that most important career, marriage.
>
> I would ask for . . . courses to teach women to be household managers and mothers . . . I would want courses in homemaking, budgeting, home nursing, child psychology, etc.[4]

Another respondent to the survey noted that while her college training was "far from a disappointment," she, too, would "trade History of Civilization for a practical cooking and nutrition course."[5] They had only themselves to blame. According to a 1940 *Good Housekeeping* article, a co-ed who forgot "the fact that the one important use of an education is to help her toward achieving a happy marriage, a home, and a family— the things which she really wants—is being a very foolish virgin indeed."[6]

Wise coeds benefited from a program run by the home economics department at Pennsylvania State College. In 1947, *Mademoiselle* magazine described how eight senior home ec majors spent a semester living in a special "home management house" with a faculty advisor and a baby.

Whose baby? Evidently they just popped over to the county home and picked out the cutest one. Ever since 1923, the home ec department borrowed a six- to eight-week-old baby "from a foundling home and kept [it] until the end of the school year, when they reach the age of ten or eleven months." Then the baby was whisked straight back to the institution from whence it came, none the worse for the wear and presumably improved, for "besides training students the houses also serve the purpose of preparing a well and happy baby for some adoptive home." The students, meanwhile, learned mothering and other lessons in housewifery. After all, "the predicament of an exam which ends at 11:50 a.m. and a lunch for nine persons to be prepared by 12:15 is not too unlike the case of a housewife at a late PTA meeting hurrying home to prepare dinner for a hungry family."[7]

There was some question, too, about whether a liberal arts education "spoiled" women for housewifery. Another *Ladies' Home Journal* panelist, Margaret Hickey, voiced a prevalent opinion that academic achievement put "outside pressure upon the gifted girl, the girl of high intelligence, to feel that she is of greater worth serving the community than she is staying home with her family." Six years earlier, writers Ernest Havemann and Patricia Salter West also wondered if college, "with its emphasis on good books and Bach fugues, [made] women unhappy and uncomfortable when confronted with such routine implements as a floor mop." Did "the college woman consider herself a little too good for housework?"[8]

According to some experts, few college women ever got the chance to practice their housewifery skills. In 1940, *Good Housekeeping* pointed to the statistic that only 80 percent of college-educated women married, as compared with 90 percent of women overall. That 20 percent percent of coeds never married seems today like little to worry about, but the experts went into overdrive in the 1940s and 1950s. Women's colleges, in particular, were derided as "spinster factories." "It's true that the 'old maid' risk for the educated woman is still a little higher than average," wrote a Vassar sociology professor in rebuttal to this slur. But, he argued, the statistic resulted from *the attitudes and faulty education of MEN!*"— the prevalent theory being that men shied away from women who were better educated than themselves, preferring instead to "marry down," intellectually speaking.[9]

A decade later, the *Time* magazine survey of college graduates pegged the number of unmarried female college graduates at 31 percent, compared to 13 percent of women overall.[10] In *They Went to College*, Havemann and West presented this and other results from the *Time* survey, as well as their interpretation of the same. By their own admission, they were not particularly objective—for example, they rated all respondents over forty years of age on a "matrimonial success" scale of their own devising. Individuals received points for marital status, number of children, and homeownership. Seven points represented the "ideal family situation," and almost a quarter of the male graduates attained this ranking. A mere 12 percent of the female graduates received the seven-point rating, and 34 percent had only two or fewer points. In a chapter called "The Ubiquitous Spinster," Havemann and West put forth a novel explanation for these findings. It was "an obvious fact, not requiring any statistical proof," that the modern man had "an undue regard for certain types of face and figure popularized by" actresses, models, and advertising. "The more privileged [a man was] by personality and pocketbook," the more likely he would "shop around for a wife" resembling one of these women, and the less likely he would be to settle for "the type of girl known today as a Plain Jane, or a stylish stout":

> [T]oday's parents, sensing that one of their daughters is less attractive by conventional standards than the other, may actually be more inclined to help her through college and into a career than they would in the case of her more marriageable sister. In many instances, the mere fact that a girl obtained a college degree may mean that her parents have already earmarked her for spinsterhood. Or that she herself, sensing her deficiencies in the present-day marital competition, has gone to great lengths to send herself through college in search of independence.[11]

College thereby became a dumping ground for unmarriageable women, whose presence contributed to the high rate of spinsterhood.

But while spinsterhood remained "an outstanding characteristic of our women graduates," Havemann and West concluded that the trend was away from it. "Among graduates the career woman seems to be giving way to the housewife, slowly but surely."

Working Outside the Home

Havemann and West defined "permanent career women" as "unmarried working women," but according to Evelyn M. Duvall, some women risked their marriages if they *didn't* work outside the home:[12]

> Some women are temperamentally so built that if they do not have a job of their own they either "blow up" or constantly meddle in the affairs of their husbands, and possibly those of other husbands as well. With them a real job outside the family meets a vital psychological need.[13]

Married or not, women's empathetic qualities were specifically useful in the business world. In 1962, Dr. Ashley Montagu noted the "great humanizing and civilizing influence" women exerted in "offices, factories and around conference tables":

> When a woman worker joins an all-male office, a miracle takes place. The men start wearing their jackets at their desks, rough swearing stops, and before you know it snarling males are smiling and saying good morning to one another. Without women, men revert to the jungle.[14]

The same "feminine qualities" that soothed an office filled with savage beasts were useful in other jobs, as well. In the mid-1960s, the Union Oil Company of California employed a unique group of women to "put a woman's touch in a man's world." Known as the Sparkle Corps, they were an all-female cadre specially trained to help "spark up the housekeeping" in Union 76 filling stations. Of course, they made sure

Sparkle Corps:

Putting the woman's touch in a man's world (for your comfort)

This young lady is a member of Union Oil's famous Sparkle Corps—a specially-trained team who help spark up the housekeeping in our service stations.

Each Sparkle Corps girl travels from station to station, rating them for cleanliness and comfort.

Our dealers never know when she may arrive. But when she does, they do know she'll conduct a thorough "housekeeping inspection" of the entire station. She checks for grease stains, dirt and litter.

And she inspects in places where you and your family may never normally visit. Such as the lubrication bay. Tire and battery storage. Service and repair areas.

Of course she pays particular attention to the restrooms to make sure they're clean and spotless.

You may never see a Sparkle Corps girl—but every time you stop in at a sparkling clean Union Oil service station you'll appreciate the fact that she's been there before you—to give it the woman's touch.

UNION OIL COMPANY OF CALIFORNIA (76)

Union 76 tires and batteries have earned the Good Housekeeping Seal

The Sparkle Corps entered a man's world armed only with their housekeeping skills, 1966.

that restrooms were "clean and spotless," but their surprise "housekeeping inspections" covered every inch of the station, checking for grease stains, dirt, and litter.

Despite the relatively messy conditions in which they worked, the Sparkle Corps had a snazzy yet militaristic uniform, not unlike the one worn by stewardesses. Pants might have been more convenient, but a skirt and blouse left no question as to the wearer's femininity. In *Plain Talk for Women Under 21!* (1956), Allen Ludden emphasized the necessity of feminine dress in the workplace:

> Your over-all appearance should be such that the people with whom you are working will be aware of the fact that you are *feminine*, not just female. . . . To be "female" at the office is a nuisance and therefore a *waste* of after-hours attractions.[15]

The hallmarks of this type of working "female" were, according to Oliver Jensen in *The Revolt of American Women* (1952), "the heavy-rimmed spectacles; the hat worn all day long; the tendency to address everyone as 'darling.' To get ahead, she generally has to work a little harder than a man. The penalty is frequent spinsterhood."

A pink slip was another penalty for women who didn't live up to appropriately feminine standards of appearance. In *Charm: The Career Girl's Guide to Business & Personal Success* (1971), Whitcomb and Rosalind Lang quoted an anonymous employer on this subject:

> We can't go up to a girl and tell her to do something about her hair or to go get a clean dress. We just look for some way to get rid of her as conveniently as possible. . . . A sloppy girl gets on my nerves. Some girls never notice annoying details like a skirt that's off center or a bow that's lopsided.[16]

Because being perceived as feminine in the working world was so important, women in nontraditionally female occupations (and their employers) took special care to make sure their femininity was beyond reproach. The All-American Girls Baseball League was founded in 1943. According to *Mademoiselle* magazine in 1947, requirements for a "sweetheart of swat" were that she be a "feminine type and have had at least two years of softball." And just in case her ball skills were better than her girl skills, a charm course went right along with training.

Even the initial training for WAVES (as women in the navy were called) included "good grooming lectures." Nor did military glamour stop there. In 1952, *Family Circle* magazine's "Teen Scene" column included a few paragraphs on joining the armed forces—sure, they personally interviewed candidates to "screen out gals with serious personality defects and emotional problems," but acceptable reasons for joining were reported to be the sentimental act of joining Dad or beau's branch, or the cut of the uniform. After all, "Mainbocher designed the slick WAVES uniform; Hattie Carnegie did the pretty WAC one."

In *How to Become a Government Girl* (1964), author Delight Hall similarly reported that there was "plenty of glamour in being a female member of one of the Armed Forces." After all, "top designers" were "consulted in the creation of complete outfits, truly handsome uniforms." If that wasn't enough inspiration, the food was "very good, the living quarters comfortable," and "pleasant recreation" completed "the daily picture." Hall made the armed forces sound rather spa-like. No wonder she urged "normal, well-adjusted, happy young women" to look into such a career. There was none of that nasty military-school type hazing in this woman's army; instead, "helpfulness and hospitality" were part of the tradition: "From the moment the new enlistee steps into her uniform, she has a readymade social life. She does not have to work hard to find new friends and be accepted. In the Services, everyone is a newcomer at some time, so there is a tradition of helpfulness and the inclusion of newcomers in all sorts of activities."

Boot camp sounded like a combination slumber party and Girl Scout jamboree. According to *Government Girl*, this was a typical "training schedule":

6 A.M.	Lights go on in the barracks. This is the up-and-at-'em signal. Amidst the chatter of a group of healthy, lively girls, the recruit washes up and dresses in a freshly laundered (by her) uniform.
6:25	Reveille formation. Snap into line outside the barracks. Five minutes are allowed so that everyone is

present and in good order—then it's off in a brisk drill step to the mess hall.

6:30   . . . Recruits stoke up on fruit, fruit juice, cereal, bacon and eggs, coffee, and probably milk. Breakfast is taken seriously as the foundation for serious effort.

7:00 A.M.   After marching back to the barracks, the recruits spend an hour putting their quarters into apple-pie order. And when they finish, the barracks are CLEAN. Many girls who escaped housework at home learn to be good housekeepers in the Services. And what might have been an unwelcome chore at home is fun when everyone is doing it—whether it be making a bed, sweeping up, or scrubbing a floor.[17]

Where do I sign up? Women didn't go into combat, of course. Instead, their "natural manual dexterity," formerly "demonstrated in lovely lace, petit point, or embroidery" was now "utilized . . . in technical fields." In fact, women "appear[ed] to be particularly talented at operating the teletype machine." Not surprisingly, when all was said and done "more girls start[ed] in clerical work than in any other Armed Forces field."

Sex and the Office

Some writers tried to protect young working women away from home for the first time from the wicked ways of the big city. Delight Hall urged parents to "arrange to have the minister of their church write to the headquarters of their religious denomination in the D.C. area . . . giving the background of the young lady and inquiring about a church for her to attend" as well as appropriate lodgings. Otherwise, a "completely unsuitable acquaintance" might result from "loneliness or innocence."[18]

Hall obviously considered the halls of good government a safe haven from such iniquity. Thus, she unwittingly sent any number of girls directly to that lion's den of unsuitable acquaintances—the Capitol:

> The Hill has the reputation of having the prettiest and most intelligent girls. Senators and Congressmen like to be surrounded by beauties from their home states. A ready smile and a pleasant personality are particularly important for the receptionists who lead a goldfish bowl existence. They are the front row ambassadors who are expected to charm all visitors.[19]

Another reason for good grooming in the office was best expressed by Munro Leaf, who, though mostly known for his charming children's books, wrote a 1938 guide for would-be career girls called *Listen Little Girl Before You Come to New York*. Leaf noted that "a sort of subdued theme song" ran though his book, one "which might be flippantly called *Find a Man*":

> . . . because if there is one angle that all of the occupations have in common it seems to be that, despite varying degrees of interest in work and careers, there is some evidence that girls are still attracted to and by boys and eventually hope and expect to find one certain one and wind up in a state of matrimony.[20]

Of course, "not for one minute" was that the whole plan, but it had "to be taken in to consideration," especially as Leaf was "trying to make it an honest book."[21]

To Helen Gurley Brown's Single Girl, the office was a smorgasbord of romance—not that other advice guides hadn't been advocating office dating for years. Remember, most of these books were written at a time when every working girl would "eventually . . . be faced with the choice of going with the job or getting married."[22] Having an affair with the boss or a co-worker wasn't quite as sticky a situation when you left the office to marry him—and that's the happily-ever-after most guidebooks assumed. True to form, the Single Girl didn't enter every office affair with pictures of a white wedding dancing in her head—but even for her, matrimony was always an option.

Helping Hubby's Career

Whether she married the boss and quit the office or wed her high-school sweetheart the day after graduation, the stay-at-home wife had a responsibility to help her husband along the path of his chosen career. Just as the home economics textbooks said, a wife's personality and homemaking abilities reflected on her husband's employment potential.

The following "case study" comes from Hazel Craig. After graduating from college, Jeff married "an attractive but somewhat spoiled" woman named Connie. Several years later, Jeff's boss noticed the quality of his work was slipping and began to doubt whether he deserved a promotion. Then came the fateful night when Connie, completely by coincidence, sat next to Jeff's boss's wife at a bridge party.

> The cause of Jeff's office behavior became evident. Connie's conversation revealed that she gave her husband no peace at home. She expected unusual attention for unimportant reasons. She complained about his long working hours and low pay. In the end, her selfish attitude was reflected in her husband's work. Another employee, with less actual ability, received the promotion.[23]

Connie would have been prepared if she had read an article called "Before I Hire Your Husband, I Want to Meet You," in the January 1956 issue of *Good Housekeeping*. R. E. Dumas Milner was a "self-made millionaire" who owned the tallest building in Jackson, Mississippi. He also refused to hire a man for a key position until he'd met the man's wife. Happy employees were productive employees, Milner stated, and if a man had "a peevish, nagging wife, if she is jealous and possessive, if she is lazy or over-ambitious or extravagant, that man is going to be unhappy." Even if a man could compartmentalize his home and business lives, an unpleasant wife was still a problem at business dinners and cocktail parties.

To avoid this, Milner and his wife took potential executives and their wives out to dinner. What made a good executive's wife, in Milner's opinion? She was friendly, a good citizen, capable. She was a "good-will ambassador" for her husband in the community. Above all, her primary interests were her husband, home, and children. This precluded a professional or creative life of her own: "There may be many successful and happily married women doctors, lawyers, artists, musicians, writers, and the like, but I believe that being the wife of an executive is a full-time job in itself."

On the other hand, Milner classified both the "wife-in-a-rut" and the "bored woman" as "real troublemakers" when they were married to his employees. The first was identifiable by her bad taste in clothing, as well as her conversation, which centered on "babies and how to wash the kitchen floor." The second had "a glassy-eyed stare," and was "frankly uninterested" in her husband's job (it seems not to have occurred to Mr. Milner that the presence of himself and Mrs. Milner at dinner might have contributed to this condition).

It hurt to discover a good man had married the wrong woman, Milner explained, but he frequently gave the man a chance anyway. If the new employee could "keep his wife successfully under control," Milner magnanimously allowed him to keep his job.

In 1967, Mirro advertised a "buffet-server" (a type of electric frying pan) using a scenario not unlike the one described by Milner. A man dressed in a business suit sits and looks at the camera, plate of food in hand, while other well-dressed men and women mingle around a punch bowl and buffet table. In the foreground is a photo of the buffet-server, with the title "What's his wife like?" "Key question, when your husband has a chance to move up. Answer it best in your home. Then they'll see. (She's modern. Smart-chic and smart-brainy.)" The appliance told a potential boss "just what kind of woman you are" and helped your husband get ahead.

By purchasing the buffet-server, the suburban wife of a junior executive—or the woman who aspired to be one—proved she could manage both household and husband (or so the ad implied). Nina Fischer's *How to Help Your Husband Get Ahead* (1964), one in a series of pamphlets comprising the Amy Vanderbilt Success Program for Woman, also reinforced the message that an important part of a wife's job was pushing her husband up the career ladder. It was sensible to be ambitious, Fischer suggested, because "a satisfying sense of financial worth" and the material goods that came with it were "very practical goals." The line between supportive wife and nagging shrew was fine indeed, however. There were *"only a few things a wife can do that directly aid her husband's progress, but there are a great many things she can do to hinder him,"* Fischer emphasized. Wives who were slovenly in dress as well as those who presented "too striking" an appearance impeded their husbands' career advancement, as did those who were never satisfied with his progress at the office.[24]

Good housewifery skills, a poised and well-groomed manner, and the ability to act as a sounding

What's his wife like?

Key question, when your husband has a chance to move up. Answer it best in your home. Then they'll see. (She's modern. Smart-chic and smart-brainy.)

All the rest they can read in that one deep-dish high-domed simply gorgeous buffet-server. It's Deluxe MIRRO. (She buys the best, to last.) Lined with Teflon. (The latest. No-stick, no-scour, super-tough Boeclad process, the new no-scratch surface.) Like any of the many Deluxe MIRRO Electrics, including the elegantly exclusive Oval Percolators, it tells just what kind of woman you are. And how else could you buy instant approval for just 24.95? At department, hardware, home furnishing stores.

"[I]t tells just what kind of woman you are. And how else could you buy instant approval for $24.95?" 1967.

board without offering advice made for an executive husband at the top of his game. It also behooved a wife to know just what to say, "Never mind, there's that stew you like for dinner," and when to meet her man at the door with a martini.[25] This was the kind of "successful womanhood" to which all pink think aspired.

Pink Redux

"Men like women. Don't act like a man, even if you are head of your own company. Let him open the door. Be feminine."

Ellen Fein and Sherrie Schneider,
The Rules: Time-tested Secrets for Capturing the Heart of
Mr. Right (1995)

When we look back at the ludicrous guises in which pink think appeared over the years, there's a certain smugness in our laughter, a belief that we've somehow progressed past such primitive attitudes. But though the aftermath of the women's movement of the late 1960s/early 1970s drove the most obvious pink think from public sight, it's never entirely disappeared.

Take the phenomenal success of 1995's *The Rules*, for example, "a simple way of acting around men" that will "make Mr. Right obsessed with having you as his by making yourself seem unattainable." According to authors Ellen Fein and Sherrie Schneider, "women who call men, ask them out . . . or offer sex on the first date destroy male ambition and animal drive. Men are born to respond to challenge." Women, therefore, should "become challenging." This means never initiating conversation with a man you're interested in, never calling a man you're dating, never paying for dates, and never accepting a Saturday night date later in the week than Wednesday. Men must take the lead, socially and sexually ("biologically, the man must pursue the woman").[1] Then again, just as Helen Gurley Brown hit the jackpot by offering up the bombshell of unrestrained female sexuality in *Sex and the Single Girl*, so too were Fein and Schneider crazy like foxes in presenting their reactionary rhetoric— like *Single Girl*, *The Rules* reached the top of the *New York Times* bestseller list. I'd like to think it was because so many women bought the book as a gag gift for their pals, but that wouldn't explain the appearance of *The Rules II* (1997) and *The Rules for Marriage* (2001), the latter of which received an unanticipated shot of publicity when author Fein's divorce was revealed just before the book's publication.

Perhaps Fein should have read *The Surrendered Wife* (2001), Laura Doyle's tribute to *Fascinating Womanhood*–style marriage. In places, *The Surrendered Wife* reads eerily like an updated, secularized version of Helen Andelin's 1960s-era guidebook:

> Respect the man you married by listening to him without criticizing him, insulting him, laughing at him or making fun of him. Even if you disagree with him, do not dismiss his ideas. . . . you will not try to teach, improve, or correct him. (*The Surrendered Wife*)[2]
>
> Cease belittling him. . . . You cannot earn his celestial love if you show *contempt*, *ridicule*, or *indifference* towards his masculine ability. . . . Don't map out a course for him to follow, analyze his problem or decision, or make a lot of suggestions. (*Fascinating Womanhood*)[3]

Of course, *Fascinating Womanhood* is still in print, and available via its own web site. This is nothing, though, compared to the marketing empires surrounding the other books. Three hundred dollars will purchase a thirty-minute phone consultation with *Rules'* authors, or they'll answer your e-mailed "quick question" for a mere $50. A *Surrendered Wife* seminar is a veritable bargain at $40 to $60 for a two-hour meeting. *The Rules*, however, remains the only book I know of to spawn its own lipstick ($15), which comes in colors like "Felicity" (cocoa brown), "Hush" (pinky-mauve), or "Utopia" (reddish-brown).

Indeed, pink think is more than ever about selling an idealized version of womanhood—or girlhood, in some cases. Via an online catalogue, a fundamentalist Christian organization called Vision Forum sells products it hopes will help families inculcate the values of the nineteenth century in their own children. The copy invokes something called "beautiful girlhood . . . alive in the heart of everyone who looks forward with expectation to a rich future of service as a woman of God, as a wife, and someday as a mother." This sounds suspiciously like the paradigm of True Womanhood, with its tenants of purity, piety, submissiveness, and domesticity. Vision Forum promotes the purchase of hope chests with model names like "The Betsy Ross" and "The Charity," which range in price from $395 to $675. Parents can fill these with keepsakes to remind a daughter "of her childhood, while preparing her for the future." Perhaps one of these mementos will be a character doll ($95.00) based on that hoary old children's book, *Elsie Dinsmore*—a bathetic nineteenth-century morality tale in which the heroine's religious faith remains strong despite a series of melodramatic setbacks. A twelve-volume new edition of the original storybooks costs an additional $150.

A more up-to-date—though no less disturbing—vision of girlhood is available online at Boy Crazy!™ "So many boys, so little time" and "Because a girl can change her mind" are two of the slogans that flash and fade repeatedly from the screen when you log on to this site. Activities include playing "Zodiac Matchmaking" or writing fan letters to one of dozens of blandly interchangeable, nonthreatening boys, aged 12 to 19, whose photos and bios make up the bulk of the page. In a twist on the usual beauty contest pattern, girls vote for their favorite boys, and one of them becomes "Boy of the Year," winning cash, scholarship, and prizes. The same boys are featured on a series of trading cards priced at nine for

$3, though girls are encouraged to collect all 363. There is also a maga-zine priced at $27.95 for a mere five issues. Articles with titles like "Most Memorable Kisses" and "Flirting Moves That Made Me Melt" could come directly from a 1950s or 1960s issue of *Teens Today*. Of course, when *TEEN* magazine asked "Are You Boy Crazy?" in 1960, the term was pejorative.

Low-tech dating games for girls remain popular. In the mid-1990s, there was the Rose Art Company's Sealed with a Kiss game, where the winning player collected the most kiss-shaped stamps on a photo of her generic-looking "boyfriend," and Milton Bradley's Dream Phone game, where players attempted to "guess who likes you." These games were rec-ommended for girls as young as seven years of age. The thought of little girls concerning themselves with heterosexual mate selection before they lose their baby teeth remains alarming—as does the thought of *adults* designing dating and marriage games for prepubescent girls.

It's not that the toy industry hasn't from time to time attempted to create toys for girls that cut across traditional gender roles. But fre-quently these attempts fail, not least because these "revolutionary" toys often serve up the same old stereotypes in shiny new packages. A hot pink box doesn't always do the trick, as Parker Brothers found out in 1990 when it released Careers for Girls, an updated version of its long-selling Careers game. While "college graduate" was one choice, tradition-ally female roles such as teacher, fashion designer, or "supermom" predominated. Players were asked to "Describe your dream husband" or "Show us how you dance with your main squeeze." When the game drew criticism from the female head of the Small Business Administration, a spokeswoman for Parker Brothers stressed that they didn't intend "to communicate that only certain careers are limited to women."

Other toys suffer less from their manufacturers' misguidedness than from the difficulty of cracking the corporate marketplace. After having been turned down by the major toy companies, Cathy Meredig used $90,000 of her own money to independently produce the Happy to Be Me doll in 1991. With measurements equivalent to 36-27-38 in the human world, the doll's proportions were more realistic than those of

Mattel's teen queen. But while Meredig's investment represented "every-thing I've ever owned in the world," Barbie alone accounted for a healthy chunk of Mattel's total retail sales ($1.4 billion in 1995). While Meredig's doll had nine outfits, Mattel's had about 100 new ensembles each year. You won't find a Happy to Be Me Doll on the shelves of your nearest toy megastore, or anywhere else, for that matter—the High Esteem Toy Company no longer exists. It's a self-fulfilling prophecy of sorts: low sales figures are used by the industry as evidence that girls "don't want" toys like the Happy to Be Me doll, when in actuality, they and their parents may never have known of their existence due to inade-quate advertising and distribution.

The venerable (and unisex) Magic 8 Ball underwent a feminizing face lift and reemerged all glittery pink and girly as the Magic Date Ball. "Will he call? Does he like me?" reads its box. Indeed, the association between the color pink and femininity is as strong as ever. For the 2001 holiday season, shoppers had a choice of "Pink," Victoria's Secret's "ultra femi-nine" fragrance, or the Gap's "So Pink" eau-de-cologne. Playtex's Gentle Glide Deodorant tampons also have a "soft feminine scent" in addition to pink box, pink-on-white wrappers, and pink plastic applicators.

Meanwhile, every few years, the fashion industry tries to make pink the "new black." "Professional Pink?" queried a *Wall Street Journal* head-line in February 1999. The article explained that "faced with stagnant sales, the fashion industry is trotting out colors typically associated with ice cream and children." In an accompanying photo, a pink-dressed woman smiles coyly as her pink-dyed poodle wraps its hot-pink leash around a pink-shirted man's legs. It's a scene particularly reminiscent of the musical number in the 1957 film *Funny Face*, in which fashion editor Maggie Prescott beseeches her staff to "Think pink!" Prescott, played by Kay Thompson, marches around the offices of the fictional *Quality* mag-azine, chanting "Banish the black, burn the blue, and bury the beige," as her staffers unroll bolts of pink fabric, and pink-suited models gad about in high-fashion technicolor vignettes.

Pink was a tougher sell in 1999—the *Wall Street Journal* quoted an apparel-industry analyst: "Never in my life have I worn a pink outfit and

I'm not going to start now." This, too, echoed *Funny Face*. Her office done over in pink, her minions dressed in pink, her magazine promoting pink to a presumably willing public, Maggie Prescott is asked why she's not dressed in the color as well. "Me?" she replies, "I wouldn't be caught dead [in it]!" Liking the color was beside the point—what mattered was consumers buying pink clothing, cars, and household items. Similarly, women's real behavior has little to do with the attitudes and ideas that comprise pink think. Yet as long as the color pink remains a shorthand for ideas about women and womanhood, you can rest assured that it's only a matter of time until we are yet again exhorted to "Think pink!"

Pink Think 101: An Introduction

1. Valerie Steele, "Appearance and Identity," in *Men and Women: Dressing the Part*, Claudia Brush Kidwell and Valerie Steele, eds. (Washington, D.C.: Smithsonian Institution Press, 1989), 15.
2. Louisa May Alcott, *Little Women* (Boston: Little, Brown and Company, 1898), 313.
3. "How to Wear Hats," by Mr. John, in *The Charming Woman*, No. 10, Helen Fraser, ed. (New York: The Charming Woman, Inc., 1950, 1952), 300.
4. "For Women Only," *The New Yorker*, September 17, 1949, 26–27.
5. "Pink Party Dresses," *Tempo & Quick*, July 18, 1955, 46–47.
6. Quoted in Frank De Ford, *There She Is: The Life and Times of Miss America* (New York: The Viking Press, 1971), 72.
7. For those too young or of the wrong sex to remember, a sanitary belt was an elastic device worn around the waist from which dangled, fore and aft, two metal clips to hold your sanitary napkin in place. They were an uncomfortable yet necessary nuisance, one which women eagerly abandoned in the early 1970s when self-stick pads became available.
8. Guus Luuters and Gerard Timmer, *Sexbomb: The Life and Death of Jayne Mansfield* (Secaucus, N.J.: Citadel Press), 114.
9. Martha Saxon, *Jayne Mansfield and the American Fifties* (Boston: Houghton Mifflin, 1975), 98.
10. Ibid., xv–xvi.
11. Ibid., 180, 177.
12. Evelyn Millis Duvall, *Facts of Life and Love for Teen-Agers* (New York: Association Press, 1956), 27–28.

Chapter 1

1. "Who Is Alan Beck?" *Good Housekeeping*, May 1957, 32.
2. Ibid.
3. Eve Nelson, *Take It from Eve* (New York: Grosset & Dunlap, 1968), 4.
4. Constance J. Foster, "Raise Your Girl to Be a Wife," *Parents* magazine, September 1956, 43.
5. Alcott, *Little Women*, 9–10.
6. L. Guy Brown, Ph.D., "Deserters from the Marriage Process." In *Why Are You Single?* (New York: Farrar, Straus and Company, 1949), 95.

7. Louise Paine Benjamin, "Is Your Little Girl a Good Wife?" *Ladies' Home Journal*, November 1947, 220.

8. Eleanore King, *Eleanore King's Guide to Glamor* (Englewood Cliffs, N.J.: Prentice-Hall, Inc., 1957), 108.

9. John Robert Powers opened the world's first modeling agency in Hollywood, California, in the early 1920s. The Powers School sold courses in charm, beauty, and modeling—its students were known colloquially as Powers Girls.

10. "Those Schools That Sell You Charm," *Good Housekeeping*, February 1960, 111–12.

Chapter 2

1. Evelyn Millis Duvall, *Family Living* (New York: Macmillan Company, 1961), 25.

2. Evelyn M. Duvall, Ph.D., and Reuben Hill, Ph.D., *Being Married* (Boston: D.C. Heath & Company, 1960), 98.

3. "The Secret of Being Feminine," *For Teens Only*, February 1963, 61.

4. Dolly Martin, *Taffy's Tips to Teens* (Englewood Cliffs, N.J.: Prentice-Hall, Inc., 1964), 110.

5. Marion S. Barclay and Frances Champion, *Teen Guide to Homemaking*, 2d ed. (New York: McGraw-Hill Book Company, 1967), 154; Nanalee Clayton, *Young Living* (Peoria, Ill.: Chas. A. Bennett Co., Inc., 1959), 38.

6. "Secret of Being Feminine," 61.

7. Bernice Bryant, *Miss Behavior: Popularity, Poise, and Personality for the Teen-Age Girl* (Indianapolis and New York: Bobbs-Merrill Company, Inc., 1948), 46–47.

8. Marcella March, "You Can Be More Popular," *Senior Prom*, January 1950, 20.

9. "Secret of Being Feminine," 61.

10. "What A Boy Notices First About You," *For Teens Only*, February 1963, 45.

11. "We Flip For Girls Who Look Like This," *Teens Today*, April 1959, 10–11.

12. "The Boys *Disapprove* Look," *Teens Today*, February 1961, 26–27.

13. Hazel Thompson Craig, *Thresholds to Adult Living* (Peoria, Ill.: Chas. A. Bennett Co., Inc., 1962), 182.

14. "Secret of Being Feminine," 61.

15. Jean Scott, "Act Like A Girl!" *TEEN* magazine, May 1961, 76.

16. "Secret of Being Feminine," 14.

17. Martin, 8.

18. Catharine Beecher and Harriet Beecher Stowe, *The American Woman's Home* (New York: J. B. Ford & Co., 1869; repr. New York: Arno Press, 1971), 13. Stowe, best known as the author of *Uncle Tom's Cabin*, was Beecher's sister.

19. Ibid., 19.

20. Ibid.

21. Sarah Stage, "Ellen Richards and the Social Significance of the Home Economics Movement," in *Rethinking Home Economics: Women and the History of a Profession* (Ithaca and London: Cornell University, 1997), 17–33. Richards was discouraged from completing her doctorate in the early 1870s because MIT didn't want to confer its first Ph.D. in chemistry on a woman.

22. Ibid., 22–24.

23. Stage, 28.

24. Clayton, 5. These "shared responsibilities" were gender appropriate, of course: in a chapter on housework, photographs showed girls washing dishes and boys doing yard work.

25. Marjorie East, *Home Economics: Past, Present and Future* (Boston: Allyn and Bacon, Inc., 1980) p. 28.

26. Not that making the classes coed helped with male attendance. In 1976, boys still made up less than 11 percent of home ec students (East, 28).

27. Quoted in East, 28.

28. Duvall, *Family Living*, 205.

29. Clayton, 309.

30. Marion S. Barclay et al., *Teen Guide to Homemaking*, 3d ed. (New York: McGraw Hill Book Company, 1972), 21.

31. Clayton, 309.

32. Margaret Raines, *Managing Livingtime* (Peoria, Ill.: Chas. A. Bennett Co., Inc., 1966) 15, 45.

33. Maggie Daly, *Kate Brennan, Model* (New York: Dodd, Mead & Company, 1957), 249.

34. Patti Stone, *Nine Grant, Pediatric Nurse* (New York: Julian Messner, 1960), 191.

35. *Ingenue*, June 1960, 11; *Seventeen*, February 1958, 32.

36. *Seventeen*, February 1958, 104.

37. *Ingenue*, May-June 1960, 9.

38. *Seventeen,* January 1959, 1.

39. *Seventeen*, May 1961, 164.

40. *Seventeen*, February 1960, 9.

41. "What Love Is Not," *Seventeen*, February 1960, 90.

42. Evelyn M. Duvall, Ph.D., and Reuben Hill, Ph.D., *Being Married* (Boston: D.C. Heath & Co., 1960), 113–114.

43. Judith D. Houghton, ed., *Miss Teenage America Tells How to Make the Good Things Happen* (New York: Abelard-Schuman, 1976), 398.

44. "Switched On," *The New Yorker*, September 25, 1965, 42.

45. "*You* Can Be Miss American Teenager," *Teen Life*, August 1964, 44.

46. In 1981, *TEEN* magazine purchased the Miss Teenage America pageant from the Dr Pepper Company.

47. In the parlance of the time, the four teenage girls were referred to throughout the booklet as spokes*men*.

48. Houghton, 393. The $12,000 scholarship would be worth close to $40,000 in 2001 dollars.

49. Deford, 215, 237.

50. Nancie S. Martin, *Miss America Through the Looking Glass* (New York: Simon & Schuster, 1985), 111.

51. "Arizona Beauty Is Chosen as Miss America," *San Francisco Examiner*, September 14,1964.

52. "Promotional Tour Centers on Phoenix-Area Teen Market," *Publishers Weekly*, March 28, 1966, 63.

Chapter 3

1. Janice Delaney, Mary Jane Lupton, and Emily Toth, *The Curse: A Cultural History of Menstruation*, rev. ed. (Urbana and Chicago: University of Illinois Press, 1988), 109.

2. Joyce Jackson [Helen Louise Crounse], *Joyce Jackson's Guide to Dating* (Eau Claire, Wis.: E. M. Hale and Company, 1957), 2.

3. Bernice Bryant, *Popularity, Poise, and Personality for the Teen-Age Girl* (Indianapolis and New York: Bobbs-Merrill Company, Inc., 1948).

4. "15 Ways to Make Boys Like You," *For Teens Only*, October 1962, 16.

5. Sylvie Schuman Reice, *The Ingenue Date Book* (New York: Dell Publishing Co., Inc., 1965), 40–41, 69.

6. Barclay and Champion, 154.

7. Clayton, 25. Emphasis in original.

8. Bryant, *Miss Behavior*.

9. "Secret of Being Feminine," 61.

10. Edith Heal, *The Teen-Age Manual: A Guide to Popularity and Success* (New York: Simon & Schuster, 1948), 90–91, 95–96, 98–101, 107.

11. Art Unger, ed., *Datebook's Complete Guide to Dating* (Englewood Cliffs, N.J.: Prentice-Hall, Inc., 1960), 99, 112, 127, 142, 154, 136.

12. Duvall, *Facts of Life*, 154, 157–58.

13. Gladys Denny Shultz *Letters to Jane*, rev. ed. (Philadelphia: J. B. Lippincott Company, 1960), 87; Pemberton, 149; Reice, 167.

14. Gladys Denny Shultz, "Of Course You Want to Be Popular," *Better Homes and Gardens*, May 1940, 54.

15. Becky Lynne, "Are You Boy Crazy?" *TEEN*, May 1961, 15.

16. Harold Shryock, M.D., *On Being Sweethearts* (Washington, D.C.: Review and Herald Publishing Association), 73.

17. Lois Pemberton, *The Stork Didn't Bring You*, 85.

18. "What Do You Mean No?" *Ladies' Home Journal*, May 1955, 32.

19. Ann Landers, *Ann Landers Talks to Teen-Agers About Sex* (Englewood Cliffs, N.J.: Prentice-Hall, Inc., 1963), 40–41.

20. Jackson, 209.

21. Ibid., 209–10.

22. Ibid., 211.

23. Brett Harvey, *The Fifties: A Women's Oral History* (New York: HarperCollins, 1993), 10.

24. Maureen Daly, ed., *Profile of Youth* (Philadelphia: J. B. Lippincott Company, 1951), 27.

Chapter 4

1. Clifford R. Adams, M.D., and Vance Packard, *How to Pick a Mate: The Guide to a Happy Marriage* (New York: Dell Publishing Company, 1946), 22.

2. Richard H. Hoffman, M.D., "I Met the Wrong Man," *Why Are You Single?* (New York: Farrar, Straus and Company, 1949), 233.

3. Patty De Roulf, "Must Bachelor Girls Be Immoral?" *Coronet*, February 1952, 60.

4. Charles Contreras, *How to Fascinate Men* (Hollywood: Chesterfield Publishing Company, 1953), 9–10.

5. Ibid, 44-45

6. Ibid, 46.

7. Alfred Kinsey et al., *Sexual Behavior in the Human Female* (Philadelphia and London: W. B. Saunders Company, 1953), 286. That 50 percent of Kinsey's sample weren't virgins on their wedding night perhaps demonstrates some of the disconnect between the idealized behavior preached in the guidebooks and the lives of human beings.

8. *House Beautiful's Guide for the Bride*, Fall and Winter 1951/52, 127.

9. Editors of Esquire, *Esquire Etiquette: A Guide to Business, Sports, and Social Conduct* (New York and Philadelphia: J. B. Lippincott Company, 1953), 284.

10. Drs. Willy, Vander and Fisher. *The Illustrated Encyclopedia of Sex* (New York: Cadillac Publishing Co., Inc., 1950), 160.

11. Millard Spencer Everett, *The Hygiene of Marriage* (Cleveland and New York: World Publishing Company, 1943), 119.

12. Quoted in Rachel Lynn Palmer and Sarah K. Greenberg, M.D., *Facts and Frauds in Women's Hygiene* (New York: Vanguard Press, 1936), 151.

13. While Zonite won the versatility crown, it wasn't the only personal care product with a multiple personality. Listerine, for example, tried to conquer another market in 1940—apparently you could gargle with it *and* massage it into your scalp to prevent dandruff. Meanwhile, a 1939 ad claimed you could *"Be* your age but *look* younger!" if

you used Phillips' Milk of Magnesia Creams. Their approach was certainly unique: "You know, of course, what Milk of Magnesia does *internally* . . . " Yes, but why would that make a consumer want to put it on her face?

14. Palmer and Greenberg, *Facts and Frauds*, 148–50. Suspiciously, these "physicians" were all of European origin.

15. Ibid., 144.

16. Ibid., 156.

Chapter 5

1. Leslie B. Hohman, M.D., "As the Twig Is Bent. XXI—Girlish Boys and Boyish Girls," *Ladies' Home Journal*, January 1941, 60.

2. Fritz Kahn, M.D. "Are You an Oedipus?" *Why Are You Single?* (New York: Farrar, Straus and Company, 1949).

3. Ibid.

4. Alfred L. Murray, *Youth's Courtship Problems*, 3d ed. (Grand Rapids, Mich.: Zondervan Publishing House, 1940), 124.

5. Thurman B. Rice, M.D., *In Training* (Chicago: American Medical Association, 1933, 1940), 11.

6. M. V. Hayes, M.P.H., *A Boy Today, A Man Tomorrow*, rev. ed. (St. Louis: Optimist International, 1961), 6.

7. Roy E. Dickerson, *Into Manhood* (New York: Association Press, 1954), 113.

8. Oscar Lowry, *The Way of a Man with a Maid* (Grand Rapids, Mich.: Zondervan Publishing House, 1940), 68.

9. Lowry, 81. Lowry noted that in the very rare cases where "an impingement of the clitoris" caused self-abuse in young women, "a slight operation" immediately relieved the "nerve tension and irritation" at the habit's root.

10. George W. Corner, M.D., *Attaining Manhood: A Doctor Talks to Boys About Sex* (New York: Harper & Brothers, 1938), 46.

11. Rice, *In Training*, 38.

12. W. Cleon Skousen, *So You Want to Raise a Boy?* (Garden City, N.Y.: Doubleday amd Co., Inc. 1962), 286. In Skousen's index "masturbation" comes immediately after an entry for *"Master Hand, The."*

13. Sheila John Daly, *Blondes Prefer Gentlemen* (New York: Dodd, Mead & Company, 1949), 147.

14. Ibid., 75.

15. Marjabelle Young Stewart and Ann Buchwald, *Stand Up, Shake Hands, Say "How Do You Do?* rev. ed. (New York: David McKay Company, Inc., 1977), 108.

16. Maureen Daly, *Smarter and Smoother: A Handbook on How to Be That Way* (New York:

Dodd, Mead & Company, 1944), 46. Daly's sister, Sheila, was the author of *Blondes Prefer Gentlemen*, and another sister, Maggie, was the author of *Kate Brennan, Model*.

17. Theodore Reik, "The Marriage-Shyness of the Male," *Why Are You Single?* (New York: Farrar, Straus and Company, 1949), 25, 29.

18. Dr. Albert Ellis, *Sex and the Single Man* (New York: Dell Publishing Company, 1963), 67.

19. Ibid., 68.

20. Ibid., 71.

21. Ibid., 72.

22. Shryock, *On Being Sweethearts*, 68.

23. Roy E. Dickerson, *So Youth May Know* (New York: Association Press, 1930), 155.

24. *Esquire Etiquette*, 257.

25. Ibid., 255.

26. Ibid., 259–60.

27. Ibid., 260. *Esquire Etiquette* didn't go into the details of technique the way Albert Ellis did, but the two books agreed on at least one thing: "[W]hatever you do, don't ask a woman if you may kiss her. There's only one thing she can say, but there are several things she can do. Make a move or don't, but don't have a conversation about it."

28. Art Unger, ed., *Datebook's Complete Guide to Dating* (Englewood Cliffs, N.J.: Prentice-Hall, 1960), 116–17. Emphasis in original.

29. Ibid.

30. Loeb, *He-Manners*, 152.

31. Ibid., 278.

Chapter 6

1. "Mind Your Make-up Manners," *Good Housekeeping*, September 1940, 77.

2. Viola and Alexander Swan, *Beauty's Question and Answer Dictionary* (Hollywood: Beauty Arts Institute, 1931), 215–16.

3. Paralee Nichols, *How to Achieve Inner Beauty and Outer Charm* (New York: Hearthside Press, Inc., 1961), 22–23; Margery Wilson, *The Woman You Want to Be: Margery Wilson's Complete Book of Charm* (Philadelphia and New York: J. B. Lippincott Company, 1942), 90.

4. Milo and Marshall, 5.

5. Milady, *The Charm Teachers Manual* (New York: Milady Publishing Corporation, 1962–1965), vi; Mary Milo and Jean King Marshall, *Family Circle's Complete Book of Charm and Beauty* (Garden City, N.Y.: Garden City Books, 1951), 302; Nichols, 24–25.

6. Edyth Thornton McLeod, *Lady, Be Lovely: A Guide to Beauty, Glamour, and Sex Appeal* (Chicago: Wilcox and Follett Co., 1955), 13.

7. Laura Cunningham, "Why I Wear My False Eyelashes to Bed," *The Cosmo Girl's Guide to the New Etiquette* (New York: Cosmopolitan Books, 1971), 28.

8. Milo and Marshall, 307–8.

9. Veronica Dengel, *Can I Hold My Beauty?* (London: John Westhouse [Publishers] Limited, 1946), 221–23, 230.

10. Milo and Marshall, 304; Nelson, 27.

11. Milo and Marshall, 304.

12. Ibid., 304–305.

13. Alma Archer, *Your Power as a Woman* (Hazel Bishop, Inc., 1957), 18–19.

14. Dengel, 24.

15. Milo and Marshall, 5; Wilson, 61.

16. Jani Gardner, "Things to Do with Your Hands That Men Like," *The Cosmo Girl's Guide to the New Etiquette* (New York: Cosmopolitan Books, 1971), 241, 242.

17. Wilson, 132.

18. Eleanore King, *Eleanore King's Guide to Glamor* (Englewood Cliffs, N.J.: Prentice Hall, Inc., 1957), 45.

19. MacLeod, *Lady Be Lovely*, 17; John Robert Powers and Mary Sue Miller, *Secrets of Charm* (Philadelphia and Toronto: The John C. Winston Company, 1954), 92.

20. Jane Russell, *My Path and My Detours: An Autobiography* (New York: Franklin Watts, 1985).

21. Jerry Hopkins, "Frederick Mellinger: The King of Cheese," *Rags,* February 1971, 32.

22. Ibid.

23. Glynne Hiller, *Put Your Best Look Forward: A Guide to Good Looks, Good Health, Good Grooming* (Garden City, N.Y.: Doubleday and Co., Inc., 1960), 53; Genevieve Antoine Dariaux, *Elegence* (Garden City, N.Y.: Doubleday and Co., Inc., 1964), 208.

24. Alice Echols, *Daring to Be Bad: Radical Feminism in America 1967–1975* (Minneapolis: University of Minnesota Press, 1989), 92–101.

25. To perform the pencil test, a woman places a pencil horizontally under a breast. If she can hold it in place without using her hands, she needs to wear a bra.

26. Rev. Samuel H. Lowther, "Beauty Through Prayer," *American Beauty,* October 1957, 10.

Chapter 7

1. Leonard Wallace Robinson, "How to Know When You're Really Feminine," *Good Housekeeping,* June 1960, 92.

2. "Should Mothers of Young Children Work?" *Ladies' Home Journal,* November 1958, 156, 158.

3. Dorothy D. Lee, "What Shall We Teach Women?" *Mademoiselle,* August 1947, 213.

4. Ernest Havemann and Patricia Salter West, *They Went to College: The College Graduate in America Today* (New York: Harcourt, Brace & Company, 1952), 65.

5. Ibid.

6. Wainwright Evans, "If Your Daughter Goes to College—Coeducation Is the American Way," *Good Housekeeping,* May 1940, 21.

7. "Campus Correspondence," *Mademoiselle,* July 1947, 14.

8. Havemann and West, 67.

9. Joseph K. Folsom, "If Your Daughter Goes to College—Many of Us Disagree," *Good Housekeeping,* May 1940, 21.

10. Havemann and West, 54.

11. Havemann and West, 55.

12. Ibid., 77.

13. Evelyn Millis Duvall and Reuben Hill, *When You Marry* (New York: Association Press, 1947), 210.

14. Quoted in Betty Hannah Hoffman, "Femininity: What Is It? Who Has It? Do You?" *Ladies' Home Journal,* July 1962, 57.

15. Allen Ludden, *Plain Talk For Women Under 21!* (New York: Dodd, Mead and Company, 1956), 166.

16. Helen Whitcomb and Rosalind Lang, *Charm: The Career Girl's Guide to Business and Personal Success,* 2d. ed. (New York: Gregg Division, McGraw-Hill Book Company, 1971), 140.

17. Delight Hall, *How to Become a Government Girl* (New York: Macfadden Books, 1964), 82–83.

18. Ibid., 172.

19. Ibid., 174

20. Munro Leaf, *Listen Little Girl Before You Come to New York* (New York: Frederick A. Stokes Company, 1938), 5.

21. Ibid., 5–6.

22. Frank, *How to Be a Woman,* 47.

23. Craig, 225–26.

24. Nina Fischer, "How to Help Your Husband Get Ahead," *The Amy Vanderbilt Success Program for Women* (Garden City, N.Y.: Nelson Doubleday, Inc., 1964), 28.

25. Ibid., 43.

Afterword: Pink Redux

1. Ellen Fein and Sherrie Schneider, *The Rules: Time-tested Secrets for Capturing the Heart of Mr. Right* (New York: Warner Books, Inc., 1995), 5, 7, 9.

2. Laura Doyle, *The Surrendered Wife: A Practical Guide to Finding Intimacy, Passion, and Peace with a Man* (New York: Fireside Books, 1999, 2001), 33, 35.

3. Helen B. Andelin, *Fascinating Womanhood* (Santa Barbara, Calif.: Pacific Press, 1963), 69, 73, 95.

Bailey, Beth L. *From Front Porch to Back Seat: Courtship in Twentieth-Century America*. Baltimore and London: The Johns Hopkins University Press, 1988.

Baker, Eugene. *I Want to Be a Beauty Operator*. Chicago: Children's Press, 1970.

Barson, Michael, and Steven Heller. *Teenage Confidential: An Illustrated History of the American Teen*. San Francisco: Chronicle Books, 1998.

Bernstein, Richard, and William Storm Hale. *After Sex with the Single Girl*. Los Angeles: Marvin Miller Enterprises, 1965.

Breines, Winnie. *Young, White, and Miserable: Growing Up Female in the Fifties*. Boston: Beacon Press, 1992.

Broadbent, Adah. *Teen-Age Glamor*. Garden City, N.Y.: Doubleday & Company, Inc., 1955.

Bryant, Bernice. *Miss Behavior: Popularity, Poise, and Personality for the Teen-Age Girl*. Indianapolis and New York: Bobbs-Merrill Company, Inc., 1948.

Campbell, Patricia J. *Sex Education Books for Young Adults, 1892–1979*. New York and London: R. R. Bowker Company, 1979.

Corner, George W., M.D. *Attaining Manhood: A Doctor Talks to Boys About Sex*. New York: Harper & Brothers, 1938.

Dahl, Arlene. *Always Ask a Man*. Englewood Cliffs, N.J.: Prentice-Hall, Inc., 1965.

Daly, Maggie. *Kate Brennan, Model*. New York: Dodd, Mead & Company, 1957.

Daly, Maureen. *Smoother and Smarter: A Handbook on How to Be That Way*. New York: Dodd, Mead & Company, 1944.

Daly, Sheila John. *Blondes Prefer Gentlemen*. New York: Dodd, Mead & Company, 1949.

Deford, Frank. *There She Is: The Life and Times of Miss America*. New York: The Viking Press, 1971.

Delany, Janice, Mary Jane Lupton, and Emily Toth. *The Curse: A Cultural History of Menstruation*. Rev. ed. Urbana and Chicago: University of Illinois Press, 1988.

Dickerson, Roy E. *Into Manhood*. New York: Association Press, 1954.

———. *So Youth May Know*. New York: Association Press, 1930.

Early, Elizabeth. *She Knows How*. Philadelphia: The Blackiston Company, 1941.

Echols, Alice. *Daring to Be Bad: Radical Feminism in America 1967–1975*. Minneapolis: University of Minnesota Press, 1989.

Editors of *Co-ed* Magazine. *The Co-ed Book of Charm and Beauty*. New York: Scholastic Book Services, 1962. Seventh printing, 1969.

Ekoos, Carl. *In High at "Sex-Teen."* New York: Vantage Press, 1963.

Ferguson, Ira Lunan. *25 Good Reasons Why Men Should Marry*. San Francisco: Lunan-Ferguson Library, 1976.

Frank, Lawrence K., and Mary Frank. *How to Be a Woman*. New York: Maco Magazine Corp., 1954.

Gordon, William J., and Steven D. Price. *The Second-Time Single Man's Survival Handbook* New York: Praeger Publishers, 1975.

Greene, Carla. *I Want to Be a Nurse*. Chicago: Children's Press, 1957.

——. *I Want to Be a Telephone Operator*. Chicago: Children's Press, 1958.

Haiken, Elizabeth. *Venus Envy: A History of Cosmetic Surgery*. Baltimore and London: Johns Hopkins University Press, 1997.

Harvey, Brett. *The Fifties: A Women's Oral History*. New York: Harper Perennial Library, 1944

Hill, Margaret. *Goal in the Sky*. Boston: Little, Brown and Company, 1953.

Holland, Hilda, ed. *Why Are You Single?* New York: Farrar, Straus & Company, 1949.

Holland, Isabelle. *Heads You Win, Tails I Lose*. Philadelphia: J. B. Lippincott Company, 1973.

King, Eleanore. *Eleanore King's Guide to Glamor*. Englewood Cliffs, N.J.: Prentice-Hall, Inc., 1957.

Landers, Ann. *Ann Landers Talks to Teen-Agers About Sex*. Englewood Cliffs, N.J.: Prentice-Hall, Inc., 1963.

Lawrence, Cynthia. "The Size 10 Dress." In *Here's Barbie*. By Cynthia Lawrence and Bette Lou Maybee. New York: Random House, 1962.

Luijters, Guus, and Gerard Timmer. *Sexbomb: The Life and Death of Jayne Mansfield*. Secaucus, N.J.: Citadel Press, 1988.

Lupton, Ellen. *Mechanical Brides: Women and Machines from Home to Office*. New York: Princeton Architectural Press, 1993.

Marling, Karal Ann. *As Seen On TV: The Visual Culture of Everyday Life in the 1950s*. Cambridge and London: Harvard University Press, 1994.

Marr, John. *(Anti-)Sex Tips for Teens: The Teenage Advice Book 1897–1987*. Self-published, 1990.

Martin, Dolly. *Taffy's Tips to Teens*. Englewood Cliffs, N.J.: Prentice-Hall, Inc., 1964.

Martin, Nancie S. *Miss America Through the Looking Glass: The Story Behind the Scenes*. New York: Simon and Schuster, 1985.

Murray, Alfred L. *Youth's Courtship Problems* 3d. ed. Grand Rapids, Mich.: Zondervan Publishing House, 1940.

Payne, Lucile Vaughan. "Good-bye, Old Laura." *Seventeen* (June 1955).

Rice, Thurman B., M.D. *In Training*. Chicago: American Medical Association, 1933. Thirteenth printing, 1946.

Richardson, Frank Howard, M.D. *For Boys Only: The Doctor Discusses the Mysteries of Manhood*. David McKay Company, 1959. Thirteenth printing, 1963.

Roget, Marie and Hector. *Swingers Guide for the Single Girl: Key to the New Morality.* Los Angeles: Holloway House, 1966.

Sakol, Jeanne. *What About Teen-age Marriage?* New York: Avon Books, 1961.

Saxton, Martha. *Jayne Mansfield and the American Fifties.* Boston: Houghton Mifflin Company, 1975.

———. *Louisa May: A Modern Biography of Louisa May Alcott.* Boston: Houghton Mifflin Company, 1977.

Schreiber, Joanne. *Here's How.* New York: Scholastic Book Services, 1967. Fourth printing, 1969.

Seruya, Florence, Susan Losher, and Albert Ellis. *Sex and Sex Education: A Bibliography.* New York and London: R.R. Bowker Company, 1972.

Shryock, Harold, M.D. *On Being Sweethearts.* Washington, D.C.: Review and Herald Publishing Association, 1966.

Sklar, Katherine Kish. *Catherine Beecher: A Study in American Domesticity.* New Haven and London: Yale University Press, 1973.

Sparke, Penny. *As Long As It's Pink.* New York: HarperCollins, 1995.

Stage, Sarah, and Virginia B. Vincenti, eds. *Rethinking Home Economics: Women and the History of a Profession.* Ithaca and London: Cornell University Press, 1997.

Steele, Valerie. "Appearance and Identity." In *Men and Women: Dressing the Part*, edited by Claudia Brush Kidwell and Valerie Steele. Washington, D.C.: Smithsonian Institution Press, 1989.

Stewart, Marjabelle Young, and Ann Buchwald. *Stand Up, Shake Hands, Say "How Do You Do?* Rev. ed. New York: David McKay Company, Inc., 1977.

Stone, Patti. *Nina Grant, Pediatric Nurse.* New York: Julian Messner, 1960.

Taylor, E. B. *Sex and Marriage Problems (From the Intimate Records of a Psychoanalyst).* New York: Hillman Periodicals, 1948.

Vance, Margaret. *Secret for a Star.* E.P. Dutton & Co., 1957.

Whitcomb, Helen, and Rosalind Lang. *Charm: The Career Girl's Guide to Business & Personal Success.* New York: McGraw-Hill Book Company, 1964. Second edition, 1971.

Wilkens, Emily. *A New You.* New York: G.P. Putnam's Sons, 1965.

Permissions/Illustration Credits

Grateful acknowledgment is made to the following for providing permission to reprint copyrighted material.

Page 12   *Health and Safety for Teenagers* cover. From *Health and Safety for Teenagers* by G. G. Jenkins, M.A.; W. W. Bauer, M.D.; H. S. Schacter, Ph.D.; and E. T. Pounds, M.A. Illustrated by Connie Moran, cover design by John Horton. Copyright © 1962 by Scott, Foresman and Company. Used by permission of Pearson Education, Inc.

Page 13   *Health and Safety for Teenagers* illustration. From *Health and Safety for Teenagers* by G. G. Jenkins, M.A.; W. W. Bauer, M.D.; H. S. Schacter, Ph.D.; and E. T. Pounds, M.A. Illustrated by Connie Moran, cover design by John Horton. Copyright © 1962 by Scott, Foresman and Company. Used by permission of Pearson Education, Inc.

Page 15   Donna Mae Mims. Courtesy of Donna Mae Mims and Bettmann/Corbis.

Page 16   *Jayne Mansfield's Wild Wild World.* Courtesy of Holloway House Publishing Co., Los Angeles, Calif. 90046.

Page 22   Quiz: "How Do You Rate as a Girl?" Courtesy of *Seventeen* magazine.

Page 37   Housekeeping toys, from Wards 1966 Christmas Catalogue. Courtesy of Montgomery Ward, LLC.

Page 41   Beauty toys, from Wards 1966 Christmas Catalogue. Courtesy of Montgomery Ward, LLC.

Page 48   Arrid ad. Courtesy of Church & Dwight Co., Inc.

Page 60   Ad for U.S. Savings Bonds, *Senior Prom* magazine, January 1950.

Page 64   *Pamela Lee, Home Economist.* Thomas Bouregy & Co., Inc./Avalon Books.

Page 69   *How to Earn the Key to Dad's Car.* Courtesy of Ford Motor Company.

Page 80   *Growing Up and Liking It* (doctor pointing at uterus). Courtesy of McNeil-PPC, Inc.

Page 85   From *On Becoming A Woman* (jacket cover) by Mary McGee Williams, copyright © 1959. Used by permission of Dell Publishing, a division of Random House, Inc.

Page 195   Femineered refrigerators. Thanks to International Truck & Engine Corporation.

Page 196   Quiz: "Am I a Career Woman?" © 1947, Meredith Corporation. All rights reserved. Used with the permission of *Ladies' Home Journal*.

Page 203   Union 76 Sparkle Corps. Copyright © Tosco Corporation 1966. All rights reserved; reprinted with permission from Tosco Corporation, a subsidiary of Phillips Petroleum Company; 76 UNION Logo is a registered trademark of Phillips Petroleum Company or its subsidiaries.

Page 210   Ad for Mirro Buffet Server, *Ladies' Home Journal*, May 1967. Courtesy of Mirro.

Insert page 1   New Pink Serena, 1958. Courtesy of McNeil-PPC, Inc.

Insert pages 2–3   Lionel Pink Train, 1958. Photo used with permission of Lionel LLC.

Insert page 4   Modess sanitary belt, ca. 1960. Courtesy of McNeil-PPC, Inc.

Insert page 5   Mystery Date Game, 1965. Courtesy of Marvin Glass & Associates Liquidating Trust. Photo by Michele Lee Willson.

Insert page 6   The Dud, 1965. Courtesy of Marvin Glass & Associates Liquidating Trust. Photo by Michele Lee Willson.

Insert page 7   Campus Queen lunchbox, 1967. Courtesy of Thermos, LLC. Photo by Michele Lee Willson.

Insert page 8   Wow! Pillow Fight Game for GIrls, 1964. Courtesy of Marvin Glass & Associates Liquidating Trust. Photo by Michele Lee Willson.